The Last Hundred Days of the Soviet Union

The Last Hundred Days of the Soviet Union

Boris Pankin

Translated from Russian
by Alexei Pankin

I.B. TAURIS
Publishers
LONDON • NEW YORK

Published in 1996 by
I.B. Tauris & Co Ltd
45 Bloomsbury Square
London WC1A 2HY

175 Fifth Avenue
New York
NY 10010

A full CIP record for this book is available from the
British Library

A full CIP record for this book is available from the
Library of Congress

ISBN 1 85043 878 1

Library of Congress catalog card number: available

Typeset by The Harrington Consultancy
Printed and bound in Great Britain by WBC Ltd,
Bridgend, Mid Glamorgan

Contents

1

The Departing
Foreign Minister

When Gorbachev phoned at four o'clock in the afternoon of Monday, 18 November 1991, was his tone a little unusual or was this just my impression, heightened by the tension of those times? That morning we had received the Amir of Kuwait. Gorbachev had been exceptionally cordial towards me. Talking to the Amir he constantly referred to 'our Minister for Foreign Affairs' and consulted me on even the smallest details. But when during a short interval between the talks and a breakfast in honour of the visitor I tried to discuss a few points with him, Gorbachev, who would usually make time to compare notes, suggested that we should talk later.

'Will you be around this afternoon? Good, I'll give you a call.' For Gorbachev, 'giving me a call' meant simply picking up the receiver of a big ivory-coloured telephone on the President's desk, marked 'Minister for Foreign Affairs'. The phone had no buttons because it didn't need them: the line was direct to my desk and completely secure.

The President was not always prompt in keeping his promises

1

to call, and anyway the matters that I wanted to discuss that day were not terribly urgent, so by the time I was back working at my Foreign Ministry office on Smolenskaya Square I had nearly forgotten about our conversation. When one of the telephones on my desk – exactly like the one on the President's desk, but marked 'Gorbachev' – gave its melodious ring I was almost surprised.

'You're not in a meeting, are you? Could you come right now?'

It took less than five minutes for my long black Zil, one of those limousines that until recently had carried members of the Politburo and so acquired the nickname 'chlenovoz' (member carrier), to sweep me from the Foreign Office to the Borovitsky Gate of the Kremlin. Again, was it just my imagination or were the Kremlin guards really saluting me with unusual zeal, had the lift going to the 'Top' (the nickname of the Presidential offices) been kept ready and waiting with its doors open, and did the secretary in Gorbachev's anteroom open the door for me with a special courtesy?

My position of Foreign Minister was already so elevated that I could hardly interpret all this special attention as a sign of yet further promotion. In that case, unless my imagination was working overtime, there was only one possibility.

Gorbachev met me in the middle of his office and offered me one of the armchairs in front of his desk. When he looked me in the eye and said: 'You know, Boris Dimitrievich, we think after all that Shevardnadze has to come back,' I wondered who 'we' might be, but I was not even surprised.

My calm response seemed to puzzle the President, who had prepared himself for a confrontation. Yet the return of Edvard Ambrosievich Shevardnadze as Foreign Minister of the Soviet Union had been broached by both foreign and domestic commentators as one of the ways in which the increasingly desperate and beleaguered Gorbachev might stem the tide of opposition against him. Given the outspoken criticism of his former leader that Shevardnadze had broadcast in the period leading up to the August 1991 putsch attempt, it was only natural that Shevardnadze – now vindicated after his warnings to Gorbachev – should be re-enlisted into the Soviet leadership. By bringing him back Gorbachev could simultaneously silence a critic, demonstrate to his opponents that he was no autocrat, and pander to the concerns of republics whose presidents viewed Shevardnadze as 'one of them'.

Obviously uncomfortable with the task of removing my Foreign Ministry portfolio, Gorbachev explained that he intended to establish for me the position of Presidential Foreign Policy Adviser, modelled on the US National Security Adviser. He wanted the three of us – himself, Shevardnadze and me – to work together. But despite his most persuasive efforts, I knew at once that I had to turn him down. The Soviet Union, even though breathing its last gasp, was still a State and still needed a Foreign Minister. But a Presidential Adviser? It was clearly a position without a function: it would only create further confusion in an already seething political cauldron, and by setting up a second power centre in the conduct of Soviet diplomacy we would be sending the wrong signals to the rest of the world.

'Of course,' he said, as if reading my mind, 'you can become an Ambassador. No problem. You understand that I can do this ...' He made an expansive gesture. 'Washington, Paris ...'

'London,' I said, with the off-hand air, it struck me later, of a person who had been expecting something like this to happen. (In those days, Gorbachev was changing the people around him as often as he changed his socks.)

Mikhail Sergeyevich was taken aback. Of course he was relieved that I was not going to make a scene, ask pointless questions or level accusations. On the other hand, who was Pankin to refuse his generous offer to convert him into a Soviet Scowcroft, Brzezinski or Kissinger? He gave me till the following morning to think his proposal over, although I kept repeating that my mind was 99 per cent made up for the London Embassy.

Why London? The British capital has always held a great attraction for me. Perhaps we Russians have a very romanticized

3

view of Britain. In Moscow, Britain is still regarded as a great power despite the obvious decline in its fortunes since the last century. Russians share with the British a certain nostalgia for the nineteenth century, and are very much aware that in that period it was the British and the Russians who helped shape many of the structures of the modern world. The results weren't necessarily always attractive, and the rivalry between the two empires was intense, but it did create a kind of bond between the two countries which has left Russians quite respectful of the British, with the result that Soviet and now Russian policy-makers continue to accord Britain a status way beyond its real power and capacities in the world. But if the importance of London as a diplomatic post rests largely on a British power that no longer exists, I have to say that the British are skilled at exploiting this illusion to good effect.

In any event, the next morning (ironically it was 19 November, exactly three months after the start of the putsch in Moscow), the 'Gorbachev' telephone rang again.

'Are you free now?'

I could only chuckle in response.

'Then come. Right now. How long will it take you?'

'It's not as far as Prague,' I joked grimly, and immediately regretted my tactless remark. 'I'll be there in fifteen minutes at the latest.'

'Shevardnadze is here,' said my bodyguard, from the front seat of my majestic ministerial Zil. He pointed to a small white Volvo parked near the Gorbachev 'porch' in the Kremlin, the President's entrance.

In the doorways, the lift, and Gorbachev's reception room, it was just like yesterday except that everyone I met greeted and saluted me with even greater zeal.

In the office I found Shevardnadze occupying the armchair I had sat in on Monday. We greeted each other like the old friends we were.

'Well, how's your ninety-nine per cent?' asked the President without further ado, but perhaps a touch more effusively than usual.

4

'It's now one hundred,' I told him, and saw what I think was a flicker of relief on his face. Today my stubbornness had made his life easier. It was easy to guess that Shevardnadze could not feel happy about having a Foreign Policy Adviser whispering into the President's other ear. Gorbachev, who only yesterday had gone out of his way to coax me into the role, would today have found himself in an awkward position had I accepted his proposal.

'Well,' he said, trying not too skilfully to show disappointment and then jabbing at buttons on the big telephone board to his left. 'Then we'll have to get in touch with Major.'

This had been agreed between us yesterday: if we settled on the UK he would immediately call the British Prime Minister and ask for his government's agreement. In such extraordinary circumstances agreements are usually granted on the spot. This would allow the Soviet government to announce Shevardnadze's and my own new appointments in tandem. And it was quite obvious that Gorbachev was anxious to announce the appointment of Shevardnadze. The switch promised to cause a considerable stir in the diplomatic world. The tense atmosphere in those days was fuelled by a constant procession of unexpected appointments, resignations, decrees, and hastily announced decisions. And the return of Shevardnadze as Foreign Minister after his grim warnings to and implied criticisms of Gorbachev in the months leading up to the putsch was bound to prompt further gossip and speculation. Hence both men wanted to be sure that the handover would be smooth and not bungled.

Gorbachev could not get through to Major immediately. The British Prime Minister was en route between 10 Downing Street and Buckingham Palace. And since I had no intention of leaving before the conversation between Moscow and London had taken place, we sat there the three of us for forty to fifty minutes, awkwardly exchanging pleasantries and small-talk in the office of the President of the Soviet Union. Despite our light-hearted banter, ranging over our common past, the increasingly complex world, and the Amir of Kuwait, who had recently arrived in Moscow together with ten of his teenage children, Shevardnadze was fidgety. He looked sheepish and embarrassed.

At last the secretary came in to inform us that John Major was on the line. Gorbachev's interpreter Pavel Palashenko was called in and took the extension.

After greeting the British Prime Minister and exchanging pleasantries Gorbachev came straight to the point. Edvard Shevardnadze was to be appointed Foreign Minister. Was Boris Pankin acceptable as the new Soviet Ambassador in London? John Major (bless the English and their good manners) instantly conveyed his congratulations to the new Soviet Foreign Minister and welcomed the new Soviet Ambassador to Great Britain, or rather, as he put it formally, to the Court of St James.

'But there is one problem,' he said. Having come to know him over the last few months I could see the expression on his face as he paused on the other end of the line. 'I have to obtain the consent of Her Majesty the Queen. I am sure she will have no objections, Mikhail, and will be only too happy to welcome Boris Pankin as Ambassador to her Court, but I do have to receive her consent.'

'How long will it take, John?' asked Gorbachev. In that moment he looked like a small child whose new toy is being taken away from him.

'Well, when would you like to make the two announcements?'

Gorbachev looked at me, at Shevardnadze, then at his watch.

'Nine o'clock this evening, Moscow time. On the national news programme that everybody watches.'

'Oh, then there's plenty of time. I'll telephone you later and I'm sure that no problems will arise.'

Edvard Ambrosievich and I made ourselves scarce. I think the President was only too glad to be on his own. Two hours later (I spent those two hours in my office not saying a word to anyone and not cancelling any appointments) Gorbachev called again.

'The Queen gave her blessing,' he said, and then managed to sound really sincere as he once again expressed his regrets that I had turned down his offer to become Foreign Policy Adviser – 'I had hoped the three of us would be making foreign policy together.'

I could only thank him politely.

After the announcements were made, naturally there was much more interest in the new Soviet Foreign Minister than in the new Ambassador. Yet, even before the announcement the ritual of messages had begun. John Major cabled: 'It will be good to have in London a representative of the Soviet Union whose commitment to reform and to democratic ideals are beyond doubt.' And from Foreign Secretary Douglas Hurd: 'I have come to respect your commitment to the democratic values we share ...'

A little later came a letter from the US Secretary of State, James Baker: 'It has been a great pleasure to work with you during this extraordinary period, particularly our close collaboration in arranging the Madrid Conference. You have done a terrific job in the face of trying circumstances and I admire you for your tireless efforts on behalf of your country.' Then from my friend, the Czechoslovak Ambassador Rudolf Slanski: 'I would like to express my admiration and appreciation of everything that you did in the last weeks for the Soviet Union, for the world and for my country.'

Ritualistic though these messages may be – rather like letters of condolence – they are much appreciated when they arrive, and they do cushion the impact and disappointment of an adverse change that it is beyond one's power to mend. But how deep was my disappointment? I immediately set about consoling myself with a pragmatic response to my new situation. Here, after all, was a chance, in the less hectic surroundings of an Embassy, to put the finishing touches to my novel based on the famous and controversial Soviet author, Konstantin Simonov. And here too was an opportunity to reflect, and perhaps even to write a book, on those turbulent last hundred days when I was responsible for the foreign policy and international relations of one of the two most powerful States on Earth.

As it turned out, those hundred days were to be the last not only for myself as Foreign Minister of the Soviet Union, but for the Soviet Union itself. The final sentence in Soviet history was to be written even before I had time to present my credentials to the British Queen. It was written in the health resort of Belovezhskaya Pusha, near Minsk, where on 8 December 1991, on the initiative of Boris Yeltsin, the three presidents of the Slav Soviet republics of Russia, Belarus and Ukraine met and decided to dismantle the Soviet Union. Their agreement was to lead on 21 December that year to the signing of the Alma-Ata Treaty that established the Commonwealth of Independent States and left Mikhail Sergeyevich Gorbachev with no Soviet Union over which to preside.

But all this still lay in the future. Neither Gorbachev in appointing Shevardnadze, nor Shevardnadze in accepting the appointment, then had the slightest inkling of what was in store for them. On the morning following the announcement of my replacement, on 20 November 1991, when I was still at my desk in the Foreign Ministry, Shevardnadze rang to say that Mikhail Sergeyevich had asked him just a few moments previously to come to the Ministry at eleven o'clock. He paused after these words, but I had already caught his drift. I told him casually that I had already heard from Mikhail Sergeyevich that he would be arriving to preside over the meeting of the Foreign Office Collegium and to effect the formal introductions and explanations to the Soviet foreign policy establishment.

At this point I should explain that the Collegium was the core of the Soviet Foreign Ministry, and has remained essentially unchanged in the new Russian State. It is a committee presided over by the Foreign Minister and consisting of the ten deputy foreign ministers and ten of the Ministry's department heads. Which of the twenty-five or so department heads are invited to a meeting of the Collegium will depend on the agenda at that particular meeting. The Collegium makes major policy decisions and discusses in policy or strategic terms all the major issues that arise in the world. During my time I had daily meetings

8

with key deputy foreign ministers and department heads. The system ran relatively smoothly, though it has to be said that in those turbulent three months we faced many disruptions from outside attempts to undermine us, and disturbing speculation on the future of our country. Some of our diplomats were already beginning to think of themselves as Russians rather than Soviets. Of course they had future careers to consider, a worry that would now be exacerbated by yet another change at the helm of their ministry.

'How do you intend to proceed?' Shevardnadze finally asked. Mentally I shrugged my shoulders. I assumed that he would arrive first, then Gorbachev, and then all three of us would go to the conference room where the Collegium was to be held.

No answer from the other end of the line. Finally Edvard Ambrosievich broke the lingering silence.

'Maybe it would be better if we meet the President downstairs at the side entrance?'

The Foreign Ministry has an entrance on the side of the yard, which is used by top officials, the Minister, his deputies and VIPs. Edvard Ambrosievich was far more experienced in these niceties than I. He had already been introduced here once before, and had gone through a formal leave-taking too. We agreed that we would meet downstairs at ten to eleven.

Shevardnadze and I arrived exactly on time as we had agreed. The President was late. This did not trouble me, since I was in no hurry, but it had been Shevardnadze's idea, and he clearly felt awkward. For twenty minutes we stood there shuffling our feet and exchanging laboured remarks, under the impervious, all-seeing eyes of the lift-operator and the militiamen on point duty.

This side entrance, like its equivalents all over Moscow, was laden with symbolism. It was the *spezpodiezd*, the gate of the mighty. This Russian term has no parallel in English, yet every ministry and government office in Moscow has its *spezpodiezd*. It is a place, and a procedure, full of meaning. Once granted access to it, an individual has attained the pinnacle of power and privilege.

Needless to say, access to the *spezpodiezd* is itself tightly controlled. One day at the Ministry, Vladimir Fedorovich Petrovsky, then my deputy and later Deputy Secretary-General at the United Nations, entered my office wearing a preoccupied expression.

'Boris Dimitrievich, there's one matter we would like you to settle straight away.' I was all attention. 'The thing is,' Petrovsky went on, 'that Andrei Vladimirovich [Kozyrev, then the Foreign Minister of Russia, which constituted one of the republics of the Soviet Union] has submitted a request to be allowed to use the entrance.'

'So, what seems to be the problem?' I asked with some surprise.

'Your ruling is required.'

The Foreign Minister of one of the world's two most powerful States had to pronounce the verdict on who might enter by the *spezpodiezd*.

Here we were, Shevardnadze and I, standing in front of the *spezpodiezd*, reformists in a new Soviet democratic order, somehow still bound by the symbols and trappings of power and privilege that became so deeply engrained upon our State during the Brezhnev 'period of stagnation'. For my part, for example, once I had been promoted to Foreign Minister it would no longer do for me to visit the tailor's workshop in the Foreign Ministry basement where formal diplomatic wear and ordinary business suits were made. Now the tailor had to visit me in my office, no matter how awkward that made me feel.

Another much-coveted perk of the Foreign Minister was his permanent buffet and bar staffed by a barmaid who was also an officer of the KGB. More dubious was the privilege of being fed by the KGB. Every day the agency's ubiquitous staff served the Minister's lunch in sealed metal lunch-pails prepared by cooks more concerned with the enemy's poisons than the Minister's palate.

At long last, Gorbachev's Zil showed up accompanied by the flashing lights and wailing sirens of the security service cars. Unlike Shevardnadze and myself, the President was abnormally

10

excited and talkative, obviously nervous. We went by lift to the seventh floor, where I proposed that we should make straight for the Collegium conference room.

'Wait, Boris Dimitrievich,' Gorbachev demurred. 'First let's go ...' He cut himself short just as he was about to say automatically 'to your office'. 'Let's go to the Minister's office.'

So in we walked. Mikhail Sergeyevich plainly needed to catch his breath and gather his thoughts. He spoke about the order of the forthcoming meeting, which he clearly was not looking forward to.

'I'll be the first to speak,' he said, 'then you' – he thrust his finger at Shevardnadze.

'Am I allowed to say anything?', I asked, rather sardonically.

'Boris Dimitrievich,' Gorbachev implored, 'don't you rub it in!' In that moment I suddenly felt a wave of enormous sympathy for this mighty leader reduced to human proportions.

Once we had trooped into the Foreign Ministry Collegium, the meeting there was quite uneventful. Gorbachev introduced Shevardnadze and expressed his gratitude towards me. He tried to be light-hearted, pointing out that he and I were born in the same year, 1931, and under the same sign, Pisces. But both audience and speakers were too aware of the momentous events rocking our country to be distracted by a jocular manner.

Shevardnadze and I then made our routine speeches, the Collegium applauded, and the handover was complete.

Arrival in London was an exciting occasion for my wife Valentina and me. We had spent nine enjoyable and eventful years living in Stockholm and Prague, but a posting to London was in a different league. Britain was still viewed as a major player on the world scene and relations between Moscow and London would be vital in my country's attempt to redefine its international role. Besides, Britain's leaders had been the earliest in the West to recognize the fundamental structural changes that were occurring in the Soviet Union in the mid-1980s, and even in the context of the old East–West confrontations Britain had subtly offered many a helping hand to the reformist elements of the Soviet leadership. As a result, Soviet policy-makers had

11

come to regard Britain as an effective conduit into Western public opinion.

Once in London one of my first tasks was to present my credentials to the Queen. Valentina and I were driven to Buckingham Palace in the usual horse and carriage, accompanied by the Marshal of the Diplomatic Corps and his customary retinue. I faced a dilemma about my style of dress, and opted for white tie and tails. Under normal circumstances I would have worn the embroidered diplomatic uniform of an Ambassador of the Union of Soviet Socialist Republics, but since that State was about to dissolve itself, there seemed no sense in wearing its diplomatic uniform. I was in the absurd position of presenting my credentials amid due pomp and ceremony on behalf of a State and a President that the host government knew were about to disappear. For a thousand miles away, in the Belarussian resort of Belovezhskaya Pusha, the relentless disintegration of the Soviet State had come to a head. The Soviet Union was to formally expire in a few weeks' time, on 30 December 1991.

As for the Queen, she took as clear and kindly an interest in what was going on back home as ten minutes of conversation allowed.

When the hour finally struck, the atmosphere in the London Embassy was subdued. As the Soviet hammer and sickle banner came down for the last time on that fateful bleak December day, not a few tears were shed – tears of no practical political significance, but flowing from a deeper source. Each individual who watched the lowering of that flag reflected on his or her own past, their childhood, adolescence, identity. For each of us this was a flag that represented more than a political idea. It stood for memories, hopes, the defeats, heroism and ultimate victory in the Second World War, and everything we had been taught for three-quarters of a century to cherish. Its lowering seemed to cut us adrift from our comfortable certainties.

While the raising of the Russian flag was of course a symbol of new hope, it also brought some immediate practical difficulties. All the diplomatic property and assets of the Soviet Union abroad, including the London Embassy sites, were acquired by Russia as part of the overall settlement with the republics where Russia assumed all the debts and treaty obligations of the former Soviet Union. Although the Soviet Embassy was staffed principally by Russians, we also had our Ukrainians, Belarussians, Armenians and others, all friends and colleagues, now turned foreigners by the stroke of a pen. Most of these non-Russians returned to their republics.

As for my own situation, Boris Nikolayevich Yeltsin, the Russian President whom I had known for a number of years, had requested me to take over in London as Russian Ambassador. This would at least provide a straightforward answer to interviewers curious to know which country I represented, and interviews now came thick and fast as the British media tried to untangle events in Russia.

It was in one of those interviews, when I was asked about my own future, that I expressed my own intentions to write a book about my experiences and sudden departure as Foreign Minister, but I could read the scepticism in the interviewer's eyes. The train had left. Who would now be interested in reading about a Foreign Minister and the circumstances of his resignation, when the President himself had gone so soon afterwards? And not only the President, but his whole country, the second superpower, vanished into thin air, like Lewis Carroll's Cheshire cat. Except that the Soviet Union left more than a lingering smile behind it. Its dissolution was a major world cataclysm whose repercussions it will take decades to evaluate. But I believed then and I still believe that the people at its epicentre have a duty to record their own impressions of its dying moments.

Still, in the face of any cataclysm, a sceptic is entitled to ask whether it is proper for an individual to focus on his own troubles and achievements, even if his personal drama is being played out before the whole world. Although a hundred days in the life of a person may count a lot for him, what do they weigh in the scale of history? But what if these hundred days are also the countdown towards the disintegration of a State – and not just any State but a colossus that for decades bestrode the world, terrifying some and inspiring others? There is bound to be a special significance in the last hundred days of the last twentieth-century empire, particularly when its death-throes coincide with the birth-pangs of a newly born creature whose adult form remains to be seen.

Expeditions now need almost a microscope to detect debris from the explosion of the Tunguska meteorite that devastated hundreds of square miles of Siberian forest in 1908. Quakes in human societies very often do not have such conspicuous immediate effects, especially in our times, when the notion of a 'Velvet Revolution' has been attached to the events in Czechoslovakia in 1990–1. The same old houses, factories, universities, towns, the same people living, working and playing there. Only the most attentive observers will delve beneath the surface and notice that although the faces may be the same, all kinds of irreversible (some would say irreparable) things have happened. And these are only the short-term effects. The roots of some events of today could be traced to a remoter past. Historians face a constant problem of changing scales of reference, changing time-frames.

Time can plod extremely slowly in a static era, but it can race if you measure it not by calendar dates but by events and happenings. The three headlong months that started with the notorious putsch launched on 19 August 1991, one week before Gorbachev's first call to me, and the Belovezhskaya Pusha meeting, two weeks after his last call, are hardly equalled in drama and tension in the history of our country. Even in terms of world history they must rank as a truly extraordinary period, a vital turning-point. And for me personally, who jumped on to this merry-go-round very much against my better judgement after nine years as an Ambassador, I hope to gain insights into those headlong days, with all their baffling twists and turns, through the effort of writing about them.

My diplomatic posts in Stockholm and Prague covered nine years from the early 1980s, and removed me from the centre of the events that came to be known as perestroika. But looking into that not so distant past, I now see that I had intimate connections – even if only as an observer – with perestroika's main actors: its hero, villains, traitors and victims. Some of my links with these actors and the clues embedded in their roles go back over several years.

Boris Nikolayevich Yeltsin I first met when perestroika was approaching its climax and he stood at the centre of lively debates and quarrels. Battle-lines were drawn between those who attempted to tame and domesticate this controversial figure and others whose goal was to batter him into submission. They tried everything to bring him to heel: Party enquiries into his 'unpatriotic' pronouncements in the United States, rumours of his mysterious bathing in the Moskva River, letters of criticism from representatives of 'the toiling masses'.

One day he came to Stockholm to take part in the launch of his book. I met him at the airport, and next day the Swedish press was filled with our pictures and columns of speculation: what could it mean that the Soviet Ambassador should go to meet a mere rank-and-file parliamentarian, especially one who was out of favour in Moscow? It may sound hard to believe, but at that time the Swedish media were more interested in the Boris on their doorstep than in a faraway Yeltsin. Was the Ambassador a long-term schemer hoping for a reward in due course, or merely a simple-minded fool who could hope for nothing more than a reprimand or a recall home?

A year later, in May 1991, I was off to meet him at another airport, this time in Prague, where I was then posted. By now he was Chairman of the Supreme Soviet of the Russian Federation and running for the Presidency of Russia with six other contenders. Only a week before he had returned from a disastrous visit to France, where he was treated mainly as a fly in Gorbachev's ointment. Here in Prague his impending arrival was also viewed as a headache for the hosts. They did sympathize with him, but could not make up their minds how to receive him. They could not afford to offend either Yeltsin, with whom they might have to reckon one day, or Gorbachev, who controlled their oil supplies.

President Havel tended towards boosting Yeltsin, whom he viewed as a dissident and therefore a man after his own heart. The Czechoslovak parliament was much more cautious about alienating Gorbachev, while its speaker, Alexander Dubcek, felt that nothing should be done to worsen the very strained relationship between the two Russians. So they turned to the Soviet Ambassador for a way out.

I for my part wanted to avoid a further deterioration of relations between the USSR and the new Czechoslovakia. After all, the protocol was clear. Yeltsin was no head of State or head of government. Gorbachev always kept an eye on what was due to his own position, and was quite capable of using an excessive breach of protocol as a pretext for cooling relations with Prague.

So together with the Czechoslovaks we suggested a course of 'tavern diplomacy' as a solution. There would be no red carpets, guards of honour and processions. Instead Havel's (and indeed the Czech people's) warmth towards Yeltsin would be demonstrated through drinking long into the night at one of Havel's favourite watering holes around town, while the press and the public looked on.

The scheme worked well. Yeltsin was pleased with his visit, protocol was preserved, and Gorbachev had no reason to take offence. In fact things worked out so well that this 'tavern diplomacy' became a feature of Yeltsin's next visit to Prague in August 1993, this time as President of independent Russia.

(I should add that I tried to introduce this 'tavern diplomacy' during Yeltsin's November 1992 visit to London, but was overruled. Yeltsin himself had expressed interest in visiting a British pub. The word 'pub' has acquired a romantic aura among Russians, calling up images of a Dickensian atmosphere with heavy oak beams and roaring fires, so it would have been quite diverting to let the President savour the real thing. But his entourage, especially Foreign Minister Andrei Vladimirovich Kozyrev, would have none of this frivolity. I had to remind Andrei Vladimirovich that on his own earlier visits to London he had been quite happy to drop into a pub or two for a drink. Pubs in Britain are after all perfectly respectable establishments. But I couldn't move him. Probably he was concerned about all those rumours circulating about the Russian leader's drinking problems.)

At the farewell ceremony for Yeltsin on that first visit to Prague, Dubcek asked me to arrange for him to have a private conversation with our guest. He had spoken Russian since his childhood and did not need an interpreter. Through the glass doors of the VIP lounge at the airport I could see the grim face of Boris Nikolayevich and Dubcek's agitated gesticulation. Eventually these two highly emotional men emerged with wet eyes.

'He promised me he would not quarrel with Gorbachev,' Dubcek whispered in my ear. 'He put his hand on mine and said that he held no grudge against him. I told him that the two of them were the guarantors of stability and democracy, and no one else.'

It struck me that this was exactly what I had been telling Dubcek about himself and Havel regarding Czechoslovakia, although in their case it was Havel who needed to be persuaded.

It will be for historians to judge whether the collapse of the Soviet Union was the result of a conflict between two stubborn, headstrong leaders, or whether this conflict was a mere by-product of a flawed and inherently unstable structure. Could a wiser, less self-obsessed leadership group have steered the Soviet ship away from Communism into a different form of union that preserved the integrity of the State, albeit a non-Communist, democratic one? Certainly on that May day in 1991, neither Dubcek nor I could dream that one day soon we would be asking ourselves whether a personal conflict between two heretics could result in the disintegration of one of the world's two mightiest States.

It was in Prague several weeks later that I saw another antagonist of Yeltsin's, but one who was truly unworthy of him. Gennadi Ivanovich Yanayev had been Vice-President of the

Soviet Union for less than a year when in late June 1991 he
came to Prague as Gorbachev's emissary to the final meeting of
the Political Consultative Committee of the Warsaw Pact.
Together with Vaclav Havel, Lech Walesa, and Zheliu Zhelev
of Bulgaria, he was to sign the act of dissolution of that ill-fated
organization. Mikhail Sergeyevich did not want to attend the
'funeral' and had sent his Vice-President. Yanayev, as the press
observed, did not applaud when others applauded and was the
only speaker at this historic wake who had anything good to say
about the deceased.

On a personal level Yanayev was quite a nice fellow, not at all
pretentious and always ready to take a shot or two of vodka, not
to mention the famous Czech beer, with the Ambassador, his
old friend from the Komsomol years. One such opportunity
presented itself when during a brief tour around Prague Castle
arranged by our hosts, I invited Yanayev and the then Soviet
Foreign Minister Alexander Bessmertnykh, who was
accompanying him, to have a beer in a bar known as 'Havel's
Tavern'. The guests were pleased to accept the invitation, and
I could only gasp in comic horror as I saw the bosses entering
the poky rooms of the tavern followed by security guards,
secretaries – about two dozen people altogether. 'No way you
can do it otherwise,' Yanayev commented, amusing himself at
my bewilderment. 'That is their duty.' If only those 'duty-
bound' people could have had a drink. But instead they just sat
or stood about and watched their high-ranking bosses blowing
the froth off their beermugs.

That night, following the tradition of hospitality, I invited
Yanayev and Bessmertnykh to my residence. This coincided
with the birthday of my grown-up daughter, who was paying
me a visit. It happened on 30 June, with less than two months
remaining before the well-known August events that made that
party even more noteworthy.

'Now, here's something for you to remember Lenochka,' a
relaxed Bessmertnykh instructed her.

'Remember this evening when the Vice-President and the
Foreign Minister of the USSR came all the way from Moscow

to help celebrate your birthday.'

I was astounded, to say the least, by the several disparaging remarks passed by Yanayev about Gorbachev. They were even more striking because it was only a few months since Gorbachev had virtually twisted the arms of the Congress of People's Deputies of the Soviet Union to force them to elect 'his best friend, the staunch Party member and a man of honour' as Vice-President. 'He isn't up to the job, nowhere near up to it,' Yanayev now kept repeating. He portrayed Gorbachev as garrulous to the point of abnormality. 'Before noon he's still capable of discussing things. In the afternoon he's hopeless, virtually incapable of listening to anybody. He just keeps talking and talking and talking.'

(When I recently heard virtually the same description of 'inadequate' applied to Yeltsin, I was equally startled. It too emanated from one of his 'close friends'.)

On that Prague occasion I tried to change the subject and told the Vice-President and the Foreign Minister about my fears of the increased activity of the intelligence services, directed within rather than outside the Soviet community. Two months later my wife and daughter had a good laugh at my expense when Yanayev landed up in the State Emergency Committee along with the heads of the KGB, the GRU and the Ministry of Internal Affairs, Vladimir Kryuchkov, Dimitri Yazov and Boris Pugo.

Yanayev and I had known each other since the mid-Sixties, when we almost simultaneously became members of the Bureau of the Central Committee of the Komsomol, the Young Communist League. He supervised the internal affairs of the Komsomol, while I was editor of the national daily *Komsomolskaya Pravda*, or *Komsomolka* as it was also known. My paper was to some extent at odds with this powerful organization. Yes, the Komsomol's own newspaper was in opposition, hard as it may be for an outside observer to imagine.

So Gennadi and I were recalling in Prague how, along with Boris Pugo, then the Komsomol Central Committee secretary for 'socialist countries', he had been dispatched to *Komsomolka*

19

to cleanse its pages of yet another heretical article by the editor, that is myself.

The fuss would usually blow up about my essays on literature. While Komsomol secretaries, and in particular First Secretary Sergei Pavlov, loved the works of such right-wing authors as Vsevolod Kochetov, Anatoly Sofronov, Anatoly Ivanov, Vladimir Firsov, Pyotr Proskurin, Georgy Markov, etc., *Komsomolka* and its editor favoured liberals like Andrei Voznesensky, Alexander Tvardovsky, Chingiz Aitmatov, Daniil Granin, Feodor Abramov and Yuri Trifonov.

Literary discussions at that time had their political undertones. Everything then had a political dimension: women's skirts and men's trousers, too long or too short, too wide or too narrow, depending on the prevailing official standard, could be viewed as politically subversive; so could long hair and beards, not to mention a crucifix worn around the neck or, God forbid, a signet ring on a man's finger.

As we were recalling this with Gennadi, we laughed and marvelled (each to himself, though) about the oddities of Soviet life: democratic reforms are underway, but a rebel of the Sixties is sidelined while orthodox figures find themselves entrenched at the heart of the process.

Boris Pugo marvelled out loud at the strangeness of life. During our youth he was a rather simpleminded fellow. (This quality of his, incidentally, may explain how he came to be among the leaders of the coup.) Two years before my move from our Stockholm Embassy to Prague, when as First Secretary of the Communist Party of Latvia he was invited to Stockholm by the orthodox local Communist Party, he paid me a visit at the Embassy. He had reminisced about earlier days, making round eyes in the clownish manner that earned him the nickname of Borya the Calf. 'I can understand why Sergei Pavlovich [Pavlov] sent to *Komsomolka* people who were responsible for ideology,' he recalled. 'But why me? I had nothing to do with that.'

Later, though, he had to do with everything. His career both during the *zastoi*, stagnation, period and in the perestroika

20

years was very impressive: Chairman of the Latvian KGB, First Secretary of the Republican Communist Party, Chairman of the CPSU Control Committee, and finally Interior Minister of the USSR. Yet much as I was surprised by these men's inexplicable rise to power during the reform years, the effect of our last meetings was such that I was amazed when I learned that it was they who headed the coup. It was so incredible that in an interview on Czechoslovak TV I called on Yanayev in all sincerity to come to his senses and correct his mistake.

Moscow's response to this unauthorized appeal was silence. Not a single word. This did not really surprise me. It was very characteristic of the way the Soviet bureaucracy responded to difficult situations – a collective reflex to keep their heads down (which is actually still apparent in Russia today). If a diplomat in a foreign posting transgressed, the reaction from Moscow was more often than not complete silence. Then suddenly they would move against you with a recall home accompanied by minders.

It also has to be said that in Moscow they had their special problems during the putsch. Soviet bureaucrats were used to obeying instructions from the Centre. When the Centre ceased to exist, or at least had its legitimacy compromised, the chickens were left headless, but rather than run in all directions, the instinct of decades was to freeze, do nothing, smoke cigarettes (maybe a bit more nervously than usual), and wait for the Centre – whatever the Centre proved to be – to reassert itself. Thus Foreign Minister Bessmertnykh's illness during the critical days of the coup was entirely true not only to character but also to tradition.

Alexander Nikolayevich Yakovlev is identified in the West as 'the architect of perestroika'. How many shades of meaning does this label now possess for people inside and outside our frontiers? (And in any case, where are 'our' frontiers now drawn?)

Oddly enough, both his and my careers got a boost with the coming of the Brezhnev epoch. In 1965, soon after the downfall of Khrushchev, Yakovlev, who was then a head of section of the

Central Committee Propaganda Department, was appointed First Deputy Chief of the Department. Some time later I became Editor-in-Chief of *Komsomolskaya Pravda*. This is only one of many indications that when Brezhnev came to power, or rather was installed there as a temporary figurehead while other Politburo members fought out the real succession, he had neither a team of his own nor clear ideas about what kind of people he needed. He was simply filling the vacancies. Later of course the unexpectedly canny new leader improved, and learnt to install his own people as skilfully as anyone before and after him. Under Brezhnev, Boris Yeltsin became First Secretary of a regional party committee.

My first meeting, or rather collision, with A.N. as I called him to myself happened because of the Spartak football team. *Komsomolka* published a critical piece on it (disrespect for supporters, patronage from big shots, that sort of thing), and felt very proud of ourselves. Yakovlev, who was a passionate Spartak fan, called me in for explanations. I insisted that facts must speak for themselves. Yakovlev had his feelings hurt, but seemed to like the stubborn editor. At any rate, when we published a controversial article casting doubt on the 'principle of the leading role of the Party in culture and the arts' (I had better remind my younger readers that this principle was one of the sacred cows of the Communist ideology) he defended us a lot more enthusiastically than he did his favourite Spartak. It was only thanks to him that I was not sacked right then.

Yakovlev got into trouble himself. Without permission from the Party leadership he printed an article in *Literaturnaya Gazeta* which, according to his more orthodox critics, 'reeked of Zionism and freemasonry'. With no one to protect him in the upper echelons where these battles were raging, he was exiled as Ambassador to Canada for nine long years.

It needs to be explained here that as well as the refuseniks who were not allowed to leave the Soviet Union there existed another category of refuseniks. These were the people who due to their high official position could not be simply discarded; often they were sent into distinguished exile abroad as ambassadors or senior diplomats. In 1982, not long before Brezhnev died, I found myself in this category. Likewise in 1973, the same year Yakovlev went to Canada, I had been removed from my editor's position and appointed Chairman of the newly created All-Union Copyright Agency (VAAP: Vsesojuznoje Agentstvo po Avtorskim Pravam).

'Get on with your new job,' growled Yakovlev in his characteristic manner as I was seeing him off to Canada at Sheremetyevo international airport. 'There's nowhere you can go in the press.'

Twice afterwards when my travels as VAAP Chairman took me to Ottawa, I went straight from the plane to see A.N. He would lock all doors and close the windows, turn on the 'noise-maker' (an anti-bugging device), a precaution not so much against Canadians as against his own staff, then unleash his tirade against Brezhnev and Moscow. Once we left his residence for a walk in a huge city park, got deep in conversation and lost our way.

Yakovlev stopped a passer-by, because it turned out that he did not remember his own address ... A.N. got on well with Pierre Trudeau, the playboy Prime Minister, but could never really adapt to alien soil.

'When Gorbachev came to Ottawa I acted just the same,' he told me once in Moscow, after his repatriation by Yuri Andropov. In spring 1985 I remembered these words, and was never surprised by his title of 'architect of perestroika' or by his rapid climb to the top.

Each time we met during my brief visits to Moscow from Stockholm, A.N. could only shake his head in surprise:

'Listen, I can't understand what the problem is. I approached him about you once ... Silence. And again ... Silence. What black cat could have run between you two?'

What could I say? Gorbachev and I attended Moscow University at about the same time, but I learnt this only from his published biography. Years ago, when he was Secretary of the Stavropol territorial Party committee, I had met his wife and daughter at a small resort where we were spending our holidays. For a month we even sat at the same dinner table in the canteen. That seemed to be my destiny during the perestroika years: each time an important vacancy emerged in Moscow, rumours would spread that 'Pankin is returning'; each time a new star rose on the political horizon he or she happened to be an acquaintance of mine.

Gennadi Burbulis and Nikolai Travkin, later respectively Secretary of State of Russia and Chairman of the Democratic Party of Russia, were rank-and-file parliamentarians when they came to Stockholm on my initiative to study the 'Swedish model'. It may well be that they developed their affinity with the market economy there. Travkin startled the people he met with caustic remarks about Gorbachev, Yegor Ligachev, Vadim Bakatin and other leaders of perestroika who according to him had lost touch with reality. Burbulis was no less radical, but his ideas were expressed in esoteric philosophic terms. 'He will go far,' some senior Soviet diplomats were saying, nodding their heads apprehensively. Later I would learn that some of them complemented their nodding with confidential reports informing Moscow about the sort of people the Ambassador was welcoming.

On my second or third month in Prague I bumped into Burbulis in the street on his way to the Aeroflot office. He said he was there privately and did not want to trouble me. At that time he was already a known 'heretic' and was siding openly with Yeltsin, although disagreeing with him on some matters. I invited him to the Embassy to speak before diplomats and the press. The diehards were still in the overwhelming majority in the Embassy. What a fuss they kicked up when the speaker made scathing remarks about a recent founding congress of the new Communist Party of Russia and its leaders. The military attaché, who was proud of being an old friend of the darling of the hard-line Communists, Colonel-General Albert Makashov, jumped to his feet when Burbulis dared to mention the name without showing proper respect. I had to remind everybody once again that we were living in the era of pluralism and glasnost.

24

I first met Yegor Gaidar when he must have been about fourteen years old. He lived in Belgrade with his father, a *Pravda* correspondent and a good friend of mine, and I stayed with them for a night on the way from Sofia to Budapest. Unusually for his age, Yegor was a keen observer of the political and economic reforms in Yugoslavia and his speech was full of fancy terminology. 'Yegor, could you use simpler language, please, so that stupid uncles can follow you,' I quipped. Many years later the First Deputy Premier of Russia told me in London that this episode had become a household joke in the family.

Yegor's grandfather was the well-known writer of children's stories, Arkady Golikov, who took the name 'Gaidar' from Siberian folklore – the word means 'a man who leads the pack'. But Yegor himself is a 'gaidar' only in name. He's an ideal committee man, a brilliant civil servant with a good mind and good ideas, but has no sense of humour, and lacks the charisma to make a leader.

Shevardnadze I first met back in 1956 in Tbilisi, when the capital of Georgia rebelled against the denunciation of Stalin at the Twentieth Communist Party Congress and Khrushchev sent tanks to quell the riots. This was the theatre of the political absurd: a nation rebels to protect the memory of a tyrant, and tanks roll out against the people for the sake of democracy! The most perverse imagination could hardly come up with such a scenario. Stalin was avenging himself from the grave, I believe. In those days Shevardnadze was the leader of the Georgian Komsomol and I was a young and promising journalist, dispatched by my editor to write stories about 'good simple Georgian folk' in the hope that this might help calm flaring passions.

My mother's father was a merchant in Orenburg, while my other grandfather was a kulak exiled from the River Volga to Vyatka in the northern Urals, so, of course, I had no kind feelings for Stalin. When I was just a boy during the Second World War I stayed with my mother and younger brother at my grandmother's house in a small hamlet, and she was the one

25

who rooted out any Stalinist sentiments I might have had. Grandma took me to a large village and showed me the burnt-out ruins where she and Grandfather once lived in a five-wall house, as they called the houses of well-to-do peasants in that area.

'This is your beloved Stalin's work,' she said, referring to my red scarf and my inclination for reciting pioneer verses. 'He has turned half our village into wasteland. Snake! Barbarian! Murderer! Just look over there.' She was pointing at more pits like the one where we were standing, overgrown with stinging-nettles and goosefoot and littered with charred planks and logs. The year was 1941, and only ten years had elapsed since the great peasant devastation termed collectivization.

Although I was shaken by the Tbilisi events of 1956, I realized already that it was not the common people who were to blame, but bankrupt politicians. Naturally, I was inclined to have a heart-to-heart talk about all those things with the Komsomol leader, but Shevardnadze skilfully sidestepped the issue and would only talk about where I should go, whom I should see and what I should write about. It was only later as I followed his zigzag career, that I realized what long-term ambitions he must already have had, that caused him to balk at being frank with some unknown sympathetic face from Moscow.

Nevertheless, when I went to say goodbye a couple of days before leaving Tbilisi he said he wanted my advice, and proceeded to explain that he had to decide whether or not to give a farewell party, or revel as they say in Georgia, to celebrate my departure. At first I thought he might be joking, but he was absolutely serious, and I recalled that after all I was in Georgia.

'All those parties with a garrulous toast-master in charge, and endless toasts,' he explained, did not appeal to him. We couldn't help recalling a joke that was doing the rounds at that time: the toast-master is toasting the guest of honour and saying what a wise, kind, generous person he is and how much good he has done for other people. When it comes to drinking

26

the toast to this paragon, the toast-maker asks him: 'What's your name, my friend?' But joking apart, Georgian tradition requires this kind of farewell party, otherwise the guest may feel offended. By now I was fed up with these performances, which had been a standing feature of my travels in Georgia and seemed alluring and romantic only at the outset. I reassured Shevardnadze that I would not feel at all offended if we said our goodbyes right there in his office over the cup of tea which had already been served, and he shook my hand with appreciation. Maybe it was exactly this moment that gave the first push to our friendship.

Even today, however, I can only guess what kind of thoughts Shevardnadze had about Stalin and the Tbilisi events: since then there have been so many U-turns in his attitude and actions. He used to say that in Georgia the sun rises sometimes in the north and sometimes in the east, and nowadays it seems it is rising in the west.

Several years later, in the Brezhnev epoch, we met once again in Tbilisi. I was the editor of *Komsomolka,* he was the Georgian Interior Minister. Shevardnadze was leading a deadly fight against the republic's Party leader, the Politburo member Vassily Mdjavanadze, who was the godfather in the system of violence and corruption that ruled in Georgia. Here I can call as a witness Teimuraz Stepanov-Mamaladze, Shevardnadze's closest friend and adviser. He was the first person invited by Edvard Ambrosievich from Tbilisi to Moscow at the end of 1985 and went with him from Moscow to Georgia in 1992. In an interview with *Ogonyek* magazine he recalled:

I was Komsomolka's own correspondent when a congress of the Georgia Komsomol was held in Tbilisi, which *Komsomolka's* editor, B.D. Pankin, attended. He began his speech with praise for the Georgia Komsomol and then turned to criticism, and then in the corridors he dared to disagree with Vassily Pavlovich Mdjavanadze about Tvardovsky's editorship of *Novymir* magazine. At once there was a vacuum around him. Emptiness. Everyone was avoiding him. And suddenly I see a grey-haired man approach him and shake his hand. It was Shevardnadze, then Interior Minister. I understood that this was not just a gesture of support, and of disagreement with pervasive servility. This was a move against the current. In circumstances where everything and everyone depended on the First Person [Mdjavanadze] this act took genuine courage.

Subsequent events showed that by then Shevardnadze had already made up his mind to challenge the satrap of Georgia. Before long, and against all the odds, he had emerged victorious in that life-and-death struggle, replacing Mdjavanadze as the First Secretary of the Georgian Communist Party's central committee, and an alternate member of the all-powerful Politburo. When I visited Tbilisi at that time I found that he had drastically changed his attitude to the famous Georgian feasting tradition. Feasts were held invariably to celebrate first nights at the Shota Rustaveli theatre, the international music symposium sponsored by the All-Union Copyright Agency which I headed at that time, as well as the republican conference of Party activists, and other public occasions. It was essential for him to show that having become 'a big shot' he had not grown arrogant, or lost contact with the people, and there was no better signal in the Georgian vocabulary to display the common touch and enlist new supporters.

Later on we often met at the Foreign Ministry on Smolenskaya Square, and one day a coded message came to Stockholm:

Boris Dimitrievich! For well known reasons the European sphere has come to the forefront of our foreign policy. Events in Eastern Europe are developing in an especially stormy and unpredictable manner. I will not conceal the fact that the standard of work provided at present by our embassies in those countries can no longer satisfy us. This is why a decision has been taken to send as Ambassadors our most experienced and qualified diplomats so that they may assist ... our country's leadership in forming and implementing policies in this important sphere. In view of this we intend to introduce a proposal to appoint you Ambassador to

28

the Czech and Slovak Republic.

Signed: E. Shevardnadze. Date: 27 February 1990.

That was the final day of President Vaclav Havel's visit to the USSR, which yielded the Declaration in which for the first time the USSR condemned the Warsaw Pact's military intervention in Czechoslovakia in 1968. It was a day when I felt the winds of history blowing in my sails.

2

After the Putsch

It all began with the telephone call that came through to the ante-room of my office in Prague on the morning of 28 August 1991. (Security regulations stipulate that ambassadors may not have long-distance telephones in their offices.) My secretary came in without waiting for permission, and said in a level tone:

'Boris Dimitrievich, a call from Mikhail Sergeyevich.'

'Which Mikhail Sergeyevich?' I asked, feeling angry because the secretary was interrupting a delicate discussion with Minister-Counsellor Alexander Lebedev.

'Mi-kha-il Ser-gey-e-vich,' the secretary repeated emphatically, overriding my tone of reprimand.

Lebedev caught on faster than I did and glanced at me intently. I rushed out of the office into a cramped booth, and picked up the special hot-line telephone.

'Pankin speaking.'

'Afternoon, Boris Dimitrievich.'

I recognized the voice at once, although in my seven years in Stockholm and over a year in Prague I had not heard it on the phone too often.

'Boris Dimitrievich,' said Gorbachev again, without waiting for my reply. 'Can you come to Moscow right now?'

'Of course I can, if you want me to,' I said, but the President could not miss the question in my tone.

'Then come today and straight to the Kremlin from the airport. You are to be appointed Foreign Minister of the USSR.'

Did I expect this proposal? Yes and no, as I will explain later. At that moment I said only:

'I'll come if you're sending for me, but I have to think over your proposal.'

'You'll have time to think on the plane,' said Gorbachev with relief, and hung up. Had he been afraid that I might refuse to come? Well, why not? At that time, on the seventh day after the defeat of the coup on 21 August, he couldn't tell what to expect from the people he was dealing with. Incidentally, he always addressed people, even those he did not know well enough, using the familiar 'you' (like *tu* in French) – an apparatchik's habit, though I never heard anyone correct him.

When I left the little booth, my forehead was running with sweat. There was no surprise in Lebedev's eyes, only questions.

'Summons to Moscow from Gorbachev. Wants to make me Foreign Minister.'

I looked around to see if there was someone else in the office. There were only the three of us. My young private secretary Igor Nikitin was never surprised at anything. At least he did not show it if he was. He was already scanning the Aeroflot timetable.

'Boris Dimitrievich, the next flight is in an hour.'

'We can delay it if necessary,' said Lebedev with unusual firmness. 'Call the car,' he said to Nikitin, and then to me:

'You have to go and pack. Will half an hour be enough?'

About an hour later, having kept the plane waiting for no more than twenty minutes, I was seated in the first class cabin of the Ilyushin 62 with a single message ringing in my ears: 'Refuse at all costs!'

31

It was the voice of my wife Valentina. When I turned up out of the blue at our home – or residence, to use the official language – she looked worried. In an ambassador's life anything could happen, and especially now, after my statement against the coup. When she learned what it was all about she started to protest, and even tried (unsuccessfully) to make me promise to refuse. In the hundred days that followed she would never change her mind.

'Well, what am I going to say to Gorbachev?'

There was only about three hours' flying time to Moscow, and then another thirty to sixty minutes from Sheremetyevo to the Kremlin.

Of course, a tide of thoughts was pouring through my mind. After all, such things don't happen too often: only an hour ago you were sitting in your office dealing with routine problems; now you are on your way to see the President who wants to make you Foreign Minister of one of the two superpowers!

As a diplomat and man of letters, or perhaps first writer then diplomat, I am used to living twice through everything that happens to me – first in reality, then on paper. It may be that my work on this book began right there in the plane, ten thousand metres high. Everything that I was to experience I looked at not only from the inside but like an outside observer too.

I began my journalistic career in the last months of Stalin's rule, as a feature writer, and I recall feeling quite envious of colleagues who wrote stories with an exciting plot, climax, and compulsorily happy ending. I was not lucky with plots. Very few optimistic stories came my way, so my features first looked like news reports and later turned into essays. Now life itself was providing a plot that any critic would call far-fetched, yet it was happening to me.

I have mentioned already that before Gorbachev's call I and Minister-Counsellor Lebedev had been dealing with a very delicate matter. It was no trivial situation that we faced that morning. On 22 August, the day after the failure of the coup, and when our statement denouncing the putsch was still in the news everywhere, I had sent an important coded message to Moscow. It drew attention to the fact that neither during the coup, when twenty diplomats expressed their readiness to sign our statement, nor later did a single one of either our 'close neighbours' (the KGB in diplomatic jargon) or our 'distant neighbours' (GRU, military intelligence) ever make public their attitude. Bearing in mind that on 19 August both of their Prague Residents sent through their own channels coded communications in the support of the coup, as someone told me confidentially, it was hard to escape the conclusion that these people were still waiting for further developments – or had received instructions to wait.

I had no intention of panicking, but I did repeat my old proposal to pack off back to Moscow a good number of these 'diplomats', especially those who in the times of Gustav Husak had been officially presented to the local secret services as KGB and GRU representatives.

Moscow was in no hurry to answer, and we wondered why. Maybe First Deputy Foreign Minister Yuli Kvitsinsky, who during the putsch had sent telegrams instructing Ambassadors to obey the State Emergency Committee (GKCP: Gosudarvenny Komitet po Cheresvchainim Polozheniyam) and now was signing recommendations on how to behave in the new situation, had not brought my telegram to the attention of the leadership. Or was it because those who like Kvitsinsky were made acting ministers after the putsch were keeping silent because their own behaviour was not impeccable?

On the evening of the day before Gorbachev's call, both chief 'neighbours' asked for an appointment within half an hour of one another. I received them with approximately the same interval. Each of them brought the written reaction of his Moscow bosses to my messages. In one case the reply was signed by Leonid Shebarshin, who for several days was acting Chairman of the KGB, in the other by the newly appointed Chief of the Soviet General Staff and Deputy Defence Minister, General Vladimir Lobov. Through 'their channels', that is through the people I had written about, they were letting me know that there was no need to worry, their officers in Prague were good experienced people, and if I thought there were too many of them – well, really this depended on one's point of view, and they were hardly more numerous than the CIA and Pentagon agents.

I let them go and sat back as if struck by lightning. The content of the messages was bad enough, but even worse was the fact that they were relayed through 'their' channels. This meant that Shebarshin and Lobov were offering me up, making me a hostage to their people in case something else happened. The most sacred rule of diplomatic service, the confidentiality of Ambassadors' correspondence with the Centre, had been broken, and by the very people who were responsible for its protection. What should I do next? Should I write to Gorbachev? To Yeltsin? But how could I be sure that my messages would reach them?

This was the puzzle that I was trying to solve with Lebedev when Gorbachev called. 'Now at least we won't have to write to anyone,' said Lebedev as he was seeing me off to Moscow. 'Just don't forget to tell everything to "Himself".'

These were the issues on my mind as I was flying to Moscow and declining the stewardesses' hospitality: 'Cognac? Vodka? Some wine? Beer?'

The young women of Aeroflot are always very attentive to their first class passengers, especially if one of them is an Ambassador to the country they regularly fly to, but this time I thought they were even more polite. Could they have learned where and why I was going?

Of course, I had no doubt that the immediate motive behind the Gorbachev proposal was the statement issued by myself and Sasha Lebedev at midnight on the night of 20–21 August.

I rehearsed that sequence of events in my mind. When everything was done, that is when the text composed by the three of us – Sasha, my wife and myself – had been written down in my terrible handwriting and dictated over the phone to my old friend, the 'Prague Spring' hero Miroslav Jelinek, who in his turn relayed it to a reliable person from the Czechoslovak news agency CTK, when we had answered all inquiries from this agency about the authenticity of the text, and whether we realized its consequences, when after that we returned to the TV set and saw Shevardnadze in Moscow coming through the crowd to the Russian White House, the time was displayed on the screen: 1.30 am.

Sasha sat down to translate our statement into English in case Western correspondents wanted a copy. He did it in longhand, since I had no Roman alphabet typewriter at home.

Sky News and CNN (we could receive both channels) were broadcasting live from Moscow, with tanks rolling down the Sadovoye ring to the White House. A terrible scene is still vivid in my eyes: two or three human figures climbed on to the armour of a tank, then like toy soldiers slipped down. The tank turned around with a screeching noise. 'Kids! They're killing kids!' my wife cried out through tears.

For some time nothing was clear in the smoke and dust, through the uproar coming from the screen. Then a reporter's voice said that the storming of the Russian government headquarters surrounded by a human chain had reportedly been called off. We could not believe our ears, but soon we saw tanks stopping and then turning back.

By that time, around three o'clock in the morning, Sasha's wife Dodo had joined us. She is an ethnic Georgian, and we used to joke sadly that she was an émigrée. Now it looked as if we too might be forced against our will to become émigrés, this time not only from Georgia but from all our vast country. Glad to see Dodo, I poured whisky for us all and proposed our favourite toast: 'To the success of our hopeless mission.'

As I flew to Moscow the events that had followed after that night were playing fast-forward through my mind.

We didn't get much sleep that night. Waking at six in the morning I turned on the radio and heard our names. It was not clear what was happening in Moscow. The tanks had retreated, but not pulled out. What would come next? The opposing sides seemed to be gathering their forces for a final showdown.

I looked out of the window. A policeman guarding the

residence was talking to two men in plain clothes. Why so early? Who could they be? Had the Czechoslovak authorities sent them to brief the guard? Were the 'neighbours' keeping an eye on us, or maybe the local ex-secret servicemen? The press had been making allegations that former officers of the secret service (STB) abolished by the new authorities continued to maintain contacts with the KGB agents at the Embassy. Once I was even called in to the Czechoslovak Foreign Ministry for explanations. And yesterday there had been press reports that former STB men were prowling around the Soviet Embassy compound. After my meeting on 19 August with Czechoslovak Deputy Prime Minister Pavel Ryhetsky, Lebedev and I had not minced our words in characterizing the putsch leaders. Next day someone in the Foreign Ministry whispered to Lebedev that a British diplomat in Prague had been asking what the Prague authorities would do if high-ranking Soviet representatives were to request political asylum. This enquiry was not made on my behalf. Valentina and I had not requested this enquiry, but we had discussed what we might do if the coup succeeded, including the possibility of seeking asylum.

What used to be the Soviet Ambassador's residence in Prague is an early twentieth-century three-storey mansion situated some way from the Embassy's main buildings, with high ceilings, balconies, terraces, lacquered dark wooden wall panelling, and parquet that creaks cosily when you walk. Everything looked special early that August morning, but as I prepared to leave for the Embassy I could not help thinking that it might be the last time I passed through these sunny rooms and halls. My wife, who got up with me although she spent the rest of the night in the room of our four-year-old granddaughter, was shaking with nerves. She begged me to take care and promised that she would not leave Alyona alone for a second and would let nobody into the house without my express permission – with the exception of Sasha and Dodo, of course. I asked her not to worry, but I myself had no idea what was going to happen next. Strange ideas were passing through my mind. What if my car didn't come? Or the gates of the Embassy

36

did not open for me? Or the lift got stuck between floors?

Fortunately, nothing of the kind had happened that morning, but a week later, in the comfort of the plane, I was thinking that all these had been possibilities. With nine years' experience as an Ambassador it was only during these days and hours that I realized for the first time how far I and anyone else in my position was dependent on the so-called 'services', and first of all the KGB. They made up a good third of diplomats, and then you must add the GRU. They were radio and telephone operators, and guards. The so-called 'security officer' was one of them. He and not the Ambassador was Tsar and God for technical personnel, as their future careers depended on what he reported through his mysterious channels. Electricity, heating, lifts, telephones, all communications, in other words every support system, were in their hands. Of course, you were aware of this in normal times, but during those critical days I felt the knowledge deep in my being.

But on that morning of 21 August, it was not only troubles that greeted me. Around eight o'clock, before I left for the Embassy, the telephone rang: it was one of the younger diplomats.

'Boris Dimitrievich, I apologize for calling so early. This is the first time I've phoned the Ambassador at home, but I can't wait. Thank you for your and Lebedev's statement, thank you for taking this burden off my soul. I am with you.'

Three minutes later comes another call. A second diplomat, similar words, enthusiastic speech. Then another call, but this time no words: silence. Frightened or sinister? Not even the sound of breathing could be heard.

The Embassy gates opened as usual. Behind them, in a doorway of the main building, Lebedev was waiting. We went to my room, followed by two or three people that we knew we could rely on.

Eight o'clock. Our traditional morning get-together, with more people jammed in than usual. As Lebedev and I had agreed, I read out our short statement and explained why we had acted as we had. I chose very cautious words and did not even invite anyone to join us. Everyone has to make their own decision. Sasha was less reserved. Only recently he had worked at the Central Committee, and met with many of the putschists almost daily: 'Crocodile' Gena Yanayev, Pugo 'the Silent', 'Office Mouse' Valery Ivanovich Boldin, for years a confidant and friend of Gorbachev. Sasha portrayed a sinister group of conspirators as a crowd of good-for-nothings and imbeciles. One after another diplomats stood up to speak out in our support. About twenty people! 'Is this the old reflexes working?', I wondered for a second. 'Aren't they simply trying to please the Ambassador, the one boss who is near them?' But no, it couldn't be that simple. No one from the 'neighbours' said a word. Perhaps it was the same tradition at work. Their chiefs were not in this room, they were in Moscow, and the residents were stubbornly keeping silent. They sat beside me and stared blankly at the wall.

My assistant whispered in my ear: the switchboard was jammed with calls. Calls from the Czechoslovak Foreign Ministry, the President's residence, the government and, most important, from the press – both local and international.

The meeting ended. In our reception hall a Prague TV crew was ready and waiting. They asked me to read out the statement to the camera, and I read:

'Mr Boris Pankin, Soviet Ambassador to the Czech and Slovak Federal Republic, and Mr Alexander Lebedev, minister-envoy of the USSR Embassy in Prague, make the following statement.

'We raise our protest against the barbarous and illegal actions of the forces acting on behalf of the State Emergency Committee against the civil population and legitimate authorities of the USSR and Russia.

'Those who have pledged to save the country from civil war are now in fact plunging our people into it.

'Ambassador and envoy continue to consider themselves as representatives of the legitimate national leadership headed by President Gorbachev.

'We stand by the hope that reason and common sense will

prevail, and that through the common effort our great country will be removed from the brink of an abyss. Our statement is aimed at achieving this purpose.'

Questions followed: What made you speak out? What do you think about your future? How will the coup turn out? I refused to make predictions but expressed the hope that the putschists would display common sense and surrender to the law in the end. I addressed Yanayev directly. He had been in Prague as Vice-President quite recently, and his signature was on the act of dissolution of the Warsaw Pact, that creature of the Cold War. Trying to sound persuasive, I suggested that his participation in the GKCP might be a mistake – a serious one, but just a mistake – and it was not too late to correct it before much blood was shed.

But what was the news from Moscow? This was the first time in three hours that I could ask myself that question. Not a word came from the Embassy's channels of communication with Moscow. The telephones of my children at home did not answer. Later I would learn that my daughter Alyona was with her husband in the editorial offices of Vitali Tretyakov's banned *Nezavissimaya Gazeta*, and my son Alexei at the barricades at the White House. Radio, the BBC World Service, was my last hope.

The news coming in was contradictory and confusing. I learned that the grim scene we had seen the night before had had a terrible ending: several people were crushed by tanks. There was conflicting information on the number of victims. Many casualties, some of them serious.

An extraordinary session of the Russian Parliament had opened, but Pugo was sending messages to the troops of the Interior Ministry ordering them to obey the Emergency Committee. A report came in that a journalist from the Czech newspaper *Studentski Listy* had been wounded. Once again this newspaper was on the front line, just as it had been in August 1968.

Kryuchkov's proposal to fly with Yeltsin to see Gorbachev at his holiday villa at Cape Foros on the Black Sea was made public in Parliament. The session decided that the Russian Prime Minister Ivan Stepanovich Silayev should go. Then I learned that his plane had taken off along with Alexander Rutskoi, Vadim Bakatin, a group of medical doctors (to examine Gorbachev?) and an American TV crew. Soon came the news that some time earlier the Emergency Committee had dispatched two planes to Foros.

The Munich-based Radio Liberty quoted a broadcast by Estonian radio of a statement from the military garrison commander of Tallinn saying: 'The military units are obeying the orders of their command and through it of the GKCP, which was behaving quite democratically, publishing decrees and, unlike the Russian leadership, not calling for violent measures.

What about the situation here in Prague? My secretary informed me about a telephone call from the police saying that a bomb had been planted in one of the Embassy's buildings and requesting permission to search the whole Embassy compound using sniffer dogs. When I asked him to check the source of the call, and find out whether the Foreign Ministry knew about it, it turned out that neither the police nor the Foreign Ministry had heard about the bomb. In the meantime we were informed officially that the Prague authorities had doubled the security on my residence and Lebedev's house. At this point I called home and tried to cheer up my wife: I told her that everything was going fine but she should still keep a close eye on our granddaughter. She said that she was keeping her almost under house arrest, and reading her non-stop fairy tales.

Lebedev complained that the consul (one of 'them'), citing instructions received through 'their' channels, was refusing to issue a visa to a Western official who was going to Moscow as an independent observer. I summoned the consul and pounded my fist on the table: 'Aren't these the same instructions that caused you yesterday to try to remove the portrait of Gorbachev from the lobby? And what kind of channels are you talking about? Only one channel exists for you: your Ambassador's orders.' The consular clerk promised that the visa would be ready in thirty minutes. Lebedev grinned: the consul was a different man today. Yesterday after the incident with the portrait he had looked like an angry wolf. Today, almost a lamb. For how long, though?

The radio brought news that communication with Gorbachev had been restored and Yeltsin had spoken to him on the phone. Later in the day came a new report: Gorbachev was on his way to Moscow.

And now in the plane the stewardess announced: 'Please fasten your seatbelts and refrain from smoking.' My time for deliberations was running out. Soon I would be walking through the VIP lounge and boarding the car. After that, the Kremlin, Gorbachev. Unless something had changed while I was flying ... But what was I going to say?

A clerk from the Foreign Ministry Ambassadors' service who was waiting for me at the airport had no idea that I was going to the Kremlin. Deputy Minister Vladimir Petrovsky, whom I called from the VIP lounge, greeted me fulsomely – 'You can't imagine how your statement was received. I was in Paris at the time.' But when I asked him to arrange a pass to the Kremlin he floundered. OK, if he didn't know anything then better not explain on the phone.

On the way, the clerk kept asking whether he should wait for me in the Kremlin or send a car to pick me up when I phoned. I didn't mind which, but was grateful for his stream of words. It distracted me from my thoughts. Meanwhile the first contacts with home realities were dissipating a rosy mist in my head, and I was turning from the green outsider back into the regular Muscovite I had been all my life before leaving for Stockholm in 1982.

The Kremlin. As was to be expected, our old Volga was stopped first at the Borovitsky Gate, where the guard suspiciously compared the dirty numberplates with what he had on his list, then on the turn into Ivanovskaya Square, and then at the 'porch' itself, the special entrance. At the entrance they also held me up for some time trying to find out who I was and where I was going. Although I felt irritated, I also nursed a secret hope that they would turn me back, but no, each time I was eventually passed on to the next checkpoint. I had gathered on the way that Gorbachev was in the Supreme Soviet, and at last I found myself in the reception room of Anatoly Sergeyevich Chernyaev – Tolya Chernyaev, Gorbachev's aide for many years and my good friend from the Brezhnev days. He was with Gorbachev in Foros, and Mikhail Sergeyevich called him 'my brother'.

Tolya's secretary went to report my arrival and came straight back to invite me into the room where Tolya was sitting in the corner watching TV. 'Hello, sit down,' he muttered, and shook my hand, as if we had last parted only a couple of hours ago.

The screen was relaying a direct broadcast from the Supreme Soviet, where Gorbachev was standing on the rostrum answering questions and comments from the people's deputies.

What we watched on the screen for an hour or two was a very strange show indeed. 'He'll finish there, then come back and receive you,' said Chernyaev in the middle of the battle. So the decisive conversation was postponed again, but my adaptation to Kremlin realities came fast.

Of course, I had been here before and met with the mighty of this world – in the Khrushchev era, under Brezhnev, during Chernenko's short term in power, and of course under Gorbachev, although I have to admit that I had never succeeded in advancing beyond his ante-room or Chernyaev's office. This has to be mentioned in order to explain to the reader the intensity of my emotions.

I do not recall in detail what was happening on the screen, in that session of the Supreme Soviet. In form it looked like a question time but in substance it was a public humiliation of the President. The people who had shown neither the courage nor the desire to speak out against the coup were now enjoying themselves. Some were trying to portray the man on the rostrum as the main instigator of the putsch. Yet Gorbachev was reacting to even the most unscrupulous attacks in a very calm and dignified manner. Chernyaev observed this ugly performance imperturbably and only chuckled at my indignant remarks. With every moment I was seeing ever more clearly how much things had changed here.

I remember the first time I saw Gorbachev in his new role of General Secretary of 'our Party', as the apparatchiks liked to say. It was shortly after his appointment in March 1985, at a meeting in a giant conference hall at the Soviet Foreign Ministry, where Gorbachev himself came to meet the Ministry staff and Soviet Ambassadors at the initiative of Shevardnadze, who was only just beginning his term there.

'Gorbachev Himself': the phrase had overtones of unchecked power – a king, a tsar, 'Stalin Himself', 'Brezhnev Himself'. I wondered how long that aura would cling to the leader who proclaimed a new course based on breaking away from the worst traditions of the past. I felt uneasy when I entered the conference hall, with all its doors controlled by security guards, and saw how just as in the good old days the audience gave him a standing ovation when he entered, or rather was solemnly ushered into the hall. And my depression deepened when Shevardnadze, supposedly a reforming new broom, began to intone from a prepared text about the great honour it was for all of us that for the first time in history the General Secretary of the Central Committee of our Party had come to the Ministry of Foreign Affairs. Only Gorbachev's response that his visit was hardly a historic event and there was no need to exaggerate its significance cheered me up.

To his credit, Shevardnadze replied with a smile that he would in future take note of the General Secretary's remark, but this time he would stick to what had been written for him. The audience livened up, there was some laughter, and all subsequent praise for Gorbachev sounded like a skit on past rituals. For me it was the first, but by no means the last occasion to marvel at the precarious blend of orthodoxy and innovation that would colour life in Moscow – and not only in Moscow – for the next six years.

I remember how during one visit to Moscow I was supposed to go early in the morning to Staraya Square (the CPSU Central

Committee headquarters) to see Alexander Nikolayevich Yakovlev. At that time he was at the height of his popularity as one of the architects of perestroika, with his prestige further enhanced by membership of the 'all-powerful Politburo', as Western journalists liked to call that body. I had some time to kill before the appointment and was strolling down Kuibysheva Street. Cavalcades of black Zils were flocking up and down the street, which was closed for regular traffic, between the Kremlin and Staraya Square. In one of them I thought I saw Yakovlev's face, so when we met I asked him half-seriously, half-jokingly, how long this outrage with the Zils was going to continue. He resented my tone, frowned, and said that he had 'raised this issue' with the General Secretary but KGB Chairman Kryuchkov had insisted on the (armoured) Zils and on the accompanying cars (assassinations were possible). 'He even cited examples, with shots fired,' grumbled Yakovlev, looking me straight in the eye, and I couldn't tell whether he was serious or joking. 'So that's how confident Kryuchkov and his KGB feel here,' I thought. 'And I wanted to complain that they're making my life impossible in Stockholm!'

Lost in reminiscences, I did not notice how the rowdy parliamentary debate had been replaced on the screen by a summer landscape.

'Let's go,' said Chernyaev and reached for his jacket. 'He'll be here in five minutes. He knows you're here.'

Our stroll along the Kremlin corridors was quite long, from one corner of a giant triangle to another, formerly the headquarters of the Council of Ministers of the USSR, only recently replaced by Valentin Pavlov's Cabinet of Ministers, now also deceased. Earlier still, this had been the Soviet of People's Commissars, and before that His Majesty's Senate. And the people changed here more often than the names. Eighteen years ago, in 1973, this was where Alexei Kosygin confirmed my appointment as Chairman of the All-Union Copyright Agency. Later, as Ambassador to Czechoslovakia and Sweden, I used to visit Nikolai Ryzhkov here. I remember hanging about in ante-rooms in the company of Pavlov,

Katushev, and Maslyukov – bosses of the past ... Former, past, ex- ... Now I was walking along this endless corridor of ghosts to meet my unclear future.

'So, what have you decided?' asked Chernyaev, brusque as usual. I startled to mumble about having told Gorbachev that I had to think.

'This I know,' Chernyaev interrupted. 'And what have you decided? What are you going to say?'

I tried another tack:

'First I have to find out how this idea occurred to him. I understand that the impetus came from our statement in Prague last week, but it can't be that alone. Who recommended me? You know that all these years he's kept me at arm's length. I wasn't received on even the most urgent matters.'

'No one recommended you,' said Chernyaev bluntly. 'This is his own idea. He sent for Yakovlev and me, said let's appoint Pankin, then started to recite your biography in detail. How you came to his home town of Stavropol, how you were often attacked for your *Komsomolskaya Pravda* articles and your campaign to preserve Lake Baikal, and how you were exiled to the VAAP – these are his own words I'm quoting.' Listening to all this, I thought to myself, that's all very well, but what was Mikhail Sergeyevich thinking of before, if he knew so much about me?

Perhaps that was the longest statement that I had heard from my old friend Tolya Chernyaev in all the years we had known each other. By the time he had finished we were already sitting in a corner of a big room swarming with people, Gorbachev's reception room.

'That's what I'm going to ask him about,' I exclaimed, inspired by the unusual eloquence of my companion.

'No!' came Chernyaev's sharp retort. 'What for? That's all past. Now he believes in you, he trusts you. He may not even understand what you're talking about.'

Silence fell. I had a feeling that I was skirting an enigma in Gorbachev's nature that only close friends could comprehend.

My last conversation so far with Chernyaev, this time about

my resignation as Foreign Minister, would take place less than three months later. It turned out that the President's closest aide and 'sworn brother' learnt about it only at the very last moment. Tolya would have felt all the more uncomfortable because literally a week before he had come to see me in the Foreign Ministry ('Chernyaev in the Foreign Ministry?' the old hands there would remark. 'Such things did not happen even when Shevardnadze was in office') and reported his view that the new Foreign Minister was making a good impression on everyone and had become a 'harmonizing personality' in such a strained and disuniting time.

I had my meeting with Chernyaev two days before leaving for London, at a time when I did not feel like mulling over these matters. Since then there have been plenty of opportunities to think about the reasoning behind Gorbachev's decision, which he withheld from his closest colleague until the very last moment, as Chernyaev reports in his book, *Seven Years with Gorbachev*.

There has been quite a lot of evidence to indicate how confused the President felt, and how much his decision weighed on him. Gorbachev met my daughter at one of the 'launches' nowadays in vogue in Moscow, and gave her a long and rambling explanation of the reasons why 'it all turned out exactly that way'. His most telling remark was: 'Well, you see, I've been through it all too, you know.' (This was after the disintegration of the Soviet Union.)

A year later, when he visited London at the invitation of several universities, the former President said roughly the same things. 'Boris Dimitrievich, don't reopen old sores,' he kept on repeating. Of course, the issue was not my own modest personality but rather the confusion in the soul of the person who initiated and carried through perestroika, his state of mind after the August putsch when the very men he relied upon most turned against him. That lesson did him no good. Having sacked the Foreign Minister who had been the sole Ambassador to back him as the legitimate President, he turned to a man who had already renounced him once. I am still wondering whether he did it of this own free will. And Shevardnadze too seemed to have lost his flair. How else to explain his accepting the position of Soviet Foreign Minister just when the Soviet Union had barely two weeks to live? I had not even presented my credentials to Her Majesty the Queen in Buckingham Palace when the bolt came from Belovezhskaya Pusha.

But I am running ahead of my story. These events lay more than three months into the future as I waited to see the Soviet President who was proposing to appoint me Foreign Minister of one of the world's two superpowers.

While I chatted with Chernyaev he simultaneously kept up brief exchanges with Gorbachev's secretary and one of his bodyguards. They in turn were keeping track of their boss's every move on his way from the main hall of the Supreme Soviet to his office. 'He's left the hall ... Stopped in the foyer to talk to some deputies ... He's in the street now ... Speaking to reporters, Western it seems ... If he comes by car he'll be here in five minutes ... if he decides to walk it'll take longer ...'

'Yeltsin supported you,' Chernyaev suddenly informed me.

'I see. I know him from Prague. He came there on his first official visit after that poor reception in Strasbourg and Paris.'

'So I hear. "I know Pankin from Prague," he said, "and I support him."'

'And what about Shevardnadze? I've been sending telegrams from Prague, and saying publicly that Shevardnadze has to be reappointed.'

'Yakovlev and I told him he'd better talk to Shevardnadze before seeing you. They must have spoken by now ...'

And at the very same moment the news presenter Tatyana Mitkova appeared on the screen and announced: 'According to reliable sources President Gorbachev has spoken on the phone today with Edvard Ambrosievich Shevardnadze. There is speculation that he invited him to return as Foreign Minister.'

Tolya and I exchanged glances.

'Didn't I tell you that he was going to speak to him?'

A sudden rise in the buzz of conversation and the changed behaviour of everyone in the room told us that Gorbachev was in his office. Now he would call me in. What was I going to say?

But it wasn't yet my turn. Alexander Yakovlev appeared in the ante-room, nodded a greeting and said Hello as if we'd last met yesterday. Actually we hadn't seen each other for three months, since he had attended a conference in Prague organized by Vaclav Havel and François Mitterrand. That was now an epoch away.

'See you later,' he added, and vanished through the doorway.

I was not shocked by his abruptness. I realized long ago that people at the top (the section of the former Senate building where Gorbachev's office was located was known in Kremlin jargon as 'The Top') live in a very special psychological climate, breathe in special high-altitude air, see everything in a special light, and behave in a style quite foreign to the uninitiated. Till then my various careers had put me on the fringes of that world. Now I was to see it at first hand, and at a time when its yawning contradictions were at their height, as generations of Soviet orthodoxy strove both to accommodate change and to protect old habits and old privileges.

It is well known that some myths are created not by heroes but by their followers. A whole tribe of secretaries, advisers, assistants and bodyguards of the leadership of the USSR did their utmost to preserve the environment of Brezhnev's time, to give the impression that the machine still ran smoothly. Nor did the Party's demise or Gorbachev's eventual defeat put an end to the pattern. When Gorbachev resigned, many of his people, including the Chief of Protocol, transferred to Yeltsin and took their status system with them: escorts of black stretch limousines, pyramids of phones, the channels of communication to the President of Russia so littered with obstacles that even the Russian Ambassador to a country as important as Great Britain often failed to get through. The logic is simple: if the chief is God Almighty, then his entourage must at least be angels. Nor were the upper echelons immune to the temptations they had criticized so harshly while in opposition. Gennadi Burbulis, for example, collected a set of high offices that included Russian Secretary of State and Secretary of the Council for State

Security. He loved the shiny Zils that drove him both on official and on private visits, insisting in answer to attacks in the press that he needed a limousine only because it contained a telephone and radio.

In general, those who live and work at 'the top' are common people whose State position no doubt requires the various attributes that help them attend to their duties, and as long as they see them in that light there can be no reasonable objection. It is when these attributes become ends in themselves that things start to go wrong. While I was Soviet Ambassador in Stockholm, the Swedish Prime Minister Olof Palme was assassinated. When Nikolai Ryzhkov, the first Prime Minister of the perestroika era, came to attend his funeral he was preceded by a cargo plane that carried two armour-plated Zils, as if two Prime Ministers could be murdered in two weeks in a city as peaceful as Stockholm. It was status that the Zils proclaimed, not security. A year later Ryzhkov made another visit. This time, no Zils. The democratic Swedish capital saw it as a sign of liberalism. Gorbachev clung to such emblems till the very end, and the present President of Russia outdoes them all: Zil cavalcades accompany him and his lavish lifestyle all over the world.

The door to the President's office swung open again. Inside, behind the desk, I saw Gorbachev, looking very like the sculpted waxwork figure then on display in Madame Tussaud's museum in London. In one of the two standard office armchairs near the desk sat Yakovlev. Him I never could perceive as a sculpture. The statue at the desk rose from its seat and turned into a man of flesh and blood. Gorbachev offered me a chair.

'Well, have you decided?' And without waiting for me to say a word he continued: 'Here I have two draft decrees.' From a half-open drawer of his desk he produced a small folder with two sheets of paper inside. 'Now I sign the first one' – he added his signature – 'and you are unemployed.' He read out cheerfully: 'Comrade Pankin B.D. is relieved of his responsibilities as Ambassador Extraordinary and Plenipotentiary to the Czech and Slovak Federal Republic ...'

Yakovlev giggled in his armchair.

'Oh, so that's why you invited me,' I said in the same joking manner. 'Maybe from here it's exile to Siberia?'

Gorbachev raised his head and smiled.

'Don't worry,' he said. 'This decree we'll put in here.' He took the signed document and replaced it in the drawer. 'Let it stay there until the Supreme Soviet ratifies this one ...' He took the second sheet, signed it, raised it close to his eyes and read out loud: 'Comrade Pankin B.D. is appointed Minister for Foreign Affairs of the USSR. This Decree is introduced for confirmation by the Supreme Soviet of the USSR.'

I looked helplessly at Yakovlev, who relaxed in his chair: 'But I haven't even ...'

'You can handle the job,' Yakovlev murmured approvingly, as if responding to my silent question. 'But mind you, they may not confirm your nomination. You know the situation.'

'Oh, they will, they will! Let them try not to,' Gorbachev growled. He looked to his left, scanned a wide panel with an array of fluorescent buttons, pushed one and said: 'Grigory Ivanovich, come in.'

We were joined in a minute by Grigory Ivanovich Revenko, the new Chief of the President's Staff, who had replaced the arrested Boldin.

'For registration.' Gorbachev handed him the second decree. Grigory Ivanovich took the paper and headed for the door, winking at me as to an old acquaintance. It turned out later that he was one. 'And publish it today,' shouted Gorbachev to his retreating back.

Revenko looked at his watch. 'In an hour it will be announced in the "Vremya" news programme.'

Gorbachev fixed his brown eyes on me: 'So you see how we do things here.'

And for the second time in the last couple of hours I had a sense of coming close to the elusive nature of this man who even in the seventh year of perestroika and on the seventh day after the coup remained a riddle to the whole world.

I thought that now we would sit at our ease with the President and discuss what he expected of me following this surprise appointment made without a chance to decline it. But not at all! The door opened once again to admit another Gorbachev aide who handed the President a sheet of paper with several lines of typing. It was a list of names, and I noticed Yakovlev's and Shevardnadze's among them.

Gorbachev pored over the paper and seemed to forget about everything. At least he forgot about me. He leaned closer to Yakovlev, crossed out one name, inserted a new one.

People were coming and going. I knew some of them. The list of names was shuttled in and out, and from a casual remark by Yakovlev I gathered that they were working on the makeup of the new Presidential Security Council. Next day it had to be submitted for approval by the Supreme Soviet.

At last in one of the pauses Gorbachev addressed me. 'Boris Dimitrievich, go and relax for a while until we're through. Ask Anatoly Sergeyevich to offer you a cup of tea. I know you are old friends.' He grinned happily, as if enjoying demonstrating that he knew all about me. 'I'll set myself free and we'll talk, just the two of us,' and he stared emphatically at Yakovlev.

I went out into the ante-room, where the TV set was on day and night. A clock was displayed on the screen, its short hand pointing to nine, the long one with only a tick to go to twelve. Then it was the 'Vremya' news programme, anchored by Tatyana Mitkova.

'An urgent and unexpected announcement,' she said. 'We have just received notification of the President's Decree. Despite many predictions and expectations, instead of Edvard Shevardnadze it is Boris Pankin who has been appointed Foreign Minister of the USSR. Until today he was Ambassador to Czechoslovakia, and distinguished himself with a *heroic* [she emphasized the word] pronouncement against the putschists.'

That was how Presidential Decrees were announced. I had never paid heed to it before, but it sounded nothing like the style used by announcers such as Igor Kirillov or other members of the old school, who used to recite these documents

51

word for word in their solemn baritones and then finish with: 'Moscow, the Kremlin,' and give the date.

This will make the world sit up, was my second thought. And, to be honest, when it struck me that my modest name would become instantly famous for the second time in the last ten days I did feel something like satisfaction. If it had to happen it was better that it happened like this: out of the blue, as if in a fairy tale.

The sensation of something improbable suddenly materializing stayed with me, and my head was spinning as I stood in the middle of Gorbachev's reception room and fielded good wishes. It cost me some effort to grasp that Yevgeni Primakov, noisy and warm in his congratulations, was already hinting that he wouldn't mind being posted as Ambassador to an English-speaking country – 'Not to the Middle East, I've had enough of that. Preferably to the UK. You'll have to replace Zamyatin anyway, he disgraced himself with his support for the coup.'

Thus the poetic moment was punctured by the prose of life.

Of course, I could not even pretend that I was capable of talking business right then. The door to Gorbachev's room was opening and closing. In a booth next door to the reception room I spotted a row of telephones and made a call home, where my son and daughter with their families were waiting for me. Yes, they'd seen it on TV. Their voices sounded happy and nervous. A new life was beginning for them too.

At last the reception was over. 'Only Yakovlev is in there,' the secretary told me, and then he too came out, and told me as he passed by that the President has authorized him to present me to the Collegium of the Foreign Ministry. 'We'll be in touch.'

What is his official position now? I wondered, but had no time to ask as I was summoned by Gorbachev.

Swiftly he rose from behind the desk, walked towards me and put his arm across my shoulder as if to take me for a stroll around his spacious office. Now he was saying something that I felt was important for him, and I too said a few words. I had had time to marshal some ideas, and was happy to find that they corresponded with what Gorbachev was saying.

'The world community came to our rescue, but it wants to know what kind of country we are today. America: Bush was the first to get through to Foros, he expressed solidarity with me, with Raisa Maximovna. John Major: we'll be receiving him soon in Moscow. He's the first of the G-7 leaders to come here after the putsch. Chairman of G-7. Talk to Primakov, he has good contacts with the Saudis. Their King is a strong supporter of our democracy. We must change priorities, get rid of prejudices. Yasser Arafat, Gaddafi – they call themselves our friends, but only because they dream of our returning to the past. Enough double standards.'

Inspired by his words, I steered the conversation towards my closer concerns: Eastern and Central Europe, Czechoslovakia. 'We untied their hands,' I told him, 'and we didn't interfere with their "Velvet Revolutions", but then it looked as if we started to regret it. We're behaving as if we want to punish them for something. Havel and Walesa had been asking to meet with you for some time.' (Hold it! This was a reproach to the President. But never mind. Even if I had agreed to become Foreign Minister, I wasn't going to change my convictions.) 'Kvitsinsky calls the new Eastern Europe a provincial hole, a parody of serious geopolitics. He talks to Ministers as if they were clerks ...'

'And what kind of telegrams did he send?' Gorbachev broke in. '"Do what the Emergency Committee tells you?" Yes, I heard about that. And Bessmertnykh wasn't at his best. Now he's trying to justify himself, giving interviews, asking to see me ...'

I begin to understand that Gorbachev is more inclined to talk about personalities than ideas.

'Many things have to change in the Foreign Ministry, many ... They just lay low and did as they were told. Nearly all our Ambassadors accepted the putsch. All this needs looking into. I'm getting signals that foreign leaders don't want to deal with such Ambassadors. In France, in Yugoslavia. But careful, we don't need any more purges. No unnecessary victims. The ones who really supported the coup, they have to be removed.'

We talked this way at some length, circling around his spacious office, at times almost embracing, then taking distance, then bumping into each other. Two fireballs in a closed space.

Before I left he showed me a telephone marked 'Minister for Foreign Affairs'. 'Direct line. You've got one just like it. You pick up the receiver, and I take it here. No one in between.'

After ten o'clock we parted as close friends. For many years I had been watching him closely, examining all his words and actions. So that's how quickly he gets close to people, I now thought to myself. Does he also part with them as easily?

Next morning, after a sleepless night spent in conversation with my children, I got up with the feeling that I had no idea what I was supposed to do.

Yakovlev's laconic 'I will present you' was the only guidance I had had.

'Present me.' What does that mean? How will he find me? Does he remember my home telephone number?

I have to admit though that this peculiar sensation felt more amusing than alarming. I turned on the radio. The 'Mayak' programme mentioned my appointment. When I picked up the BBC it was first on the news. Radio Liberty was broadcasting a repeat of a week-old interview I had given in Prague in connection with my recent statement. I tuned in at the point where I was saying that the 'Velvet Revolution' in Prague would have been impossible without perestroika in the USSR, and popular resistance to the coup would not have been so strong and effective if the 'Velvet Revolution' hadn't happened. I called these August days in Moscow 'the feast of the Transfiguration'. You don't have to be religious to see a kind of symbolism in the coincidence that the decisive battle between the old and the new started on 19 August, the feast of the Transfiguration of Jesus Christ.

The step from sublime to ridiculous is notoriously short. The man at the centre of so much attention was sitting in his pyjamas by the radio, wondering if there mightn't have been some mistake about his appointment.

From time to time the telephone would ring, and it would be a relative or friend, congratulating me on my appointment but surprised to find me at home. People here were ready for anything, and it occurred to me that my fears might not be so very vain.

In the afternoon I decided to call Yakovlev, but where could I locate him? Should I call him at home? But if I reached him there he might be embarrassed, and if I didn't, his family might start worrying. In my telephone pad I found an old number of his. I called it, and the phone was picked up by Yakovlev's secretary of many years, Stanislav Konstantinovich, Stasik.

'Alexander Nikolayevich?' He repeated my question in surprise. 'Don't you watch TV?'

A strange question in the middle of a working day.

'Certainly I do. They're showing cartoons.'

'Switch to Channel 2! They're showing the Supreme Soviet session.'

Oh, yes! I keep forgetting that I'm in Moscow. In Prague we had only one channel of Soviet TV. Here it was, and all exactly like last night. The Supreme Soviet sitting, Gorbachev on the rostrum. The list they'd cobbled together yesterday was under discussion.

The telephone. Now it was Stanislav Konstantinovich calling me. He'd got in touch with Yakovlev, who was sitting there on the right-hand balcony. Yakovlev asked me not to worry. He had set the Collegium appointment for five o'clock. A car would pick me up, we would meet at the Kremlin and then go to Smolenskaya Square. Only now did it strike me that he was marking time, waiting for the Supreme Soviet to approve Gorbachev's proposal of a Security Council. The President wanted to make Yakovlev a member of this Council, and it was in his new capacity that he meant to present me to my colleagues.

I need hardly say that my attention to events on TV redoubled, though soon it turned to disgust. Last night's performance was continuing. It was not the Security Council

55

that was being discussed, but the President who, by 'allowing' the putsch, had obliged our poor people's deputies to make a choice. From the speeches of those deputies who still commanded my respect, I concluded that I was not alone in feeling some distaste.

It was almost five o'clock when the list of candidates was voted down. Not because of its composition – only yesterday the President had been attacked for having got rid of all the initiators of perestroika and surrounded himself with untrustworthy people. So today it would be inconceivable to oppose the return to key positions of figures like Shevardnadze, Bakatin or Yakovlev. No, it was the right of the President to have a Security Council at all that was being questioned.

The President's people were watching TV as closely as I did. As soon as there was a break in the broadcast my telephone rang. It was Grigory Ivanovich Revenko, the jovial but highly organized new Chief of the President's Staff, calling to say that the President had asked him to present me to the Collegium, and could I collect him at the Kremlin? The car was already waiting for me downstairs.

When Revenko greeted me outside his office, he told me he had already informed the comrades at the Foreign Ministry that we were going to be late. I wondered how these 'comrades at the Ministry' would react when they saw that the new Foreign Minister was to be presented, not by the President or at least his closest associate, Yakovlev, but by a more or less unknown Chief of the President's Staff, who might need introducing himself.

Revenko, however, had no qualms at all about our forthcoming mission, and on the way he reminisced about when and where he, 'a modest First Secretary of the Kiev regional Komsomol committee', had met the famous Editor-in-Chief of *Komsomolskaya Pravda*. I tried not to betray that I did not remember either these occasions or Revenko himself, but of course it was good to find out that I was still remembered as the *Komsomolka* editor.

Smolenskaya Square. For nine years I had been coming to

56

this building as an Ambassador. Like all ordinary people – at any rate those of them who had access there at all – I used to enter the building by the main entrance. Like everybody else I would present my ID or diplomatic passport to militiamen at the entrance and then at another checkpoint. Like them, I waited for one of the old-fashioned lifts with their big cages bearing signs of past grandeur – shabby wooden panelling, tarnished bronze hand-rails. Only two of the six lifts stop at the 'ministerial' seventh floor, others go straight to the tenth. Today, for the first time in my life, I was to get into the building by the 'porch', the VIP entrance, and use the special lift.

Downstairs, at this very entrance, Deputy Foreign Minister Vladimir Petrovsky was already waiting. I have no great fondness for the outward signs of power, but this time I must confess that it gave me a strange sensation to see a saluting militiaman and Petrovsky hurrying to greet us. How many times had I had to wait in his ante-room to be received? Not that he wasn't the politest person in the world, with a friendly way of dealing with Ambassadors. But to be met by the Deputy Minister!

The human brain is a versatile instrument! I was reminded of that fact once again in the course of that memorable evening, with a flood of images surging through my mind as I entered the crowded Collegium meeting room. How many times had I had to wait outside till it was the turn of my item on the agenda, or to sit among the 'other ranks', or speak either from my seat or from the rostrum, wary of tricky questions from snobs for whom you were always an amateur, an outsider, because you had not climbed up every rung on the diplomatic ladder, starting from the lower ranks. It made no difference where you had come from. If you hadn't emerged from within their diplomatic world, it was never good enough.

But there was no room here for doubts. I knew that above all these people appreciated self-assurance: it was a trait that our diplomats had to demonstrate under all circumstances, that they imbibed with their mother's milk. You'd better not show signs of uneasiness, or even worse, timidity. It follows that I entered the room with a nonchalant air, nodded to the audience that rose to their feet to greet me, listened through brief and businesslike compliments from Grigory Ivanovich, and tersely declared that I regarded this appointment as a great honour. I went on to say that I saw no need for an inauguration speech. Our task was crystal clear. We needed a foreign policy that spoke for democracy victorious. There would be time enough later to discuss the details.

But there were two announcements that I made on the spot. They came as a surprise even to Revenko. First, Vladimir Fedorovich Petrovsky was appointed First Deputy Minister. Accordingly, Yuli Mikhailovich Kvitsinsky would no longer exercise these duties. Why Kvitsinsky? This, I hoped, was clear to anyone. Why Petrovsky? I needed a person experienced in the inner workings of the Foreign Ministry, and he was better suited for this role than anybody else.

From the meeting room Revenko and Petrovsky conducted me to my office and there left me. I looked around with the same feeling as in the meeting room. This was the centre, the citadel of the Soviet diplomatic service. A portrait of Lenin on the wall; a small, more intimate portrait of Gorbachev on the desk, like those I'd found in a dozen other offices in the last years.

My eyes alighted on the row of telephones, and I located the one marked 'Gorbachev'. After a brief deliberation I picked up the receiver. Two or three buzzes, and a voice with a southern Russian accent said:

'Afternoon, Boris Dimitrievich. How's it going there? Firmly in charge?'

'Not yet,' I joked. 'Just looking around.'

'OK, go ahead. And don't forget, Major is coming soon,' he reminded me in his already familiar energetic manner.

And hung up. As quickly and abruptly as he would do throughout the three months that we worked together, practically hand in glove. Few people, I suppose, knew that the man so often criticized for being too hesitant, and always late

58

with his decisions, lived at such a frantic pace. The thought occurred to me, that from now on I was doomed to live at much the same pace too. And so I was.

3

First Impressions

That night I left the Foreign Ministry at about eleven o'clock carrying a folder stuffed with papers. Three months later in London I discovered that 'homework' was a regular thing for government ministers there, and they carried their papers in a container called a 'red box'. What was in my 'red box' on the evening, or rather night, of my first day at work? Metaphorically speaking, the whole country was in that red-hot box. And not only my country: the whole world was waiting for my words and decisions.

Or so I thought at the time.

Here was a memo from Petrovsky. I wondered he'd had time to write it. Initially, I presume, it had not been addressed to me. Now it fell to me to make the decision.

The Moscow Conference on the Human Dimension of the Conference on Security and Cooperation in Europe (CSCE). The name had become only too familiar since the decision taken in Vienna three years previously, to hold three conferences on Human Rights: in Paris, in Copenhagen and, to crown the process, in Moscow. I had lost count of the telegrams I sent from Stockholm and Prague with my proposals and ideas on the subject.

The Soviet proposal to hold a closing conference in Moscow met a reaction of surprise and even indignation at first. The 'prison of nations', the 'evil empire', wanted to host a conference on Human Rights? Wasn't this just another public relations gimmick? To tell the truth, I sometimes shared this feeling. The passion for crowded public platforms, especially 'in defence of peace', was in the blood of our foreign policy makers. It was quite normal for us to campaign for goals that had nothing to do – as many people knew – with the real intentions or sentiments of our leaders. Take, for example, the Helsinki accords of 1975, which ratified the final act of the CSCE, an idea that the Soviet Union pushed hard for many years. Under the Brezhnev regime our leaders had no intention of living up to the Helsinki provisions, especially those in the Human Rights third basket. But what a wonderful opportunity it presented for them to go solemnly along to Helsinki, to pose in front of the cameras with the leaders of so many nations of the Northern Hemisphere, and to put their signature under a document that was bound to enter the history textbooks.

As I watched TV in 1975 I found myself drawing analogies with the notorious film, *The Fall of Berlin*. As a figurehead, I dare say Leonid Ilich Brezhnev could compete with Yosif Vissarionovich Stalin, although he was by far outstripped by the latter in the skills of murder, sadism and perfidy. Not one of all the cruel and hypocritical actions of the 'leader for all times and all nations' ever turned against him during his lifetime. And from his grave he could still watch with a grim satisfaction how our country, our people and the rest of the world were painfully struggling with the system and problems that they had inherited from him.

As for Brezhnev, he did run into a lot of problems with the third basket. To take its provisions seriously would mean having to carry out a democratic revolution and undergo a transformation from hawk into dove. To do that, he would have to ban censorship, permit a multi-party system, and release political prisoners. To do that, he would have to start by admitting that we *had* political prisoners.

Perestroika was in its second or third year when the idea of holding a conference on Human Rights in Moscow emerged. The world was still looking for a gimmick in this seemingly generous proposal, and many people thought that to stage such a conference in Moscow would be like holding a feast in the midst of a famine. But long live the mighty inertia of negotiations, conferences, bilateral and multilateral meetings. Once put forward, the proposal of a Human Rights conference acquired a life of its own: there was nothing that could stop it, just as two decades ago nothing could stop our drive towards a conference on security and cooperation in Europe.

Eventually a three-stage formula was worked out, with the last stage to be held in Moscow. There is an old eastern fable about a man who promised the Shah of Persia to teach his donkey how to talk in ten years' time. When his friends asked how he intended to fulfil the promise, the man answered that by that time either the Shah, or the donkey, or he himself would be dead. Perhaps all the parties relied on the same wisdom when they came up with Moscow as a conference site. Over the years both from Stockholm and from Prague I had been reporting the lukewarm responses to the Paris and Copenhagen stages of the conference. It had never entered my head that one day the decision on whether or not to convene the Moscow conference would fall to me. Now a decision was urgently required. Three years ago, the opening had been scheduled for 9 September 1991. Tonight was 30 August.

Either the Shah, or the donkey ... The whole world had been sent reeling first by the putsch and then by its defeat. The President of a superpower suddenly snatched from the scene, and then to rescue him another President, the President of Russia, a land stretching from the Baltic Sea to the Pacific Ocean, had to use a tank – one of the many that flooded Moscow – as a rostrum. And the first freely elected Parliament in our history froze in impotence and fear, as if hypnotized by

62

the ranks, the positions and the names of the conspirators: Vice-President, Prime Minister, Minister of Defence, KGB Chairman. This was the same Parliament, the same Supreme Soviet, that over the last couple of years had adopted law after law granting human rights to Soviet citizens. Hardly any international covenant on human rights remained unacknowledged.

The first cold wind simply blew away all these rights and guarantees like autumn leaves.

Nevertheless, tonight was 30 August and the conference was to open (or not open) on 9 September. From the practical, normal, bureaucratic point of view this was just an unfortunate coincidence, an extra burden. Was this the time to receive guests as high-ranking as the Foreign Ministers of the European States, the USA and Canada in a capital not yet fully recovered from the shock of the putsch, a country not fully aware of its present condition, let alone what lay in store?

But on the other hand, from the angle of Human Rights could any better time and place be found for such a conference than Moscow, which had just thrown off the last chains of totalitarianism? Could a better chance present itself to a born-again country, to inform the whole world of its plans and intentions in this traditionally sensitive sphere?

But what about the organizational side of things, the logistics? I went on reading Petrovsky's paper.

This was not the only homework my deputies had waiting for me. Another file was titled simply 'Ambassadors'. Even before opening it I knew that this was going to be the most unpleasant part of my duties. How often in the days and weeks to come did I look into it with the same mixture of pain, disdain and regret.

Twelve days had passed since the coup began and nine since it failed. In its aftermath, the behaviour of our Ambassadors during those fatal and heroic days was attracting the close scrutiny of the Soviet and international press. Why had they behaved so disreputably? The press clippings were full of familiar diplomatic names beneath biting, acrimonious headlines. Yesterday's proud representatives of their country

63

became today's targets for caricatures and pamphlets, contrasted with favourable mentions of me and of our statement – 'The only Ambassador ...' But if I was the only one, it meant that the rest ... What were we to do now? Replace the whole ambassadorial corps? Even in 1917, Lenin and the Bolsheviks had not had that much nerve.

I leafed through the file and realized that several ambassadors had already been recalled to Moscow. Of course, not thirty, as the foreign press was reporting, but only seven. London, Paris, Belgrade, Stockholm: Zamyatin, Dubinin, Loginov, Uspensky. The bread always falls butter side down. Why did it have to turn out that among so many of my colleagues, these were people I knew quite well? Memories of meetings, conflicts, sympathies were associated with each name.

Take Nikolai Nikolayevich Uspensky – Kolya – who had succeeded me in Stockholm only fourteen months before. In 1984, as First Secretary of the Soviet Embassy in London, he was Gorbachev's interpreter during his first visit abroad as Secretary of the CPSU Central Committee. Margaret Thatcher then pronounced her famous 'We can do business with Mr Gorbachev.' Uspensky made a favourable impression on Gorbachev, in contrast to the then Ambassador, Victor Popov, who presumed to tutor the future General Secretary on how to deal with foreigners. As a result the Ambassador was soon replaced, and Kolya returned to Moscow to become deputy head of department at the Foreign Ministry.

A year later, in 1986, came Gorbachev's 'historic' visit, as Shevardnadze called it, to the Foreign Ministry. At that time speakers were carefully selected from above. So who was to speak before the General Secretary on behalf of aspiring young diplomats? Who else but Nikolai Nikolayevich. Our Kolya soon became head of a reorganized department that, as well as dealing with the UK, Canada and Ireland, was now to supervise relations with Scandinavia. That was how we got acquainted, and I must admit that at first it was much easier to deal with him than with his predecessor in the Scandinavia office, Georgi Nikolayevich Farafonov, an unreconstructed Stalinist whose career began under Andrei Vyshinsky.

When I moved to Prague and Uspensky went to Stockholm, rumours spread at the Foreign Ministry that he had changed his tune. I had a chance to observe this personally. Several days before the coup, my wife and I went on vacation to Sweden at the invitation of some old friends. We got together with Uspensky for a couple of hours, and it was impossible to recognize him: he seemed depressed and even frightened. I accounted for this by the effect on him of the hard routine of ambassadorial duties, seldom appreciated by outsiders, but one of my former colleagues hinted that he had been got at by 'the neighbours'.

The report in front of me showed that during all three days of the coup, our Nikolai Nikolayevich – a scion of perestroika and a favourite of Gorbachev and Shevardnadze! – tried hard to convince the Swedish press that the Yanayev–Yazov putsch was a constitutional undertaking, and defended their right to adopt drastic measures. In the bureaucratic language of the memo: 'On 21 August 1991 he gave an interview to a Swedish newspaper which was interpreted in Sweden and other countries as support for the conspirators. He concedes that one statement of his could justify such an interpretation. His actions undermined the prestige of the Soviet representative in Sweden.'

The Swedish *Dagens Nyheter* commented: 'To shy away from expressing one's personal position does not always represent the high art of diplomacy. There are moments when a person who finds himself in a quandary from the standpoint of his official role must judge things from a moral standpoint and take the line of honour.' According to another newspaper, when asked why, unlike his predecessor, he had not come out against the coup, Uspensky answered in all seriousness that Pankin must have been better informed.

No, I refused to go on reading this folder, with its further dozen similar cases. Although I understood very well that sooner or later I would have to come back to it. That night, the first after my presentation to the Collegium and the last before routine work began (if 'routine' applies to the state of affairs in Moscow and in my Ministry), I could not go through more than one document from the 'red box'. But papers or not, my head was throbbing with apprehension of the problems to come. As one of the Soviet newspapers (I think it was *Megapolis-Express*) observed: 'The drama of Soviet foreign policy is that it is living through extreme turmoil at home, that coincides with the accelerating temp of world politics.'

In Prague, where I had spent the previous fifteen months as Ambassador – the Prague of Vaclav Havel, Jiri Dienstbier, Alexander Dubcek and Vaclav Klaus – their surging energy had turned the city into one of the hubs of international activity. Who could fail to visit yesterday's prisoner of conscience, the playwright and philosopher who had almost literally stepped from prison cell to Presidential Palace? Not President Bush, nor Prime Minister Margaret Thatcher, who in her speech at the national Assembly called for the ultimate crusade against Communism. Then there was Helmut Kohl, concerned with the Sudeten Germans to whom Vaclav Havel, not yet clad in the thick skin of the politician, had made haste to apologize in his first days in power. François Mitterrand, with his idea of European Confederation, found ardent supporters in the new Czechoslovak leaders. Europe, as opposed to the Soviet Union, sounded like music to their ears.

There was hardly an initiative from the West that they did not support, and they fizzed with their own ideas. There was hardly an international event, let alone a conflict, in which they did not deem it absolutely necessary to intervene, or at least to express their radical position. The Iraqi invasion of Kuwait, events in Yugoslavia, tensions between some Latin American states and their totalitarian neighbour Cuba ... everything found a response in the country whose past rulers knew only one policy – to wait for instructions from Moscow.

Was it any wonder that Prague and Moscow developed such a tangle of relations, notwithstanding, or perhaps even reflecting, the fact that now they had to deal not with Brezhnev or Chernenko or Gromyko, but with the fathers and initiators of perestroika, men like Gorbachev, Ryzhkov, Shevardnadze ... Everything in our relations at that time was under strain: economic ties, withdrawal of troops, the ownership of remaining military property, the role of the KGB in the 'Velvet Revolution' ...

By virtue of my position and temperament, during my tenure in our Prague Embassy I was in the middle of this relationship, and now that the Soviet Union no longer exists I can confess that often I was at a loss whose side to take. Every now and then, someone in the Soviet Foreign Ministry, the Central Committee, the Embassy (behind my back, naturally), or in orthodox circles in Prague, would imply or publicly ask the question: whose interests does he represent? I remember that at the Foreign Ministry Collegium three months before the coup, Yuli Kvitsinsky – Kvitsinsky the Magnificent as his friends called him – reproached me only half-jokingly that I could not 'give these new leaders in Eastern Europe a punch in the face when necessary'. He himself, I must admit, was very good at that. The smack of his diplomacy resonated all over the former socialist Europe.

How many telegrams were dispatched, how much ink expended, on efforts to convince Moscow, in the person of Prime Minister Valentin Sergeyevich Pavlov, not to cut off the oil supplies to Czechoslovakia that kept their economy alive. How painful for the new democratic leaders was Gorbachev's flat refusal to meet with them.

When in June 1991 Gorbachev sent Gennadi Yanayev to stand in for him at the closing meeting of the Warsaw Pact countries in Prague, where all the East and Central European political leaders were gathered, I don't know who was more disappointed – the hosts, Havel and Dienstbier, who had been looking forward to meeting the initiator of perestroika, or myself, who had spent more than a month trying to persuade Gorbachev to come. At one point I even had Alexander Nikolayevich Yakovlev sign one of my numerous cabled appeals when he came to Prague for a couple of days. All was in vain.

Someone – I think it was Kvitsinsky – succeeded in

persuading Mikhail Sergeyevich that he ought not to preside over the funeral of the Warsaw Pact. The opposing argument, namely that his presence might have turned the funeral into the birth of a new era in relations between the former empire and its former satellites, cut no ice with him. Contrary to his image of the decisive innovator, reinforced by his bold gestures and expressive body language, Gorbachev was actually a very hesitant and unsure individual. He successfully pulled down the old structures that he recognized as worthless, but it embarrassed him to be seen doing it. When he should have been taking credit for some of his actions, the ghost of the old apparatchik inside Gorbachev saw him as being saddled only with the unpredictable kind of responsibility that no bureaucrat enjoys. So my pleas for his attendance put me in a dubious light. What did the Ambassador want? Why was he meddling? It looked as if he wanted to lure the President to Prague.

After an unfortunate incident at the Paris CSCE summit, some of my so-called friends advised me to quit before I was fired. I had managed to talk Gorbachev into meeting with Havel in Paris – France was a third country, and it solved the problem of who goes to whom. The intentions were most serious and constructive, as Shevardnadze would tell me in a telephone conversation later when everything failed. But it happened that right before a meeting with Gorbachev it was Havel's turn to speak at the plenary, and he – *o, sancta simplicitas*! – proposed to grant observer status at the conference to the Baltic republics, then still Soviet dependencies. As if he did not know that Gorbachev objected even to their presence in the audience!

The reaction of the Soviet delegation was quick. The long-awaited meeting was cancelled thirty minutes before the scheduled time with no explanations offered. Later on at a gathering in front of all the other leaders, Havel, the gadfly of the Pankraz Prison, asked Gorbachev what was going on. Nothing to do with politics, had been the condescending reply, just a schedule change. Even Shevardnadze felt uncomfortable when he deemed it necessary to explain to me what had happened and asked me to reassure the Czechoslovaks. What was I supposed to feel, as an Ambassador whose first duty was to communicate the actions and intentions of the leaders of my State? Whose side was I to take, at least in my own soul? How was I to answer questions from the Prague political establishment and the press?

And on top of everything, what was I to say on the issue that became decisive between the two leaders, the question of Baltic independence?

This problem had been haunting me ever since my term in Stockholm. The Social Democrats who had been in power there since before the Second World War had a deep-seated guilt complex towards the Baltic States. Years ago the Swedes had recognized de facto their entry into, or rather annexation by, the Soviet Union, and immediately after the war they agreed to deport from Sweden a large number of repatriates accused by our country (often with good reason) of collaboration with the Nazis. Ever afterwards they longed to make up for these actions, and when perestroika began they decided that their time had come. Geographically, the Baltic region was the closest part of the Soviet Union to them. Historically, in the epoch of Sweden's great-power aspirations which ended with the defeat of King Charles XII by Peter the Great at Poltava in 1709, most of the region was in Swedish hands. During the late 1980s Swedish emissaries skimmed across the Baltic Sea, and the leaders of the newly-born popular fronts were frequent visitors to Stockholm.

Both of these interest groups were striving to convince me (they never shyed away from visiting the Embassy) of something that I was already convinced of myself: that Moscow was lagging hopelessly behind in implementing the principles that it itself proclaimed. For example it promised but failed to grant to the Baltic republics at least a degree of economic independence.

At an Embassy reception Mariu Lauristin, one of the founders of the democratic movement in Estonia, told me: 'If the Centre had put the Union Treaty on the political agenda at least a year ago, no one would have been talking about separation from the Soviet Union. And now anyone who would just dare to hint at not supporting full independence would be swept away. Swept away,' she repeated.

This is what actually happened to many of them.

Similar messages were reaching the ears of the Swedish Foreign Minister, Sten Andersson. During an official visit to the Soviet Union he went to Tallinn, Riga and Vilnius on his way to Moscow, and then brought these impressions, coupled with his own ideas, to the notice of Soviet Prime Minister Nikolai Ryzhkov. His words were welcome to me because they echoed what I had been writing repeatedly from Stockholm, both on my own behalf and on that of my contacts in the Baltic republics.

Vaclav Havel and his team had enough reasons of their own to flirt with the Baltic States. It was a meeting of rebellious hearts and minds, for in those States, as in Prague, many of the leading figures in government and parliament came from dissident circles. It pained me to acknowledge that Moscow, the birthplace of perestroika, appeared to them as a monster that ignored the deepest aspirations of their countries and peoples.

Until the last year of the Soviet Union it was never conceived at the top that the Baltic States might one day be detached from a Soviet Union whose formation was seen as an irreversible reality, its fifteen republics integral parts of the whole. Not even in their wildest dreams had the Baltic dissidents conceived of absolute independence, and in spite of all the rapid shifts of events and attitudes in the last two years of the Soviet Union, divorce was never considered a serious option.

It was only in the kaleidoscopic world of post-coup Moscow that the inevitability of Baltic independence dawned on Gorbachev and the rest of us, and no sooner had this new reality taken shape in our minds than we swung wildly in the opposite direction to write off those republics altogether. Obviously we recognized that Baltic independence had become a plank of American and European foreign policy, and we aimed to use the Baltic question as a bargaining chip with the West in dealing with financial and aid issues, but the value of this card kept dwindling as events forced the pace.

For my part, I always felt that the Soviet Union would happily accept the Baltic republics as three more Finlands – buffer States, culturally and economically Western-oriented but politically neutral in the international arena and sensitive to Moscow's defence concerns. Both in my Stockholm and Prague posts I had floated such ideas with Moscow (in the guise of reports on conversations with Swedish and Baltic exile interlocutors), but the awkward suggestions of a Soviet diplomat abroad fell as heresy on Moscow ears, and were ignored in the usual manner.

Once I became Foreign Minister I was anxious to accelerate moves towards Baltic independence because I felt that Soviet interests would be best served if we retained the initiative: I did not want to lag behind, but rather to anticipate the inevitable and steer a course towards it, rather than being dragged there.

The context of my thinking took up the broad logic of Soviet foreign policy in the past few years, which was a shift from defence and rivalry with the Americans to doing everything possible to further the economic reconstruction of the Soviet Union. We looked to the US for economic assistance, and were prepared to make many concessions to achieve it – hence our compliance with independence for the Baltic States. Our retreat from the Third World and downgrading of our relations with Cuba fit the same pattern. On the one hand we could no longer afford to maintain these kinds of relationship; on the other we strove to present their abandonment as badges of good intent. Both the Americans and we dressed up our statements in terms of détente, but for our part it was the economic imperatives that drove us, as the Americans perfectly well understood.

As for Europe, it was plain that it was the Germans who were going to be of the greatest economic use to us, so it was they who received the most careful attention there. The irony of seeing the former aggressor now transformed into the potential saviour was not lost on us, but policy had to be based on immediate pragmatism, not on some form of nostalgic and obsolete romanticism.

71

The importance of Germany as the focus of our European policy had obviously tended to marginalize Britain and the other European countries. Russians have always had admiration for Germany, respect for France and affection for Britain. In the present conditions of Russia and Britain, the potential of Britain's role in the restructuring of Russia's economy in terms of investment, know-how and sheer economic power, is clearly more limited than Germany's.

On Japan, Gorbachev was always very cautious in seeking to expand economic relations, even though Japan's role as a source of investment and assistance is potentially enormous. But Gorbachev did not want to open up the issue of the Kuril Islands, ceded to the Soviet Union after the Second World War by the Yalta Conference, an arrangement since challenged by Japan, which has called for the return of the four southernmost islands in the group. My own idea as Foreign Minister, again determined by economic necessity, was to remove the Islands as the first items on the agenda of any negotiations with Japan, but to encourage their economic development with Japanese assistance. But the Japanese were adamant: no Kurils, no assistance. Actually I believe that two of the four islands could be returned quite easily, and this was decided in principle by the Politburo way back in Khrushchev's time, but later dropped again. It is the obvious first step.

It was a disorienting experience to look at these broad issues from the perspective of the Foreign Minister of the USSR. I am sure that anybody whose career has undergone a sudden dramatic rise will recognize the sensation that I call the 'inverted-binoculars effect', as when you look through the reverse end of a pair of binoculars and find things that just now looked big and important suddenly growing small and insignificant. An uneasy feeling crept into my mind. What if it turns out that while you were there as Ambassador, there was something very important that you didn't know? Now you will learn it, and understand why your own ideas differed so much from the policies of your government. And once you realize this, you'll be doing the things you used to disagree with.

This thought vanished as quickly as it came. Of course, it was not the first time that it had crossed my mind, but although I was hardly a beginner, I had never stood at such a turning-point before. Not that there hadn't been more than enough temptations to change my mode of behaviour when circumstances changed. Sometimes I even yielded to them, as human beings do. But even defeats can teach good lessons.

Who were the men who knew this important something that was not open to me? If Prime Minister Pavlov, Vice-President Yanayev, KGB Chairman Kryuchkov, Defence Minister Yazov, or Boldin kept top-secret papers locked away, where did this knowledge take them? And not only them, but the whole country? Both as individuals and in their official capacity, they held the keys to many of the problems that I as an Ambassador had wanted to see resolved. Together with Gorbachev. And now he had called for my help. Had he done that because he understood something important in himself, in life, in my own past appeals to him?

It was on this inspiring note that I completed my first day and night as Minister for Foreign Affairs of the USSR. I remember feeling surprisingly strong in body and spirit at that late, well after midnight, hour. And the Soviet Union, which had gone through so many dramatic changes during the three days of the coup, had no more than three months left.

4

Taking Bearings

The gruelling routine began. That memorable night I went to bed around two o'clock in the morning and got up before six. This was to become the usual ratio of sleeping to waking in the next three months. It was not a conscious decision, just a reflex that I needed to develop unless I wanted to be overwhelmed by the flood of everything that had to be done. I don't know what kept me going but throughout those days and nights I lived as if by a special inner timetable, in a special mood. As I got up each morning I feared I would collapse by the end of the day and each night as I went to bed I was not sure that I could muster the strength to get up in the morning. Yet the spirit inside me burned so strong that the moments of weakness never lasted for more than fifteen minutes, day or night.

One minor incident illustrates the pressures I was dealing with. It happened after a visit to the Middle East, where I signed with my Israeli counterpart David Levy an agreement on restoring diplomatic relations between our countries, and where James Baker and I announced that invitations to the Madrid

74

peace conference on the Middle East were being sent out. Despite all my spiritual and physical commitments, I arrived home from Jerusalem, Damascus, Amman and Cairo with an upset stomach — not unusual for those who return from hectic travel.

This happened on a Saturday evening. On Sunday afternoon I was scheduled to meet the President of Cyprus, George Vassiliou, at the airport. The following day I was to fly with Gorbachev to Madrid, where we were to alternate with James Baker in chairing the sessions of the Middle East conference. Such were the historic tasks awaiting me while I dashed from bedroom to bathroom every fifteen minutes, wondering whether, if the intervals grew longer tomorrow, I might use one of them to get to the airport and meet the distinguished guest. For the very first time, it occurred to me then that maybe there was something more to speeding Zils and exemption from traffic lights than just pampering their passengers' egos.

They say that God gives strength to a man if he blesses his mission, and I do believe that this applied to me during those hundred days. But on that cloudy Sunday morning in October, God clearly had other business than helping the Soviet Foreign Minister to go out and greet the President of Cyprus.

In the old days it was no problem to substitute one high-ranking official for another. But who could be my replacement now? The Union Centre that was still used as a bogey by 'democrats' — who did it consist of? The President, in accordance with protocol, would be receiving his counterpart in the Kremlin. Ivan Stepanovich Silayev, the Chairman of the Inter-Republican Economic Committee, a de facto provisional government, was in Brussels, trying to obtain humanitarian aid and credits from the European Community. As for ministers, the list was short: myself, the Minister of Defence, the Interior Minister, and the KGB Chairman. For any one of those to show up at the airport to greet the President of Cyprus would cause unwelcome speculation. What would Turkey say, or the Turkish community in Cyprus? The United States and the Muslim states of the Middle East might also misinterpret the gesture. We did have Yakovlev, with his worldwide reputation as the architect of perestroika, but his official position was unsuitable for a protocol role. And I could not send any of my deputies to the airport, because this might offend Vassiliou.

So, I believe it was the mere absence of room for retreat, rather than prayers, that helped me through that painful day. And once I had summoned the strength to meet the visitor I managed to go to Madrid too.

The episode may be quite comic and marginal, but this unusual angle demonstrates the strain on the Union's governmental structures at a time when the situation was changing every day, if not every hour.

When I was appointed Foreign Minister I did not really have time to ponder about it. An inertial belief that power, at least in its outward attributes, is unshakeable was until recently deeply engrained in the minds of every Soviet citizen, including the most radical dissidents. And how could it seem otherwise if the President received you in the Kremlin, and if on the day after your appointment the notorious black Zil was waiting at the entrance to your house, its front seat filled by a broad-shouldered man with sharp eyes, a dark overcoat, and well-pressed trousers – your bodyguard. The private secretary inherited from your predecessor meets you at the gate of your personal lift. In your office the schedule for the day is already waiting for you, typed in block capitals – a tradition that dates back to Gromyko. The schedule contains your departure to the airport to meet the British Prime Minister, John Major, who comes accompanied by his Secretary of State for Foreign and Commonwealth Affairs, Douglas Hurd. It seems just like the old days that you know mainly from TV reports.

The two British visitors arrived only a few days after my appointment, en route to China. Britain was chairing the G-7 group of leading industrial nations, and spoke on their behalf. The crowd of people waiting to greet these visitors was thinner than it used to be. Absent, for example, was the Ambassador to the United Kingdom: he was in Moscow, but not invited to meet the PM. Absent was the Soviet Prime Minister: he was in prison. The head of the Russian government, Ivan Silayev, was to meet the British Prime Minister. This was his first experience of such an occasion, and he plied me with questions.

But the chief surprise awaited us in the Kremlin. When our cavalcade reached the Kremlin and solemnly drove through the Borovitsky Gate, when the Prime Minister was escorted through the ceremonial entrance of the Great Kremlin Palace to the Hall of St Catherine, where his face-to-face talks with Gorbachev were to start, it turned out that Gorbachev was – missing.

'He's been delayed,' an embarrassed presidential aide whispered to me.

Major and Hurd sat calmly in their armchairs, and there was nothing for it but to make conversation – the architecture of the Kremlin, my experiences in Prague, and – since they were British – the weather. Both of them recognized the historic nature of these days, and were not put out by the delay, though in the world of diplomacy it would normally have been interpreted as a slight. They were very supportive of our decision to go through with the Human Rights Conference, and knowing that Gorbachev was in two minds about it, they encouraged me to persist. I in turn felt it permissible to hint that Gorbachev's resolution could be bolstered by support from G-7.

Both men were very self-assured, with Major leading this and the subsequent conversations while Hurd played the consummate diplomat, nodding gravely at the right moments and making intelligent interventions. Major was dressed like a successful British executive, but one who had acquired his taste in the school of upward mobility. Hurd's suit looked hand-tailored, but not by an expensive hand, and his white cotton pochette clearly had a practical use, as opposed to the silk variety that some Britons sport as a kind of foppish affectation. (I should add that during my subsequent service in Britain I noticed that many middle- and higher-ranking civil servants, especially in the Foreign Office, often preferred hand-made suits of inferior quality to the better made and better quality off-the-peg variety. I have often wondered whether this was a relic of status consciousness in Britain, or had some other exotic socio-cultural explanation that was beyond me.)

At last it was as if a breeze blew through the place, and we knew Gorbachev was coming. He burst into the hall, embraced Major, shook hands with Hurd, apologized for being late, but hinted to the visitors that it was not his fault.

A quick photo break, then a conversation began with Silayev, Hurd and myself participating. Gorbachev extracted from his pocket several sheets of paper with notes in his large, hardly readable, handwriting.

'Here!' he said, and shook the papers almost in Major's face. 'We were working on that all night. Just finished. Made a deal. I believe we came up with a very serious document. A historic document,' he repeated, trying to convince himself more than his interlocutors. Major and Hurd – splendid English composure! – sat nodding politely, waiting for clarifications. Major did try to squeeze in some words of greeting, but Gorbachev hardly noticed in his eagerness to reveal what his sleepless night had produced. He reminded me of the boy who, having thought that all his toys had been stolen, is ecstatic to discover that the thief has dropped a few on the way out.

From Gorbachev's explanations to the British Prime Minister, I learned what was really going on in the country, and how close to the edge we stood. Gorbachev was talking about a meeting of the leaders of Soviet republics (the three Baltic countries and Moldova were not present) some of them had already declared their independence and sovereignty. (The statement became known as the '10+1 Declaration'.) In that meeting they created a Gossoviet (State Council), a committee of republican leaders, whose aim was to abolish the Congress of People's Deputies and the Supreme Soviet and to function as a kind of holding company board that would oversee the interests of all the republics. The reason for Gorbachev's excitement was that by agreeing to the creation of the Gossoviet the republics' leaders had ensured the survival in some form of the Soviet Union, now in the guise of a Union of Independent States (not the Commonwealth of Independent States that was to come later).

I don't want to give my readers the impression that I was more naïve than I really was, but a measure of bracing naïveté may yield a more vivid account of the general picture.

Of course, in Prague and for the last two days in Moscow I had been keeping the closest possible watch on developments during and after the putsch, and I had discussed them with Gorbachev and Yakovlev. Like everyone else, I was waiting for the opening of the Congress of People's Deputies.

Back in Prague days earlier I had noted that the reaction of the Ukrainian leader Leonid Kravchuk to the coup had been rather slow. What else could be expected from a Party functionary of such long standing! The same applied to the head of the Uzbek Parliament, Islam Karimov, whom I did not know at the time. It didn't surprise me that he, just like Kravchuk and various other republican leaders, had resigned from the governing bodies of the Party, and then from the Party itself, after the coup. In some places they even followed Russia in banning it. That's the way we are – always trying to catch the departing train.

But what was I to make of the series of republics that proclaimed their independence? Almost each one of the last ten days of August brought a new declaration of independence. Before the coup there had been a 'parade of sovereignties'. One after another, republics of the Union of Soviet Socialist Republics, including Russia, had proclaimed their sovereignty. But although they were beginning cautiously to call themselves 'States' or 'countries', no one – apart from the Baltic republics – would make serious mention of secession. Now came a 'parade of independences'. The coup and its defeat accelerated the process. It was not an escape from the Union, but from the threat of totalitarianism restored. What better proof could there be, that such a danger still existed?

The position of Russia was puzzling me. I could see why Yeltsin had taken control of the Union structures, including the armed forces, during the coup. In fact he had acted like an officer who had to replace a wounded general in the thick of battle, and this had helped to bring victory. But what did these decrees mean, now that Gorbachev had been released from house arrest and returned to his duties? Moreover, the Soviet President too had displayed genuine courage. Judging from the press, and its reports from the USSR and Russian Supreme Soviet, I was not the only person to be intrigued by this. Questions were put both to Yeltsin and to Gorbachev. Yeltsin preferred to keep silent. Gorbachev brushed them aside.

I had had no time to think through any of this, either in Prague or here in Moscow, so I listened very attentively to what Gorbachev was now explaining to Major about the outcome of his all-night session with republican leaders. He had arranged to meet them again after his talks with the British Prime Minister.

Over the past week the sittings of the republican Parliaments had ended. The Soviet one had decided to convene an Extraordinary Congress of People's Deputies, which would have to decide the future of our gigantic country and its people. According to tradition the Congress must open with a Presidential Address, but what was the President to report on? He had already reported, and even engaged in self-criticism, at the sessions of the Soviet and Russian Supreme Soviets, in reply to those who wanted to know how it happened that his closest friends and colleagues had turned into traitors and conspirators. To certify his deepest disappointment in his friends and past convictions, he had resigned from the post of General Secretary of the Communist Party, and disbanded the Party.

Hence came the idea, Gorbachev was explaining to Major, of a joint address to the Congress by the leaders of the Union and all of its constituent sovereign and independent republics. This statement would contain the basis on which to build a new, democratic, humane and prosperous Union of the people of our country, rising out of the ruins of totalitarian order.

This country of the future was contained in the sheets of paper that Gorbachev held in his hands as he was speaking to the British visitors. Our two guests seemed thoroughly impressed. I too was impressed, and inspired.

80

To look reality in the face – that is what the document was all about. Earlier in his historic career, this was not Gorbachev's forte. His fatal gift of leaving pressing problems to the very last minute – or even later – had become notorious in the eyes of his fellow citizens. What he was saying now, and what would be announced to the Congress next day, was a dramatic breakthrough. Instead of taking issue with republican declarations of independence, he meant to allow them free rein. Let them have as much independence as they wanted, if that was what it took before they could start to come together again. As they would need to do, for they could hardly survive on their own, so close and organic was their historical, political, economic, cultural and ethnic integration.

The Union was a single organism, and there was no getting away from that fact. Its various parts would have to reassemble, but let them do this of their own free will, not through pressure, or by orders from above.

To translate these ideas into constitutional language meant working out a new Union Treaty. It was pointless to return to the previous version that had been ready for signing on 20 August. Here, the conspirators had done their worst: they had broken the country apart. But the old system was not worth mourning. Each republic would have a chance to work out its attitude to the Union Treaty completely on its own. They would be free to choose whether to join it or not. And while the work on the Treaty was under way it was necessary to create an economic union based on the principles of a single, open, economic environment and a market economy.

In order to safeguard national security, the republics would need to sign an agreement to maintain the armed forces of the Union and an integrated military-strategic environment. And a transitional period would be required, in order to cast today's hastily-made decisions into sound and durable forms: a Constitution, executive bodies, legislature – 'Just like what you have in England.' Gorbachev was smiling triumphantly, as he concluded his long emotional presentation.

I did notice that the Foreign Ministry went unmentioned by

81

Gorbachev, that there was no reference to it in his papers, and that the words 'foreign policy' were used only once or twice, but at that moment I did not pay much attention to it. Like everybody present I was swept along by the logic of his words. I felt an urge, familiar since my early journalistic years, to roll up my sleeves and get straight down to work.

After Gorbachev had concluded his story, and our guests had made their sympathetic but cautious responses to it, Major asked Mikhail Sergeyevich if they might talk confidentially in private, naturally with interpreters participating. Along with the President's aides I was about to vacate my chair, but he tugged insistently at my sleeve: stay here. When Major saw this he gave the same sign to Douglas Hurd. So there were six of us left in the room – the President and the Prime Minister, two Foreign Ministers, and two interpreters. To Gorbachev's surprise, and probably even to his displeasure, since he was looking for a more detailed response to his story from the guests, the talk focused on biological warfare. The information furnished to the British as well as to the American leadership, by sources that the Prime Minister chose not to divulge, suggested that the Soviet Union was continuing to conduct research and development in that area, in violation of its international agreement, and in particular of the Convention on Bacteriological Warfare signed by the USSR in 1972. Moreover, we had maintained and even expanded our production capacities, which could be put into operation at any time.

John Major suggested that considering everything that the failed putsch had exposed, there must be a possibility that such work could be carried out, and such facilities remain and be developed, even in defiance of the will of the innovatory democratic leadership of the country – Gorbachev, in other words. Speaking this time also on behalf of his American counterpart, President Bush, the British Prime Minister expressed a hope that the information he had referred to would be thoroughly investigated, and the breaches eradicated. The concrete case in point were certain facilities in Leningrad and its vicinity.

Gorbachev's sour expression displayed his obvious disappointment over the unexpected turn of the conversation, but he assured the honoured guest that his allegations would be thoroughly looked into, and the results reported at a proper level.

I have to admit that in the whirl of events and problems that crammed each and every one of those memorable hundred days, I did not have the chance to revert to the biological warfare problem. It was Yeltsin who raised it again when on 30 January 1992, he stopped off in London, while en route to New York to attend the UN Security Council. The programme of the London visit also included a private meeting with John Major in which I participated, this time in my capacity as Russian Ambassador to Great Britain.

Yeltsin said that he was aware of the conversation with Gorbachev in Moscow. He said he knew that Gorbachev had later repudiated the idea of proceeding with any of the country's programmes of biological warfare development.

'But what Gorbachev said was not true,' the Russian President went on. 'Most likely they flannelled him. I now have accurate information. Research and development *has* been carried out until very recently. I have issued a clear-cut order to halt it, and to dismantle the installations – in other words, to eliminate any possibility of further so-called progress in this area.'

Major, who as it turned out had been intending to raise this subject, sighed with relief. The visitor had saved him the trouble of awkward explanations. But the awkwardness arose all the same later on, when in the oval room at 10 Downing Street defence ministers Tom King and Yevgeni Shaposhnikov joined us to report about the outcome of their negotiations. It was clear from what they said that King had asked his Russian counterpart the same sticky question about biological weapons, and Marshal Shaposhnikov had rejected out of hand the slightest possibility that R&D work had continued in Russia. Major and Yeltsin looked at each other. It became obvious that the President had either had no time or no inclination to notify his minister about what he intended to say to the Prime Minister. Now he spoke in a conciliatory manner and assured those present that, come what may, there was nothing to worry about. Things would be put in order.

He spoke too soon. More than once while I was in London the Western leaders reverted to the question. The first time was in August 1992, when Russian-American consultations were held in London at foreign minister level in connection with the forthcoming signing of the START II Treaty. Another was when James Baker's successor, Lawrence Eagleburger, and Douglas Hurd sent a message to the Russian Foreign Minister.

The negotiations between Yeltsin and Major also started with that issue in November 1992, when the Russian President was in London again. The arguments set forth were the same. Yeltsin recalled his first assurances, when he had insisted in all sincerity that there would be no further breaches of international agreements. His counterparts insisted that their information indicated otherwise. No one, naturally, admitted the possibility of the Russian leader telling deliberate lies. It simply seemed that both he and Gorbachev had been deceived, and sometimes even disobeyed.

Here is what was written in black and white in one of the documents handed over to the Russian side: 'Individual aspects of the military-biological programme the existence of which President B.N. Yeltsin acknowledged in the past and the one he banned in April are in fact being covertly implemented without his knowledge.' This also gave rise to grave concern that 'the senior officials who for a long time took part in the development of the offensive military-biological programme of the former Soviet Union still hold positions of authority in the sphere which they are now called upon to curtail.'

So what was going on? On the one hand, Russia under Yeltsin met halfway all the British and American proposals aimed at putting things in the field of biological and chemical warfare in order. In particular, a trilateral Russian–British–American agreement was signed, and mutual verification begun of the facilities concerned. On the other hand, judging by more new talks held in private, it was the West's view that things remained essentially unchanged. Finally, there was a series of leaks to the press, including *The Times*, about the sources of this information. One of them turned out to be a former Russian scientist called Vladimir Pasechnik, who claimed to have been involved in a programme code-named 'Biopreparat' ('Biopreparation'), which had facilities in Moscow, Novobirsk, St Petersburg and elsewhere. He had become frightened of his 'brain-child', and defected at the first opportunity. Two other turncoats, probably from the intelligence service, were not named in the press, but apparently it was they who supplied the up-to-date information to the West.

Finally it emerged that pursuant to a decree by the President of Russia, Major-General Anatoly Kuntsevich, chairman of a committee that dealt with chemical and biological weapons, had been relieved of his duties. The indications were that he was the 'senior official' who had sabotaged the Presidential orders. Western leaders sighed with some relief, even though this incident said something about the enormous resistance encountered by the Russian leader on the path towards 'civilizing' the country.

The subject of our meetings with Boris Nikolayevich Yeltsin in the course of the one hundred days which I depict here, and those that took place later in London, raises other perspectives on Gorbachev's successor, and this may be the moment to digress a little on the personality and makeup of this extraordinary yet flawed individual. In one of his speeches Yeltsin himself provided the key to understanding one side of his character. He was outspoken in telling TV viewers that in order to get things moving he required some powerful stimulus, often of a psychological kind. It was essential for something or someone either to highly inspire him or, on the contrary, to provoke him to anger. During the first few days following the meeting between Yeltsin, Kravchuk and Stanislav Shushkevich in Belovezhskaya Pusha, immediately after the break-up of the Soviet Union, it was Gorbachev who provided much of that 'negative inspiration' for Yeltsin. It was purely to spite Gorbachev that on 30 January 1992 Yeltsin told John Major in London that promises made by the ex-President of the USSR concerning biological weapons had not been kept. During the same talk, incidentally, he also told Major about another 'big deception' that Gorbachev practised more than once, and in public. Having pledged to reduce the armed forces of the Soviet Union unilaterally by half a million troops, the Soviet leadership intentionally exaggerated their true strength by approximately that many troops, so that they could reduce this fictitious strength, but not the troops as such.

On the way to the royal suite at Heathrow Airport, more than a month after the Soviet red flag was lowered over the Kremlin, the distinguished guest of the British State told me excitedly in the armour-plated Zil about his last meeting with Gorbachev at the end of December 1991. As he spoke it was clear to me that Yeltsin drew inspiration from the contempt in which he held his defeated adversary. This last meeting with Gorbachev had apparently dragged on for nine hours: six hours talking in private, the other three spent with the nuclear codes experts. 'So, for those six hours he turned over his last duties and affairs to me. Top-secret papers from the most secret safes. You know, the things that previously were turned over from one General Secretary to another. These were foreign policy matters, one more sordid than the last. I said: "Stop! Please! Just hand in these papers to the Archives, and they'll make you sign for them. I don't intend to be held responsible for them. Why should I take charge of all those matters? You are no longer the General Secretary, while I have not been one, and will not be."'

Some of the above 'matters' Boris Nikolayevich depicted in his book *Memories of the President* (in English, *The View from the Kremlin*), which was published two and a half years after our conversation took place. The most dreadful was the Katyn case, the atrocious shooting of tens of thousands of Polish servicemen who were taken prisoners in 1939–1940 following the conspiracy between Stalin and Hitler, when in keeping with the secret protocols of the Molotov-Ribbentrop pact the Soviet Union proceeded to 'liberate' Western Belarussia and Western Ukraine.

It happened that shortly after Yeltsin flew from London to New York on 30 January 1992 I met a Western publisher who was trying to secure a book from the Russian President, having been involved in the publication of his first book – written while he was still a Soviet member of parliament in disgrace. We had met for the first time when I was Chairman of the All-Union Copyright Agency, and we met again when he accompanied Yeltsin to Stockholm for the Swedish launch of the first book, entitled *Against the Grain,* while I was Ambassador there.

Now my companion – let's call him Peter – told me that he was working on Boris Nikolayevich to continue writing his memoirs. In July of 1991, when Peter was in Moscow, Yeltsin had brought up the question himself – 'But I told him that it was too soon for that,' bearing in mind that his first book had not yet exhausted its potential.

They agreed to meet again in September, and in the meantime came the putsch. Immediately after it, Peter called Ilyiushin, one of Yeltsin's senior advisers, and suggested: 'Perhaps you have other more urgent things on your plate?' Ilyiushin said: 'Come on over. It's down in his diary.' So Peter went to Moscow.

'We met in the "White House",' he recalled, 'then left for some State dacha. We sat, spoke, ate and drank. Yeltsin talked on and on about the putsch, and Gorbachev, and I realized that all this was rooted for him in the autumn of 1987' – the date of the Party plenum when Yeltsin criticized Gorbachev and the Politburo of the Communist Party Central Committee, and was stripped of his posts in the ranks of the Party elite. 'This is what became his principal driving force' – and here Peter made the gesture of wringing a cock's neck.

'Later that night,' Peter went on, 'he asked me whether I needed to go to Moscow. I said I had an early morning meeting. He promised to send a car to get me there, and gave me an alarm-clock which had been a gift from the Japanese. A cheerful roar woke me up in the morning. It turned out that I had overslept my rendezvous: the alarm-clock hadn't rung because the batteries were dead. It was still showing 2 am, which was the time we'd said goodnight.'

They agreed to revive the idea of the book, and in December, shortly after the events at Belovezhskaya Pusha, Peter was in Moscow again: 'It's time to start writing the book. Start it on the first of January.'

'No,' Yeltsin objected. 'On the second. On the first I'll be celebrating the New Year.'

They met a few hours before Yeltsin departed for Alma-Ata, where the treaty establishing the Commonwealth of Independent States was to be signed. He had just returned from a meeting with Gorbachev – probably that nine-hour tryst.

'I said that it was all over,' Yeltsin told Peter. 'No more meetings. I won't be seeing him again.'

'Maybe that's not the best way out. Maybe it's better if you do call on each other in future?'

'What for?'

'Well, you know ...'

'No, never! For my part I shan't be in touch with him again.'

Maybe it is this sequence of fiery outbursts fuelled by topics that enthuse or outrage him, alternating with typically Russian bouts of bear-like hibernation, that offer the key to understanding Yeltsin's character, and the moods and actions of the man about whom it can be said – as it was said about Peter the Great – that he 'brought Russia to its feet'. Just as more than two and a half centuries have not settled the debate about the outcome of the transformations forced by Peter, so too may our descendants dispute the activities of the first freely elected President of Russia.

Supreme power has not altered Yeltsin. He has always been a direct man with spontaneous, often petulant, responses. When he writes it is to get things off his chest. It is for him a cathartic therapy which relaxes him. Whenever the psychological pressures build up, his release is to go to ground somewhere, to think and write – this explains some of his mysterious disappearances. Maybe he gets to drink a little at the same time.

This pattern may also explain his lack of leadership during such episodes as the Chechen crisis, while Grozny was under attack by Russian forces.

But let us return to those fateful one hundred days.

The events that followed the visit by John Major, notably during the Extraordinary Congress of People's Deputies, did not diminish my early enthusiasm for our attempts to put the country back on track. Gorbachev's radical proposal to alter the agenda of the Congress and to debate the 10+1 Declaration stunned the deputies, and they recovered only after the new agenda had already been voted on. The Declaration itself was read by Nursultan Nazarbayez of Kazakhstan. It expressed the readiness of these republics to redefine their relationship within a continuing but reformed Soviet structure. The whole situation on the Congress, the collisions between the deputies and 10+1, reminded me of trying to start a car during a freeze – all the tricks you resort to, from just pushing the starter again and again to pouring hot water, lighting a small fire under the engine, and eventually pushing the car in desperation.

At times the deputies would assemble for the session, only to receive a new draft of this or that document and adjourn to study it. Or they would be sitting idly, waiting for a quorum. There were occasions when, after the unfavourable results of a vote became known, the Chairman – often it was Gorbachev himself – would declare that if the Congress did not vote again it would be dissolved.

As leader of the democratic forces, Boris Yeltsin was labelled 'usurper', and the spokesman of the right-wing forces, Lieutenant-Colonel Victor Alksnis, accused the Presidium of violating elementary democratic norms.

A crazy mixture of orderly behaviour and anarchy, pluralism, authoritarianism, and God knows what else – such was our new democracy, and it hasn't grown much more harmonious since then. But as a driver does usually manage to start his car, so after a series of pushes, pulls and skids, the Congress of People's Deputies did start, and began to move forward. As a result it signed the death sentence on itself, and gave life to the new Union.

In contrast to the Constituent Assembly of 1917, it was not dispersed before it completed its historic mission. I am sure that scholars, historians and writers have yet to gauge the full significance of this epoch-making gathering. As for me, I remain convinced that the structures envisaged by Congress deserved a longer life. They might have ensured a smoother, less painful transition to the democratic regime that is so longed for by most people in our country, whether they live in Moscow, Kiev, Alma-Ata, or Belovezhskaya Pusha.

Certainly, I was transfixed by the events of the Congress, as I observed how from session to session the documents acquired substance. Ever more sharply, like images on photographic paper, the structures and coordinating bodies essential to the survival of any social organism were emerging. Among them was the Ministry for Foreign Affairs, one of the four remaining central agencies. For me this was more important than simply a safeguard of my personal political future. It opened the way towards fulfilling my calling – that is how I was increasingly viewing my job. Now, without further ado, I could get on with my task as I saw it. The formal necessity to sit through the sessions of the Congress gave me an excuse to postpone dealing with the inevitable routine of ministerial affairs, and provided an opportunity to ponder the longer view.

A term often used in world politics is 'doctrine' – philosophical, military, foreign policy ... But what does it amount to? Is it something like, say, Moses' Ten Commandments? The Monroe Doctrine could be squeezed into only three words: America for Americans. In our political language, this word 'doctrine' became exceptionally popular during the perestroika years in relation to disarmament policies. We proclaimed then that from 'the doctrine of active defence', that is repelling attack and then defeating the aggressor on his own territory, we were shifting to 'the doctrine of sufficiency'. I remember two visits to Stockholm by Marshal Sergei Akhromeyev, the Chief of General Staff of the Soviet Army, an energetic man in his sixties, who looked like everybody's jovial uncle. The first was to attend a conference on confidence-building measures, the second to deliver a lecture at the Stockholm International Peace Research Institute (SIPRI).

The Swedes, and diplomats from other countries, bombarded him with questions on the meaning of sufficiency: how ICBMs would be targeted, what change was implied in the ratio of offensive to defensive capability in our ground forces, air forces and navy. Akhromeyev answered eloquently and with obvious relish. He drew diagrams, produced charts, and promised that verbal formulas would soon be translated into action.

On the third day of the coup, Akhromeyev committed suicide. Neither he nor his successor, Mikhail Moiseyev, had time to fulfil their promises. Akhromeyev's death also killed off a doctrine – the doctrine of sufficiency. As for our previous doctrine – the one on 'active defence' – documents that the Bundeswehr inherited from the People's Army of the former German Democratic Republic graphically demonstrated that defence was the last concern of the Warsaw Pact forces. As the press used to report until very recently, our military were trained for offensive operations rather than for defence. Terms like 'breaking through defence installations' or 'combat in the rear of enemy defences' were liberally used. Plans were made for the first use of nuclear tactical weapons 'if necessary'. In other words, not every doctrine means what it says. Some States consistently keep their word, others cheerfully break it.

During my one hundred days we banned doctrine at the Foreign Ministry. My approach was to proceed from my own observations and experience. Certainly, I benefited from advice from the press – there was no shortage of that during this period – except that my rule was to listen closely, and then do the opposite. The press required me, for example, to identify our priority zones. Could I point on the map? Were they the same as Shevardnadze's, or, God forbid, Gromyko's? Or somewhere else? The United States? Europe? Cuba? Japan? India? Maybe South Africa at last, which my predecessors had refused to talk to? The Middle East? Israel?

But I could not conceive how this or that region could be definitively declared the zone of primary interests. Doesn't that depend on a number of variables, rather than on fixed principles? Could my former counterpart, James Baker, ever have anticipated that he would soon be a visitor to the eastern republics of the former Soviet Union? That he would be going to saunas with the Presidents of new States, drinking kumiss, and as an honoured guest sharing boiled head of lamb with other participants at a *sabantui* (feast), around the *dostarkhan* (low table)? This one receives an ear to help him listen better; this one a tongue so that he may hold his own, another a portion of brain he might find useful.

So did Baker's travels throughout the former Soviet territories represent a change of doctrine? No, circumstances changed. If yesterday the Americans had only to deal with Moscow to prevent leaks of nuclear weapons, technologies, or personnel to totalitarian or fundamentalist regimes, today they go to Alma-Ata, Tashkent or Ashkhabad, and exchange Embassies and Ambassadors.

Eastern and Central Europe – the same countries, the same geography, the same sun and stars over our heads. But the relations are new! And thank God, they will never be the same. Alexander Dubcek repeated to me more than once: we have to give up an 'eternal fraternity', but never friendship. You can't choose a brother, but you are free to make friends.

De-ideologization, humanization, pragmatism: it was these very ordinary words and principles that spurred on my work at this time. So I opted for quick tactical moves that would eventually build the ground for strategy, rather than slow and laborious redefinition of strategies. All the experience that I had accumulated in nine years of diplomatic service cried for expression, but why give voice only to my recent career? Was there an impregnable barrier between that, and the things that guided me in my previous life?

Meanwhile all around us the public debate rang with complaints that the Soviet Union was falling apart, and the realities of everyday life seemed to confirm this. Yet I felt that only now was my country rising from its knees, all over the huge territory stretching from Kaliningrad to Nakhodka and the Kuril Islands. It was the task of diplomacy to speak for this country, and to tell the puzzled world what it stood for now, not only with words and declarations but with concrete deeds. It was not only my personal convictions, but the zeitgeist itself, that was pushing me in this direction.

So it was as Foreign Minister of a born-again State in search of new ways and a new calling in the world – that was how I perceived my mission as the long hot Moscow summer faded.

5

The Human Rights Conference

Let me recall that the top folder in the 'red box' that I took home on my first night as Foreign Minister was entitled 'Moscow Conference on Human Rights'. My foreign colleagues said in their congratulatory letters that holding the conference now was extremely important, but they would understand if it was postponed. After weighing all the pros and cons of convening it at the designated time, I concluded that everything depended on our state of organizational readiness.

In the last couple of weeks, organizing the conference had hardly been anyone's priority, especially since the Chairman of the Organizing Committee, Gennadi Yanayev, was spending his second week in the Matrosskaya Tyshyna Prison. But there was always the General Secretary of the conference, Vladimir Petrovsky, my new first deputy.

'What shall we do?' I asked him. He said there was no need to worry. Of course the preparatory work had slowed down, but it could be speeded up again if we didn't waste time.

'So?' I asked.

'So you have to write a memo to the President. Phone him up, and be insistent.'

Petrovsky was more experienced in dealing with Gorbachev, and I soon understood why he had spoken these last words. He confirmed that the first deliberations after the coup had already taken place, and that the prevailing inclination was to stall. Kvitsinsky was for delay, and Anatoly Kovalev, the other First Deputy, had called from hospital to express the same opinion. Now Alexander Nikolayevich Yakovlev was to consult the Ambassadors of interested countries and elicit the mood of their leadership – in other words to obtain their consent for postponement.

'By the way,' continued Petrovsky calmly, 'there was a call from Yakovlev. He's expecting the Ambassadors tomorrow morning, and you are invited. Do you want to go?' A quizzical look in my direction.

My first impulse was that of course I would go. It was after all Yakovlev asking. My second was to think again, and this relieved Petrovsky. Why should the Foreign Minister go to Yakovlev? What would the Ambassadors make of that?

'No,' I replied. A.N. would be unhappy. But friendship is friendship, and business is business.

I picked up the receiver and pushed the magic button. When Gorbachev answered, Petrovsky slipped out of the office. This was the tradition: if the President called the Minister, or vice versa, no one else would be present.

I outlined my position. There was a brief pause at the other end.

'We discussed this. The conclusion was to delay.'

'We too discussed this.' I tried to inject a cheerful note. 'Our conclusion was to go ahead.'

'Who did you discuss this with there?' Gorbachev picked up my tone.

'With Petrovsky. He is General Secretary of the Conference.' Without waiting for a reply, I began to outline our reasons. I emphasized the opportunity for him and for Yeltsin (he chuckled) to address the world, not through the media but directly, to meet with other leaders, to deliver our message.

He listened attentively, and I felt that he agreed with what I was saying, but still he concluded: 'Let's wait for the Congress and see how things go there.'

The opening of the previous Congress of People's Deputies sprang to my mind (I had watched it on TV in Prague), with its hysterical intervention by a delegate named Umallatova, a highlander from Dagestan, demanding Gorbachev's resignation. Was that what he was thinking about?

'Let's see how things go there,' Gorbachev repeated. 'Views differ a lot. It can be unpredictable. Anything can happen there. And you'll have guests ...'

'Perhaps the presence of guests will restrain them,' I joked.

He laughed. 'Don't you know our people? Have you forgotten them in all your years abroad? I see your point, Boris Dimitrievich, but let's do it like this – we won't make a final decision now, but wait for the opening of the Congress. And then we'll see.'

'We can cancel any time, Mikhail Sergeyevich. But if we want to convene, then every day is important, every hour.' I began to explain how difficult it was, now that no one knew who was responsible for what.

Finally we reached agreement. I would send telegrams to the embassies informing them that the conference would open as scheduled, but we reserved the right to confirm this after the opening of the Congress. Now all sides were satisfied, and I had been introduced to the ways of Mikhail Sergeyevich.

The telegrams were sent out at once, and the final decision was quick to come. Gorbachev announced it during his meeting with John Major, when he was telling him about the 10+1 Declaration. The night's debates must have reassured Mikhail Sergeyevich that the Congress was under control, and he must also have been bolstered by the support for the conference from the visitors. I can confess now that when we were riding with Douglas Hurd from the airport to the Kremlin, I briefed him on my discussions with Gorbachev, and asked him to support my position. Which he did with obvious pleasure.

The President's decision was immediately transformed into memos, orders and instructions. The fly-wheel began to spin. And as host I had the honour of opening the conference at the precise hour, day, month and year that had been agreed in Vienna.

So began the international Human Rights Conference in Moscow – an idea that seemed so preposterous only three years ago that the British Foreign Secretary, Sir Geoffrey Howe, described it as being 'like a whisky-distillers' convention in Riyadh'. World opinion was still astounded that it could happen, and the assembled Foreign Ministers kept repeating one after another that when three weeks ago they had learnt about the coup, they couldn't imagine in their wildest dreams that the conference would open on cue.

The principal players from abroad were – with the exception of Douglas Hurd – people I was meeting for the first time. Here was a group of Foreign Ministers, bearing the title of high office but in reality a collection of quite ordinary recognizable individuals, certainly not as remarkable as I had expected. My first meeting was with Hans-Dietrich Genscher, who loved his role as the avuncular sage, self-assured and dignified, doyen of the Foreign Ministers' club in which I was the new boy. He affected a degree of familiarity that verged at times on the patronizing, and tended to throw his not inconsiderable weight around, though this had more to do with his own nature than with any politically deliberate attempt to bludgeon a weakened Soviet Union.

The French Foreign Minister, Roland Dumas, was pleasant and polite, despite his heavy charge of personal vanity. Easily the most colourful member of the group was the Italian Foreign Minister, Gianni De Michelis, whose operatic and clownish manner masked a very sharp native intelligence. I can't say that I was terribly surprised when I heard that he was under investigation in Italy's anti-corruption drive.

James Baker was much the most remarkable of these men. Always radiating self-confidence, he behaved like a dignified gentleman, much more the courtly Southerner than a stereotype of the garrulous Texan. He was very good with his aides, and displayed a remarkable degree of self-control, though I often felt that there were few emotions in him that would make that a difficult task. He was a smooth-running American machine, one-track-minded, goal-oriented, and that goal defined by his role as a professional politician rather than a diplomat. He was continually aware of the domestic political dimension of everything he did or said, and kept one ear pricked for the effect of his actions on the image of President Bush and of the Republican Party. While he appeared obsessed with his country's role as undisputed world leader, and did all he could to sustain it – as was to be expected from an American Secretary of State in the post-Cold War era – I always saw that obsession as subservient to the basic aim of securing the re-election of George Bush and the power base of the Republican Party.

When he welcomed the conference participants, Gorbachev said that they were visiting the capital of a State that had turned a new leaf in its thousand years of history. The first events of the conference confirmed his thesis. Before the official opening, the Foreign Ministers of all the European countries, plus the USA and Canada, held a session of the Council of Ministers of the CSCE, and admitted to their ranks as full members Latvia, Lithuania and Estonia. This was made possible by the decision taken three days earlier by the State Council created by the Congress of People' Deputies, to recognize their independence. What neither the government nor the Supreme Soviet had had the courage to do in the previous two or three years, was enacted at the first session of this new governing body of our country.

Sergei Kovalev, for many years a Gulag prisoner and one of the closest colleagues and associates of Andrei Sakharov, became co-chairman of the Soviet delegation. (He was later to achieve prominence through his protests concerning Russian intervention in Chechenya.) Sakharov's widow Yelena Bonner, in her address to the conference and in an article proclaimed 'It was not Mikhail Sergeyevich we defended, we defended the law', and drew attention to a new danger, the spread of ethnic

98

conflicts that lay dormant in quieter times and ignited under pressure, in places where the drive to independence led to neglecting the rights of minorities.

Her warning turned into a prophecy. Not far removed was the day when CSCE representatives would go to Nagorno-Karabakh armed with the mandate of the Moscow conference. For the moment, the Moscow participants were discussing only Yugoslavia, Albania, Cyprus.

I asked Sergei Adamovich Kovalev to prepare two passages for my speech. The first stated that we in our country must look into the conditions in our prisons, and needed to reform our penitentiary system. Those who violated the law still had a right to see their human dignity respected. What better expert could be found on that, than Sergei Kovalev? The second passage dealt with the fate of those who were convicted on criminal charges but claimed to be politically motivated – hijackers, or people illegally circulating classified information on the desperate situation of this or that region or person.

The *New York Times* twice – as if fearing that it might not be believed – reported that the new Soviet Foreign Minister had said in his speech that national guarantees might not be adequate to protect human rights, and the USSR was reviewing the principle of non-interference in the affairs of other countries, which for many years had served totalitarian States as a cover for crimes they committed against humanity and freedom.

The reporter certainly grasped the main point: that no matter how important the principle of non-interference might be, it could be superseded by the supremacy of human rights and basic liberties. First the individual, second the State. The fact that this maxim was uttered in Moscow, which had only recently cast off totalitarianism, made the world listen even harder. And as if inspired by this attention, the participants resolved to reinforce their principles with a special mechanism of control, to transfer to the humanitarian sphere the system of confidence-building measures, inspections and verification tested in military affairs. Wishes and declarations now took concrete, institutional form.

We were so full of proposals that sometimes the Western countries were unable to absorb them all. And no wonder. Established over centuries, and becoming commonplace for them, their adherence to democracy there was now faced by the raw proselytizing of new converts from Eastern and Central Europe.

So went the early days and hours in a post-putsch Moscow. Sometimes it seems to me that contemporaries are incapable of perceiving the unique nature of the events that happen to them in their own times, their tragedy and greatness – two sides of the coin. We are so used to turning obediently to the past in our search for historic deeds and heroes.

The conference was the first significant international event after the coup. It reminded us and the world that life went on. Reports in the press and on television and radio kept Muscovites informed on what was happening in the Hall of Columns of the Dom Sovietov, House of Soviets – the location where fifty years ago, Stalin had staged his sinister political trials.

Black Zils in unprecedented numbers (each Foreign Minister, including our new colleagues from the Baltic States, was provided with one) shuttled back and forth on those early autumn days along Moscow's spacious avenues and boulevards, but people in the street no longer looked at them with hatred and disgust. The number of political bosses in Moscow significantly diminished, and everybody knew the Zils were now used mainly by harmless foreign visitors.

On the Sadovoye Ring, the underground entrance where the three defenders of the White House had perished, you could always see flowers and hear foreign languages spoken. At the Embassies of European countries there were bright lights, and lively gatherings in the evenings.

I said in my speech at the conference: 'In order to qualify for membership of a previous conference that dealt with the humanitarian aspects of the CSCE process, Moscow had to revisit the experience of Berlin in 1953, Budapest in 1956, and

Prague in 1968, where people fearlessly confronted the tanks with their bare hands, and unconditional commitment to the ideas of democracy. The fact that this time in Moscow people had to fight their own tanks, not foreign ones, serves as further confirmation that the borders of freedom do not coincide with the borders of States, and that the defence of freedom is just as indivisible as are such fundamental concepts as conscience, truth and morality, and cannot be subject to political expediency.'

Whatever the crafted rhetoric of that moment, the sentiments were genuine. But little did I know how difficult would be the course we had set ourselves.

6

James Baker and His Five Principles

The Moscow Human Rights Conference represented both an opportunity and a further burden. Thirty-five Foreign Ministers, plus my counterparts from the Baltic States and the republics of the Soviet Union, came to Moscow and were supposed to meet me individually – with only three of four days at our disposal. Only with a few of them, like Douglas Hurd, for example, had I had time to get acquainted earlier.

Even now, my head spins when I look at my schedule of those days. Six, seven, eight, ten meetings in a day. All this, as well as attending the conference, meetings of the State Council, receptions for the ministers by Gorbachev and Yeltsin, where I also had to be present. 'Had to ...' I would never have imagined that accompanying Hans-Dietrich Genscher, Roland Dumas, Hans van den Broek or Sten Andersson to see the President of the USSR would one day turn into a chore! And all this went on under the sleepless gaze of the TV cameras, in a barrage of questions.

It is not customary to speak about such things. The Foreign

Minister has to generate the impression of an all-knowing, all-understanding sage, and I did pay my dues to that tradition. But now that the ordeal is behind me I can confess how heavy power can weigh, even for a mere Foreign Minister, let alone a Prime Minister, or a President.

In the extraordinary situation of those times, it is obvious that attention would be focused on our forthcoming meetings with James Baker. First came his letter. It was delivered to the Foreign Ministry on 3 September and was dated 30 August, the day of my appointment. Was it just a standard letter of congratulation, one of those that were piling up on my desk? Yes, and no. Congratulating me, and expressing the hope of 'meeting you soon and working with you to improve the strong cooperative relations our two countries have enjoyed for the past several years', the Secretary of State wrote about the solidarity of Americans with the Soviet people when they stood up against 'attempts to crush their newly won political freedoms'. He wrote that 'Americans will continue strongly to support progress towards democracy and a market economy.' Touching upon foreign policy, he called for 'a true partnership between our peoples, based on democratic values and a free market system'.

This conventionally worded letter of congratulations thus proposed the agenda for negotiations and prospects for cooperation in times to come. But perhaps he was not sure that his new colleague would pick up the signals, so Baker soon made public his 'five principles'. This was before his visit to Moscow to the human rights conference. I don't recall now how I first learnt about them: whether by means of a telegram from our Ambassador, or from the CNN reports, or from Soviet radio, but almost immediately my response to Baker's five principles was in great demand. When the chief of the CNN Moscow bureau set up an interview with the generous intention – so he told me – of introducing me to the world, he hinted that he was going to ask me about the 'five principles'. The problem was that no one in the Foreign Ministry or in the US Embassy in Moscow had yet seen the text of those principles.

103

Baker was on his way to Moscow, news was accumulating about his plans and intentions, but still we had received no official messages – an unusual diplomatic tactic, to say the least. At his press conference in Washington on 6 September, just before he set out, he said that he would spend two days in Moscow, meet Gorbachev and Yeltsin, his new colleague Pankin and the Russian Foreign Minister Andrei Kozyrev, and before that would visit Alma-Ata, Kiev, Bishkek, and another one or two republican capitals.

First of all, Baker said, he would make known to the Soviet leaders and public the five principles that would guide his country's diplomacy in judging political developments in the USSR, and in particular relations between the Centre and the republics. Baker's behaviour (or was it the style of his aides?) reminded me of the methods of Solovey Rasboinik (Nightingale the Brigand), one of the heroes of medieval Russian folk sagas: he would lie quietly in ambush, then make a sudden charge. Baker's declarations certainly took us by surprise. Petrovsky and the other experts on the United States shrugged their shoulders in resignation, as if to say: 'Americans! That's just their style when they think they've got the upper hand. They rev up the diplomatic bulldozer and push their views and policies through.' Not that we were in any mood to feel humiliated. On the contrary, we longed to be accepted. In those days the common obsession that gripped our entire leadership was with the idea of becoming a 'civilized State'. The issue of being patronized or humbled did not arise. In fact giving advice to the Soviet Union was a pastime that had been positively encouraged by the highly sociable Shevardnadze, who in all his contacts with the West seemed more ready to be polite and accommodating than to stand firm.

For my part I was aware that this dissolution of old-style Soviet intransigence was often seen in the West as a lack of confidence. If Gromyko had acquired the nickname of 'Mr Niet', Shevardnadze came to be seen as 'Mr Da'. The striking contrast in Shevardnadze was that he could be tough as a street-fighter, but as a poker-player he was weak. He had been hard and ruthless as Georgia's Interior Minister, when he never shrank from sacrificing people who stood in his way, and even his friends. But he was not a man of ideas, and could never stand up to a tough opponent with a mastery of detail. Details made him impatient, even the important ones. One consequence of his accommodating manner and its reception abroad was that at the upper levels of the Gorbachev regime the West's largesse with advice and the occasional sermon was positively welcomed as a sign that the Soviet leadership was accepted as potential partners in the new world order.

This obsession with Western reactions to us was baggage that I now had to carry and handle. And shrugging our shoulders about Baker's ambush was now part of the price we had to pay for membership in the club of civilized States.

At long last, Baker's principles arrived. They came almost simultaneously in a coded message from our Embassy in Washington and through the TASS wires. It was a good document, and wholly unobjectionable: the Soviet people must themselves decide their destiny in a peaceful way, and in accordance with the democratic values, practices and principles of the Helsinki Final Act; existing borders, both internal and external, democracy and the rule of law had to be respected and change should only be made through due democratic process – namely, elections. Of course, I fully agreed with Baker. I just couldn't make out whose principles he had in mind: America's or ours. I sensed that I must prepare for our meeting not only in substance, but in style too. I would be presenting and defending not only our own positions, but myself as a person. While principles and national interests are permanent, the experience of a Minister is something that comes with time (remember Shevardnadze in his first year in office).

By then I had more or less clarified the most important issues I had to deal with, in the framework of my own three principles: de-ideologization, humanization and pragmatism, all subject, of course, to the continued support of the Soviet and Russian Presidents. I had no problems with either then.

A new folder had appeared in my safe box, ten typed pages

under the heading 'Some International Problems'. The Contents page listed the following topics:
- The UN General Secretary
- Afghanistan
- The Middle East settlement
- Relations with Israel
- Cuba
- The northern territories
- Renouncing the regime of closed territories
- Erich Honecker
- The Soviet–Czechoslovak Treaty, and the treaties with Hungary, Poland and Bulgaria
- Relations with the Republic of South Africa

I took a similar folder to Gorbachev, and held my breath as he looked at the contents and began to leaf through the pages with obvious interest and eagerness.

What I proposed was:
- By mutual agreement with the Americans, to stop arms and military materials supplies to the Kabul regime and the mujaheddin;
- to step up our efforts in preparing the Middle East conference, and to this end restore diplomatic relations with Israel;
- to complete the process of de-ideologizing our relations with the Fidel Castro regime, and to this end to begin negotiations on withdrawing our military training brigade from Cuba;
- to sign a consular agreement during the pending private visit of South African Foreign Minister R.F. ('Pik') Botha, and then, during a stay in Moscow by President De Klerk to establish full diplomatic relations;
- in negotiations with Czechoslovakia and other Central and East European nations, to drop the demand to control the content of their treaties and alliances; and to negotiate and initial these treaties at Foreign Minister level, and then to have them signed by the Presidents. To this end, to accept the invitation of Vaclav Havel for Gorbachev to visit Prague, and to invite Lech Walesa, Josef Antal and Zheliu Zhelev to Moscow.

The problem was that previously such proposals had either not been raised with Gorbachev, or did not get through to him, or were rejected out of hand, like the issue of the new generation of treaties with the States of Central and Eastern Europe. The points that got on to my list were those where a dramatic reversal of our previous positions was needed. One vital factor that made all this possible was the low profile nowadays maintained by the Soviet military. Defence Minister Shaposhnikov was a gentle, civilized man, not at all in the tradition of the old-style muscle-bound top brass. He discouraged his generals from taking up assertive postures, and seemed genuinely sympathetic to the idea of ushering in a new era. It also has to be said that after the putsch of August 1991, many of the military were embarrassed by their own tacit sympathy for its aims, if not active support. So the quiescence of the Soviet military made it easier for us to be imaginative.

Gorbachev read the memo through, flipped the file shut, and handed it back without a word.

'Well?' I asked.

'Well, what?' he said, pretending to be surprised. 'Go ahead.' And then he smiled.

'So I can follow this line, particularly in negotiations with Baker?' I enquired.

'Yes,' he said, with the same enigmatic smile.

'Incidentally, Baker is asking for a meeting with you. Can I confirm?'

'Yes,' he repeated. 'Check the time with Chernyaev.' He paused for a second. 'And leave your folder here. I suppose you have a copy?'

'Yes, I have.'

'Good.' He smiled again and stretched out a hand to say goodbye.

That's how we made foreign policy. I was content, but still couldn't help wondering why Gorbachev agreed with me so easily, without discussions, although what I proposed contradicted his past beliefs. Later, I think I understood why. As a statesman who had become known for his constant hesitations, he did not like either this reputation, or this trait in his own character. So when after long and painful deliberations he came to a decision, he preferred to stick to it. He had made his choice in me as Foreign Minister, and despite having kept me at a distance for several years, now he was prepared to make me his Foreign Minister and rely on me absolutely.

Returning from his Foros imprisonment, Gorbachev, despite all that he had been through, spent one more day insisting on his continued trust in the Party and Central Committee, which could purify and consolidate their ranks after the putsch, and lead the people and the country along the new path. He even talked about convening the plenum of the Central Committee. Next morning he resigned from the post of General Secretary, left the Party, and suspended and in fact outlawed it. Such was his disappointment in his 'comrades', after all he had learnt, that overnight the father of perestroika burnt all he had cherished and renounced all the illusions and prejudices he once had.

My thoughts were preoccupied with Baker's visit. Even if I had wanted to forget about him, the press and TV would not have let me. Baker was already on our country's territory, and was flying from one republic's capital to another. Soviet and American newspapers were full of him – news, speculation, and many questions, a lot of them quite caustic, especially from the Soviet side.

Caustic comments from newly liberated Soviet commentators were the price we all had to pay for the emancipation of the press. Freedom made their heads spin faster than young wine. The lethargy in which most of our press had always wallowed is well known, and things were particularly bad for journalists writing about international affairs or international trade. There were so many more bans and taboos in those areas than in domestic coverage that they amounted to a blanket of silence. I remember that twenty years ago *Komsomolka* made an attempt to interview the Minister of Foreign Trade, and thus to open this closed sphere. The Minister, Nikolai Patolichev, virtually went into hiding from our reporter, on the pretext of restrictive regulations, but I told the reporter that I would sack him if he didn't produce the interview, and after that he intercepted the Minister somewhere in the corridors of his ministry and said to him: 'Nikolai Semenovich, you come from Rostov and I come from Rostov. If we don't stick together we'll be trampled by the Muscovites.' This at long last made Patolichev, who had a sense of humour, crack, and he let us into his sacred domain.

Even at the stage of perestroika when the journalists covering domestic news already had the bit between their teeth, their colleagues in the international field still had to confine themselves to recycling official information and rehashing Foreign Ministry press releases. They continued to rail at the crimes of imperialism against Cuba and Ethiopia, and to laud the heroic labours of the people of fraternal Czechoslovakia and the even more fraternal Bulgaria. Now newcomers to freedom, they went to much greater excess than their colleagues working the domestic beat. No one was spared their scorn – not Baker, not me, not Gorbachev, nor even 'People's President' Yeltsin. The presumption of guilt or at least incompetence was all-pervasive.

'Soviet foreign policy strategy: does it exist?' read one headline in a respected paper, which suggested that before sitting down at the negotiating table with Uncle Sam it might help to figure out what we wanted to talk about. Obviously we were too stupid to grasp this ourselves. 'Whose foreign policy have we got?' exclaimed another serious newspaper. And a popular weekly concluded the discussion by asserting in a banner headline: 'Diplomacy is closed for stock-taking.'

Some people wanted to see Shevardnadze at the negotiating table, convinced in advance that Pankin was too soft. And a few tears were even shed for Bessmertnykh. But it was not all criticism. A report in *Nezavissimaya Gazeta* on one of my press conferences was headlined 'Minister's answers were good, newsmen's questions were bad'. During that press conference the reporter had appealed to his colleagues: 'What are we asking questions for? To get information, or to show how smart we are?' I was not much bothered by this, or, rather, less bothered than many politicians at that time. After the schooling I had received from the press in Sweden and Czechoslovakia, it was an amusing spectacle. Following the old proverb that the cleverest of all is he who will take a fool's advice, in the midst of all this questioning and carping I was finding food for thought.

Questions about the 'obsession' of our foreign policy with the West, and above all with the United States, came up again and again in the wake of my meeting with Baker. Aren't the States that border the USSR more important for our interests, because they are close neighbours? This preoccupation with the West was understandable while the Soviet Union was doing its best to look like a superpower, although our presence in that company was due mainly to nuclear weapons. But what are we thinking about now? The economy is in ruins, the republics are trying to break loose. And meanwhile the new Minister who invited guests from all over Europe spends hours with Uncle Sam.

It might sound convincing, but what did it really amount to as I pored over my list of priorities? Of course that list was not compiled for Baker, but for Gorbachev, for Yeltsin. But could you avoid any of these questions in conversations with Baker? In each of the issues – let alone disarmament, which didn't even need a special message in any list – our interests were very closely intertwined. Why should America be concerned about Afghanistan, our neighbour? But if it came to that, what was our business in Cuba, America's neighbour? This confrontation started well before our entry into Kabul.

The Americans would no doubt be happy about our readiness to agree on the reciprocal cessation of arms supplies to the warring sides (the so-called negative symmetry). Some time ago we had made a breakthrough by withdrawing our troops from Afghanistan, and calling the invasion a mistake, and even a crime. But why did we feel we had to go on supporting the Najibullah regime? Of course, you can't abandon friends, but wasn't it clear by now that this so-called friend was nothing more than a puppet of the now imprisoned Kryuchkov? (Formally Afghanistan had been run by the Central Committee,

110

but in reality it was a KGB operation. Other than the Ambassador, almost the whole of the Kabul Embassy staff was either KGB or GRU, military intelligence.) Why should millions of people on both sides of the border suffer because we were slow to correct our mistakes? Of course, we could not overthrow the Najibullah regime, as the mujaheddin wanted us to – this would amount to a repetition of the original intervention – but it was our obligation to withhold military support without further delay.

My own approach to Afghanistan was one of intense relief at the prospect of getting out. On New Year's Eve of 1979/80 I had been on holiday in the North Caucasus, and out driving with Valentina and my friends Victor Nikolayevich Poliakov (Minister for the Automobile Industry) and his wife, when we heard the announcement of the Soviet invasion over the car radio. We sat in our chauffeur-driven limousine and I whispered: 'This is a mistake. This will be our Vietnam.' Poliakov nodded agreement. Valentina – never one to stay silent in front of chauffeurs – agreed in no uncertain terms. From that moment I had always been sceptical about our Afghan policy, and this often caused rows with my friends.

On Eastern Europe we had had longer to draw the lessons of our actions, but we had started to draw them. Yet here we tended to give the impression of being ashamed of what we ought to be proud of: that we had allowed events to develop according to their inner logic. So it turned out that George Bush and Margaret Thatcher were received there as saviours, while we were regarded with suspicion, to put it mildly.

So I came to two conclusions. First, that in order to develop priorities in foreign policy, we had to think in terms of problems, not regions. Second, that right now our priorities were all in one way or another connected with the United States, and there was nothing to be done about that. A great power is a great power, and Soviet foreign policy had to recognize how much we now depended on the United States for economic assistance.

Many times I caught myself thinking as if I were in front of a microphone, or a camera – as I often was. I really enjoyed knowing that my thoughts, new ideas and improvisations would immediately become public knowledge, and sometimes this thinking on my feet turned out to produce better policies than those that under different circumstances would have been hammered out in endless sessions for months and months. The harsh necessity of living under spotlights for twenty-four hours a day gave me a welcome opportunity to address the public at any time.

For the meeting with Baker arranged for the early morning of 11 September 1991 at the Foreign Ministry reception house on Alexei Tolstoy Street, I arrived three minutes ahead of schedule, with the press already crowding the main entrance.

Baker was late. Only by two or three minutes, but in the circumstances this was long enough for me to conclude that it was unlike him. Normally, he was very punctual. Was this a hint of his attitude towards us? 'Okay,' I said to myself, 'it means that my plan for the evening is correct.' The more I had to recognize the weakened Soviet position in the world, the more I felt I had to stand up to Western statesmen such as Baker, and not appear as the raw newcomer. I approached the press and tried to look as calm and good-natured as possible as I answered their questions about what we were going to discuss. Should they expect something new? Wait a little, I told them. We'll meet right here after the negotiations and a working breakfast – if you're patient enough to wait. Yes, the meeting will take three or four hours, as scheduled.

Here was Baker at last, announced by the wailing of sirens outside the mansion's walls, and a general commotion in the hall. The Americans had suggested that we spend fifteen to twenty minutes talking in private, and then have a plenary session. I had different plans. With a smile, I proposed to Baker that we should get better acquainted, since we had only had a chance to meet briefly at the Human Rights Conference the day before. I added that we were in an unequal position. For obvious reasons I knew much more about my counterpart than he did about me. He protested politely. So, I added, I was ready

112

to correct this asymmetry. Another protesting gesture from his side – did he think I was going to tell him the story of my life? I reassured him: it would be about my political, not personal beliefs – about the problems that we had to discuss. As he would see, a lot would coincide with his ideas about the agenda. I was also convinced that we would be able to agree not only on procedural questions, but on issues of substance too. And I anticipated that the press would start speaking about new Soviet concessions, and might explain them by our desperate position, and our need for further assistance from the US.

At this point I showed him the summary in English of the memo I had handed to Gorbachev, and I saw him raise his eyebrows.

'I hope we can come to a common understanding on many of these issues,' I went on, pleased with the effect it had on him. 'But I want to make one request: even if the agreement we reach is closer to your initial position than to ours, please avoid the temptation to tell the press that these are concessions extracted by you. All this stems from the ideas and positions of the people who are running our foreign policy today. If you wish' – I ended on a joking note – 'you can consider me a co-author of your five principles. I shared them long before I heard about them.'

I felt that this beginning both intrigued Baker and pleased him. With a touch of confusion he put away some sheets of paper he had been shuffling in his hands, and conceded that he had been intending to give me something like an introductory lecture, but now felt slightly awkward about it. Now he was eager to know what lay behind the agenda I had shown him. Why didn't we sit together and go through it?

Our conversation ended when it was time for breakfast. We skipped a plenary and had a truly working breakfast, informing other participants what we had agreed upon and authorizing them to prepare the appropriate documents. In the course of our conversations I told Baker that we could not tolerate being presented with a *fait accompli*. His unilateral actions would not help to put Soviet-American relations on a fresh footing. He

113

was polite in his response, but knowing the strengths and weaknesses of both our hands, I fear that he was not much impressed by our ruffled diplomatic feelings.

Next day we held another round of talks, and then a news conference. Then a meeting with Gorbachev and another news conference. To give Baker due credit, never once during our meetings (and we were to meet in New York, in Jerusalem, in Madrid, in Paris) did he allow himself a hint of a condescending tone. But once during his visit to Moscow he did behave in a presumptuous way on a ticklish issue, and it might have turned into an international scandal.

As I mentioned, during our first meeting I informed Baker about our intent to start negotiations with Cuba concerning the withdrawal of our military training brigade, numbering three thousand servicemen. I did not need to explain to Baker the significance of this measure: it was a new step in de-ideologizing our relations with Cuba. Nevertheless I did make it clear to him that he should regard this as a point of information, not as a subject of discussion between us. It was not our habit to discuss bilateral relations with third parties. I also said that by taking this step we wished to reduce tensions in the Caribbean and to enhance confidence-building measures in the region, and we expected the US to reciprocate.

'We know you've suspended reconnaissance flights over Cuba, and that is good,' I told him. 'But why not go further? Why not, for instance, reduce the number of your units at the Guantanamo military base, reduce the number of visits by your warships to its harbour, and introduce the practice of giving notifications, perhaps even unilateral, of significant military exercises, troop movements, and so on ...'

Baker was listening very carefully, nodding and asking questions, but I could see that he meant to postpone till later any comment on my suggestions about confidence-building measures. The unexpected news about our troop withdrawal really enthused him. Later, of course, he went over this with Gorbachev, and Mikhail Sergeyevich, who had my memo on the desk in front of him, confirmed what Baker was longing to hear

114

about the troops. On the way to the press conference (his meeting with Gorbachev was in the Kremlin's Hall of St George), Baker looked around and with a conspiratorial air asked Gorbachev not to forget to mention the news about Cuba. I was taken by surprise. We had only just sent instructions to our Ambassador in Havana, and to the best of my knowledge the latter could not have had time yet to meet with any senior Cuban officials. It would be tactless and amateurish to spring the news on Cuba out of the blue, and there was no point in embarrassing Castro.

Unfortunately I did not have time to counter Baker's ploy. We were already passing beneath the solemn white arches of the Hall of St George, where a crowd of journalists waited.

Gorbachev mentioned our decision about the brigade in Cuba, and said that its withdrawal in the foreseeable future was yet another proof of our intention to build relations with that country on the basis of internationally recognized principles, and 'to free them of elements that were formed in a bygone era and under different circumstances.'

The news was given much coverage, particularly because in his statement Baker was quick to thank the President for the withdrawal of the brigade in Cuba, which would no doubt have a positive impact on the American public.

This set a wave of conflicting interpretations surging around the world. Time after time I had to explain to the Third World media the true implications of our decision. Castro was surprised and hurt, and let fly at us with speeches, press conferences, and severe reprimands to the Soviet Ambassador in Havana. His Moscow Ambassador protested vigorously and demanded to see me, but I asked a lesser official to handle the problem – the equivalent of telling Castro to stop bothering us. Later he tried to play the whole thing as a gaffe on our part, but the reality was there for all to see. In a broad perspective, we needed to reassure Third World leaders that despite our intensive contacts with the Americans and the West after the putsch, the USSR still had their interests at heart – after all we had over forty years and a wealth of political capital invested in

115

our contacts and influence there. At the same time, it was now clear how much of our support for the Third World had been a product of Great Power rivalries, and once those had evaporated, so did the automatic quality of our support.

Yet our relations with Castro had always had an emotional and romantic content over and above the politics of the situation. In the eyes of the Soviet elite he was a true hero who reminded us of our Soviet traditions of heroism. His appeal was not unlike the appeal of Nelson Mandela in some Western circles: here was a leader fighting for the rights of little people against gigantic forces. All this had to give way to the recognition that we could no longer afford either to sustain him economically, or to exacerbate the American obsession with Cuba. The faithful Fidel had to be sacrificed on the altar of Soviet self-interest.

One question that I asked myself was whether, if I had had time to introduce a word of caution before the news conference, I could have prevented Gorbachev from being bounced into making this announcement. Judging from the obvious pleasure with which he made it, I don't think so. He was happy to have the opportunity, and wasn't going to miss it. And he was not at all embarrassed by the rumble of angry comments about the deal between the USSR and the USA that continued to be heard for some time from what we used to call the 'Island of Freedom'. When I pointed out to him that we had mishandled the whole gambit, he did hesitate for an awkward moment, but then he shrugged his shoulders, as if to say: 'Come on, Boris, we have bigger problems than Castro to contend with.' In any case he had taken a dislike to Castro, whom he considered an egregious windbag, and an expensive luxury who had become a dangerous burden.

It was in the nature of Gorbachev, I persuaded myself. He was very slow in taking a decision that involved something that was really dear to his heart – and who among us, future left or right, democrats, conservative or reactionary, was not infatuated with Cuba: Comrade Fidel, the storming of the Moncada barracks, the *Granma* schooner ... ? But having made a decision,

116

Gorbachev acted quickly and without reservations.

Yet there was also another explanation for Gorbachev's actions. He needed to be active – perhaps even hyperactive – on the foreign affairs front and Cuba had presented him with an ideal opportunity. Because of the dynamics of his relationship with Yeltsin, Gorbachev was no longer able to control the domestic affairs of the country during the last three months of its life, and this virtual isolation on the home front caused him to look to foreign affairs for opportunities to assert himself. This exclusion from domestic affairs also left him with plenty of time on his hands to receive foreign visitors some of whom would never have crossed the threshold of the Kremlin in normal times, let alone the General Secretary's office. For my part, I found myself the captive audience of an increasingly desperate man expounding his ideas and explaining the events of the coup over and over again to each of these visitors. Gorbachev's monologues took up so much time that the visitors seldom had time to get to their own points.

Yet after all, Gorbachev's analysis of the paramount importance of restructuring the Soviet economy and society was fundamentally correct. And if this meant making political concessions to the West, then it was a price we had to pay – and a price Castro had to pay too.

The statement on Afghanistan was not yet ready by the time of Gorbachev's press conference. Baker and I made it public on the following day. This time it really was a bilateral decision, announced as a joint statement by the two ministers. Ironically enough, the first person to support it was the Afghan leader Najibullah. He knew how to put a brave face on things. Besides, unlike Fidel Castro, he had learnt about the document six hours before it was made public.

The joint Soviet–American statement also attracted much attention. It was perhaps the chief event in our first negotiations with James Baker in Moscow, and all the more so because neither Baker nor the US administration had expected an agreement on that subject. 'The Afghan war is over for the Soviet Union,' proclaimed one of our newspapers. It called

117

Najibullah 'another victim of the August revolution'. The press in those days compared the statement to the Geneva Accords of 1987.

This story too has a prehistory. Only a month before our meeting with Baker, the chief Foreign Ministry expert on Afghanistan, Special Envoy Nikolai Kozyrev, stated in public that the decision to call a simultaneous halt to the supply of arms and war materials both to the mujaheddin and to the Kabul regime was impossible to implement because it did not apply to Pakistan and Saudi Arabia, and the 'negative symmetry' would in fact become an asymmetry. But, as Ambassador Kozyrev confessed to me later, he had said this only because he had to. He knew that the text of the document had been prepared about a year before at the Shevardnadze–Baker talks in Houston, but KGB Chairman Kryuchkov refused to give his consent, and this automatically killed the agreement – never mind that the President was obviously inclined to support it. But now Kryuchkov was gone.

The position of Pakistan and Saudi Arabia was worrying me too, though, so at my own insistence we gave a stronger emphasis to those paragraphs of the statement in which the hope was expressed that third parties (meaning Pakistan and Saudi Arabia) would follow our example. The Secretary of State assured me that he would bring all his influence to bear on these countries, and time confirmed his promise. Of course many factors were at work there, but several months later when our commitments were already in force (the USSR had ceased to exist by that time), Pakistan relinquished its position of unequivocal support for the extremist wings of the mujaheddin. Riyadh had done so even earlier.

My concern was not so much with prolonging the Najibullah regime as with preventing further bloodshed and ensuring an Afghan solution to the conflict. There was risk, of course, but in the end it justified itself. The vicious circle was broken. One decision brought new ones in its wake.

Two weeks later in New York I met with representatives of the mujaheddin. This would not have been possible without the

Moscow statement.

The delegation from the Afghan opposition was headed by Professor Sibghatullah Mojadedi, who represented the moderate wing of the 'Peshawar Seven'. We met in one of the reception rooms of the Soviet Mission to the United Nations in New York. The visitors greeted our UN representative Yuli Vorontsov as an old acquaintance. Only recently he had been our Ambassador to Afghanistan, and the first to start talking with the 'armed opposition', or 'bandits' as they were called for many years in our country. As for the Soviet Foreign Minister, it was the first time those present or any of their colleagues had met one. So it was no wonder that they darted some sharp and quizzical glances in my direction.

A flurry of thoughts and feelings blew through my mind as I watched these men clad in their chalvars and cummerbunds come trooping into the room – national costume clearly intended to make a national statement. And it was natural for the mujaheddin to feel cautious and suspicious, for in the past the Gorbachev–Shevardnadze position had given Najibullah unquestioned backing. We stood around awkwardly at first, before eventually shaking hands. The difficulty of doing so was more than political: their cloaks were not designed to make handshakes easier, so there was a certain amount of fumbling before our hands could meet. How many horror stories, true and false, had I read about these people in the Soviet press? Yet the press that packed the room was much taken by the sight of the Soviet Foreign Minister mingling with leaders of the armed opposition. In any case the Soviet media had already made an about-face, and the very same people who once vilified the Afghan opposition were now demanding something not far short of crucifixion for Najibullah.

In a meeting that lasted for an hour around a conference table, I was surprised how articulate these leaders of mountain fighters were, how gentle their manners. Mojahedi was a shrewd and outstandingly intelligent man. Had he remained in a leadership position events would have turned out very differently.

The intentions and demands of these visitors were of a

moderate nature. They did recognize the obligations of the superpowers, gratefully accepted the intermediary role of the UN General Secretary, and were even prepared to talk about a transitional government, but not with Najibullah. My assurances that we did not 'stick by Najibullah, although we do not feel it proper to demand his resignation – this must be decided by the Afghans themselves' made an impression on them.

Without hesitation this Afghan delegation expressed a readiness to enter into a dialogue about the fate of our prisoners-of-war. They agreed that it was immoral to make them, as soldiers of a country no longer fighting in Afghanistan, hostages to the political interests of the warring sides. But they warned that it would not be easy to bring about their release in practical terms – the boys were scattered in dozens of field units, camps and bases, and no one really knew how many there were. I said that our figure was 306, but we did not know how many were still alive. I added that we did not insist on their return to the USSR. Those who wished could go to any country in the world, or stay in Afghanistan, but their parents, wives and fiancées must know what happened to them. I had met with some of our soldiers' mothers before leaving for New York, and could well understand their pain. I saw that I was saying the right words to the mujaheddin, and that brought us a little closer. As a first step, they promised to provide us with a list of all prisoners-of-war who were alive and well.

Further proof of this came soon afterwards in Moscow, when negotiations with the mujaheddin resumed as agreed. The head of the new Afghan delegation, Professor (another professor!) Burhanuddin Rabbani, Foreign Minister in the provisional government formed by the opposition in Peshawar, in no way resembled my first interlocutor, the leader of the National Salvation Front. Rabbani was a slippery creature and tried to play off the Soviet and Russian delegations against each other.

This he found quite easy to do, for in manipulating the race between the Soviet and the Russian power structures to find a way out of the Afghan quagmire – and, it has to be said, to earn credit for doing so – Rabbani was able to play the Soviet prisoner card quite effectively. In our discussions with Mojadedi in New York we had quickly obtained some assurances in principle about the rights of our prisoners. The discussions had then focused on the continued Soviet support for the leadership of Najibullah which plainly the mujaheddin would not brook. This was a predictable and understandable position, though one that we were in no hurry to resolve. But now in Moscow the discussions led by the wily Rabbani centred more on the issue of prisoners. Rabbani knew that this would be an emotive issue, and so it proved. And more importantly there were Russian reputations to be made. If securing the return of our boys meant deposing Najibullah and handing him and his presidency over to the freedom-loving mujaheddin, there were many who felt it was an acceptable price to pay.

As we attempted to clarify to ourselves our negotiating position with the mujaheddin, I could not help thinking sadly how much grief, bloodshed and suffering we had caused with our armed intervention in the affairs of a neighbouring State, what tribulation of mind and soul, let alone loss of life, this insane action had brought up on us. Yes, we had to bring back each and every one of our soldiers, both the army still serving there and those taken prisoner, but we could not turn them into heroes, they had not fought for a just cause. They were more like the American soldiers in Vietnam than the GIs and fighters of the Red Army who had defeated fascism in the Second World War.

As prisoners of our tormented past, we constantly made new myths. The myth of the Afghan war veterans as knights without fear or reproach is particularly galling. How can we condemn that unjust war and glorify those who fought it, soldiers and generals alike? We condemn those diplomats and apparatchiks who did not oppose the August 1991 coup, but we tend to overlook the fact that they had only three days to make a decision, whereas the dirty war in Afghanistan lasted for nearly a decade. There was more than enough time to observe and understand. Equally unsavoury was the attitude of the new

121

converts to a revised Soviet policy on Afghanistan – especially people like Alexander Rutskoi, who spotted the opportunity to make political capital out of the prisoner issue and played straight into the hands of Rabbani, the clever maximalist waiting for him in ambush.

During my watch at the Foreign Ministry, the Afghan issue remained sadly unresolved, still log-jammed on the status of Najibullah. It needed voices of reason, moderation and compromise among the mujaheddin to prevent their country sliding into the appalling mess in which it finds itself. These qualities were sadly lacking. In the event it was the force of arms after the Soviet withdrawal that decided the country's bloody fate.

If the Afghans needed an example, they had only to look in the direction of South Africa, which once looked like a powder-keg waiting for a spark, but whose recent moderation has not devalued the virtue dictated by necessity. For years the African National Congress received much covert support from the Soviet Union – money, arms, training – both through the Communist Party of South Africa and through Angola. This happened chiefly in the Brezhnev–Andropov–Chernenko period. Once Gorbachev came to power our assistance was gradually scaled down. Towards the end the ANC, like so many other Third World friends, fell victim to Soviet economic difficulties. We could no longer afford to help, and we needed to show the West that we were uncoupling ourselves from areas in which we had competed.

Meanwhile the South African Government, in the person of Foreign Minister Pik Botha, was very active in courting the Soviet Union. Botha was a very energetic individual with a driven, almost eccentric, manner. He was like someone from the Caucasus: gregarious, assertive, back-slapping, but unmistakably shrewd. His pursuit of the Soviet Union was so single-minded that he arrived there one day quite unannounced and uninvited, having obtained a private tourist visa, and proceeded to show up first in Kiev, then in a grand tour of Riga,

Vilnius, Tallinn and Leningrad/St Petersburg before showing up in Moscow. Obviously I knew about his visa application, which I approved, and also about his movements in his private chartered jet, which we had also approved, but it was still a bizarre situation. I agreed to meet him, and without preparation on either side we quickly progressed to an agreement on consular relations. In fact it all happened so fast that Botha himself seemed as taken aback by the speed of our response as my own staff was. But with hindsight I wonder whether his buzzing about the Soviet Union was not actually intended to give us time to formulate a position before his arrival in Moscow.

Hans-Dietrich Genscher was also in Moscow for the Human Rights Conference, along with James Baker and other Foreign Ministers. To say that he was the Foreign Minister of the Federal Republic of Germany would be an understatement, no matter how well he coped with his duties. In 1974 he had become the leader of the Free Democratic Party of Germany, which by choosing its coalition partner – either the Social Democrats or the Christian Democrats – was able to determine who would rule the country. Genscher was one of the pillars of post-war German democracy.

Genscher had left Moscow in September, but he was back in several weeks. It could be said that it became a kind of outing for my counterparts to visit Moscow and travel across the vast territory of the Soviet Union. They were given a truly royal reception in the capitals of republics that were not blasé about such visits, and everybody tried to familiarize them with the local customs.

Genscher was one of the most frequent visitors of that period, and he never came empty-handed. At the end of October, when I was just back from a trip to the Middle East and had set about preparing for the opening of the Madrid Conference, he shared with me an idea that he and Baker intended to put forward. They wanted to explore the possibility of setting up a North Atlantic Cooperation Council, which as well as the NATO countries would comprise the Soviet Union, the newly independent Baltic States, and the Eastern and Central European nations.

As a participant in the ceremony that dissolved the Warsaw Treaty Organization I found the idea attractive. Back there in Prague I had been convinced that the liquidation of one bloc would inexorably result in a drastic transformation of the other. A sentry stays awake when he is sure that the enemy is somewhere close out there, and gets drowsy when the danger fades. It seemed to me that the proposal floated by Genscher and Baker was a step in the right direction. It was another scenario for achieving a united Europe with flanks reaching from ocean to ocean, all the way to the Far East, with a stiffening of military cooperation. Since the Cold War and the great ideological confrontation were over, such cooperation would be aimed willy-nilly against the new risks – separatism, savage nationalism, terrorism, drug-trafficking, and so on.

I had previously arranged a meeting between Genscher and Gorbachev, so we went straight from the Foreign Ministry to meet him in the Kremlin. I now discovered that someone from Gorbachev's entourage had already put on his desk a 'briefing paper' according to which the initiative from Genscher and Baker was nothing but an outright attempt to deceive the naïve perestroika democrats of the Soviet Union.

Mikhail Sergeyevich was quick to echo what it said, but his voice lacked conviction, and Genscher's arguments and my own remarks quickly resulted in a reversal of his position. I pondered once again about the reasons for such metamorphoses, and the moment brought a flash of insight. Each and every task he faced during that unique period he regarded as a multi-layer cake. It was essential not only to resolve the matter on its merits, but at the same time to please a very fluid constituency, either winning the maximum number of necessary persons over to his side, or keeping them with him. He would connive with the die-hards who prowled about him, then having departed from his initial position he would reach out to the liberals, while at the same time he threw up his hands to the 'hawks' as if to say, well, you see, I have tried your line of reasoning and it doesn't work.

Still another sobering idea occurred to me on that occasion. Even in the old days, the impression that because he was the General Secretary, and head of the omnipotent Politburo of the Communist Party Central Committee, he could do as he pleased was a superficial one. The KGB, the top military brass, and the powerful regional clans (he himself emerged from one of these) kept him firmly entangled. But now those strongholds were no more. They had vanished into thin air, and yet the reflex was still there. He could still not – and probably would never be able to – pronounce a simple 'yes' or 'no'. He had lost his way for ever, as the poet Yevtushenko put it, between the town of 'yes' and the town of 'no', and this vacillation was becoming common knowledge.

In a word, he gave the go-ahead for Soviet participation in the military and political structure we were discussing, and the North Atlantic Cooperation Council was safely born. Incidentally, the fact that the President and I did not immediately participate in the Council did not prevent us two years later in London from claiming it as our brain-child. In December of 1993 Mikhail Sergeyevich came to Great Britain with Raisa Maximovna to give several lectures and to receive an Honorary Doctorate from one of the Scottish universities. Impeccably tactful as usual, John Major and Norma invited the Gorbachevs, myself and my wife to lunch at 10 Downing Street. Prior to that, the Gorbachevs had called on me at the Embassy.

At the outset the conversation with the Prime Minister was simply social chit-chat, when Raisa Maximovna suddenly complained that warnings had been issued from Moscow – implying from the Kremlin – to the Russian Embassies in the capitals that the Gorbachevs were visiting: they were not to be received or helped. The result was that except in London and a couple of other countries, Russian diplomats would not even see them. We in London had received no such instructions, and I doubt that anything so explicit had been said. But no doubt hints were dropped, and diplomats know which side their

125

professional bread is buttered. Before Gorbachev's visit we had asked Moscow on behalf of the British Foreign Office and security services whether they had anything to recommend. The response was the orthodox Foreign Ministry reply to awkward questions – total silence.

After the awkward pause that followed Raisa's outburst, we turned reluctantly to talk of high politics. At that time, the most popular subject of conversation in the political salons of Europe was the manifest wish of the former satellites of the old Soviet Union to join NATO. Gorbachev spoke stridently against this, and even scored a point off his successor, who allegedly had whetted appetites in Warsaw by saying that the autonomous republics in Russia could do whatever they wanted, but when push came to shove had made a U-turn. It was in this connection that Gorbachev warmly recollected the North Atlantic Cooperation Council that 'we established together with Boris Dimitrievich'.

When I managed to get some words in edgeways – which, I have to admit, was rather difficult to do – I was going to remind Mikhail Sergeyevich of his initial response to that idea. Then it occurred to me that I would be left with no time to make my second remark, so I proceeded immediately to it. I said: 'It's not that individual countries should have to join NATO to protect themselves from some mythical threat, but rather that NATO should join the CSCE, and become an instrument, a military arm, of this common European organization which is the only one that actually exists today.' No immediate comments followed. Both Major and Gorbachev couldn't work out whether I was speaking in earnest or simply playing with a paradox that had crossed my mind.

Yet I am confident that events are developing in precisely this direction, even if it is not always evident at first sight. The NATO ultimatum issued in February 1994 regarding the siege of Sarajevo, and reinforced by Russia's vigorous action in sending military units to that area, was the first instance when NATO acted in the final analysis on behalf of both the CSCE and the United Nations. This was done for peacemaking rather

126

than for defensive purposes. The same thing happened a little later at Gorazde.

So what about the entire 'Partnership for Peace' programme? At first glance this is a step towards expanding NATO, creating a kind of waiting-room for membership. In reality, however, it is a transitional structure on the road to a collective security system, and while the candidate countries are qualifying for admission it may well turn out that NATO is just unnecessary. These are, in fact, the same issues we discussed with Genscher and Gorbachev in the Kremlin at the end of October 1991.

Alas, there was one more topic to be discussed with Genscher at that time, and a far less pleasant one. The issue was Erich Honecker. A few months previously, when the process of German reunification – or to be more precise the liquidation of the GDR – reached its apogee, the world had learned that the former long-time head of that 'first socialist state of workers and peasants in the history of Germany' had been flown to Moscow aboard a Soviet military cargo aircraft. This feat was naturally attributed to Gorbachev, and for good reason. The leaders of the Federal Republic called it an act of betrayal, claiming that by then the territory where the Soviet troops were stationed was already under the jurisdiction of the united Germany, and hence removing Honecker was an infringement of its borders and a violation of its laws. Technically speaking, this was the case. Others said that Gorbachev simply wanted to atone somehow for having abandoned the former leader of the GDR, and was obeying his own ever-present impulse to kow-tow to the unreconstructed champions of the fading communist order. Honecker was in any event now living in a small dacha outside Moscow.

During one of the first talks we had, Gorbachev told me frankly that he did not know what to do with Honecker. In the course of their regular contacts he had more than once warned him: 'The one who is late off the mark becomes a prisoner of history.' In this case the danger of imprisonment had become real rather than figurative for Honecker, but it had not been allowed to happen. Gorbachev's position could be read between the lines. It went something like this: 'What's done is done. Erich Honecker is not the case in point any more. The question is how to save face. I haven't had a meeting with him and I don't intend to. I don't even know exactly where he is right now. You are a newcomer. Your hands aren't tied. Think!' Obviously my task was to persuade Honecker to contact the German Embassy in Moscow and strike some sort of deal.

We knew by then that Genscher was going to raise this subject when he attended the Moscow Human Rights Conference. On the very eve of his arrival, Helmut Kohl brought it up again in a telephone conversation with Gorbachev. In addition, it turned out that the Germans were bringing pressure to bear on Yeltsin. One could understand their tactics. Yeltsin was a democrat. He had faced down the forces that were closest in spirit to the leaders of the former socialist Europe, people like Honecker.

They were also relying on a certain naïvety of Yeltsin's in the field of foreign policy, quite natural for that period, a feeling that since he had 'signed on' as an opponent of the totalitarian communist system, he had better come out actively against everything and everyone with links to that regime. Erich Honecker was a most suitable target in this respect since he was the supreme icon of the old communist institutions. Lastly, the Germans were counting on Yeltsin's chronic dislike of Gorbachev – here was a convenient opportunity for Yeltsin to score off Gorbachev. And they were right. Yeltsin did raise the 'Honecker case' almost the first time we met. 'This case should be thoroughly looked into,' he pronounced gravely.

Genscher stayed on after the Human Rights Conference and made a blunt request for us to extradite 'the former leader of the former GDR who was illegally brought out of Germany and whom the German authorities have charged with the manslaughter of some fifteen persons: in accordance with his orders, the guards on the border between the two Germanies in Berlin opened fire on GDR citizens who were trying to escape to the FRG.' By the time we met Genscher, I had reluctantly

128

scanned the whole bundle of materials that had accumulated from the mass media and the official correspondence. The situation was tricky. Naturally, no one was going to set about justifying the fact that people had been killed, but even the most respectable Western lawyers expressed doubts about whether Honecker could be held personally responsible, as the leader of a State which had gained official international recognition. *Dura lex, sed lex* was the ancient Roman legal maxim that they kept on recalling: The law is hard, but it is still the law. Every State protects its own borders, according to its own legislation. In the case of the GDR, it was also faced with its international obligations. Article 5 of the Warsaw Treaty obliged all the participating countries to 'ensure the inviolability of their borders and territories'. A uniform system of border control stretched across the whole of Europe, from the Baltic to the Black Sea, so, if they wanted to make someone answerable it was not only Honecker they must arraign, but also all those who established and strengthened the Warsaw Treaty Organization. And this was a matter of political rather than criminal responsibility.

The German authorities issued a warrant of arrest for Honecker. And since they had been aware of the killings on the border from the moment they took place, it followed that at the time of the enthusiastic rapprochement between the FRG and the GDR, both Helmut Kohl and Hans-Dietrich Genscher had socialized, concluded treaties, and hence exchanged kisses with a notorious criminal. In which case they had to be called to account for acquiescing in Honecker's crimes.

Genscher of course was aware of all these arguments, and he could not listen to what I had to say without a perceptible awkwardness. I tried to obtain guarantees that Honecker would not be imprisoned if he returned voluntarily, but in keeping with the political decision taken in Bonn, Genscher stood his ground: Honecker had to be extradited unconditionally and then put on trial. Not that he would have to serve the sentence: almost certainly he would be granted a pardon because of his age and ill-health.

Trying to break the deadlock, I suggested that the Germans might cancel the hastily issued arrest warrant so that the representatives of the Embassy could meet with Honecker or his wife like any other citizens of their country and together work out a mutually acceptable solution.

Both Gorbachev and Yeltsin liked the idea – especially Yeltsin, who was about to pay a visit to Bonn and hoped it would enable him to bring back as a souvenir the solution to this sore subject for everyone. Honecker and his wife said that they would think about it.

In the meantime, someone from Gorbachev's or Yeltsin's team – I cannot now say who – was careless enough to mention in the press that a compromise had been reached between Pankin and the Foreign Minister of the FRG. A vigorous response from Genscher followed. I found this out when my aides told me that the German Ambassador had been instructed to call on me.

'You mean, instructed to ask to call on me?' I corrected, for it was not up to Genscher to decide whether or not I should meet his Ambassador. I then asked Deryabin, my new deputy, to receive the Ambassador. After the meeting he gave me Genscher's letter, in which, as expected, the German Minister expressed his concern over false rumours doing the rounds in the Soviet press that Germany stood ready to make concessions.

It was quite clear that the letter was inspired by domestic political considerations. In fact our reports from contacts with lower-level German diplomats indicated that Honecker was a hot potato that they were actually anxious not to have to handle. Certainly there was never any question of linking his return to German economic ties and assistance to the Soviet Union, and since they did not play their strongest card – a threat to our economic ties – I feel entitled to conclude that the German government did not look forward to his return. The letter nevertheless consented to a meeting between German representatives and Honecker. This was precisely what we needed. Shortly after that, the first in a series of these meetings took place.

During this period Yeltsin had taken a keen interest in the Honecker affair, not least because it afforded him the opportunity to express opinions. On one occasion he declared, with that splendid sincerity which, to my eye, sometimes verges on simple-mindedness: 'You have to realize where I stand. I'm in a position to tackle a lot of problems without consulting Gorbachev. In fact, almost everything. But there are several problems which I'm not in a position to deal with. I can't drag Honecker out from where he is [he meant the State-owned dacha where Honecker was staying], pack his bags and deliver him to you. The world would then reprove me morally for this move. But I'm working on the question, and I'm not saying that there is no way out under these circumstances.'

These words were published on 13 November 1991, and the way out was found three weeks later. After the meeting in Belovezhskaya Pusha the President of Russia was placed in a position to solve all problems, including that of Honecker, who was told that he was no longer under the protection of the State of Russia. He then took refuge in the Chilean Embassy in Moscow, whose head, Clodomiro Almeido, along with other left-wing figures who had escaped from Pinochet, was at one time given asylum in the GDR. The old man was moved to the Embassy in December of 1991. The following July the Chilean Ambassador had to inform Honecker that he could no longer give him refuge. Representatives of the Russian security services walked Erich Honecker and his wife Margot from the gates of the Embassy into a car, and from there aboard a plane departing for Germany.

What happened next is well known. The Germans succeeded in making a martyr of a man who had loyally dedicated himself in word and deed to the Marxist-Leninist doctrine condemned by his people. When he was brought to Berlin, they sent him straight to prison – the same one where he had languished as an anti-fascist when Hitler was in power. At that time, many of those involved were hoping that he would be dead soon, which would offer the best way out for everyone from an awkward situation. But as luck would have it, Honecker would not die.

131

He made speeches at his trial, each one more rousing than the one before. Eventually the highest judicial authority in Berlin rebelled, and came to the decision that it was a violation of human rights to continue the trial of an old man with a terminal disease. Eventually, in January 1993, he was deported into the care of his daughter and her husband in Chile, where he had longed to go ever since Moscow, and he died after seventeen months.

7

Inside the Foreign Ministry

On the night of 29 August, when the Chief of the President's Staff, Grigory Revenko, introduced me to the Ministry, the first person to enter my office after the session of the Collegium was Yuli Kvitsinsky, once my immediate boss in Prague, whom I had just dismissed from the post of First Deputy Minister. My decision could hardly have come as a surprise. Ever since the dismissal of Alexander Bessmertnykh when I was in Prague I had been using all the resources of the spoken and written word, both public and confidential, as well as in coded telegrams, to broadcast my view that it was dangerous to leave the Foreign Ministry in the hands of a man like Kvitsinsky even for a short while. My last desperate appeal on that theme had been made in an interview with the *Izvestia* correspondent in Prague, Leonid Kornilov, which I gave as it happened only a day before the call from the President.

While I was packing to go to Moscow I telephoned Kornilov and asked him to shelve the interview for the time being, but it was too late for that, and the text was carried in the *Izvestia* weekly supplement *Soyuz*.

'The Foreign Ministry has received no replacement for its dismissed head,' I told Kornilov. 'In fact it is now run by Y.A. Kvitsinsky. This is a surrealistic situation: the very man who in the dark days of August sent telegrams to our missions abroad with orders to follow the instructions of the putschists now appeals to us to act in the spirit of the new documents. On top of that, he reports that the Foreign Ministry – under his guiding hand – is conducting intensive investigations into the activities of the Foreign Ministry staff in Moscow and in the Embassies, during the putsch. One can imagine what results it is likely to yield if the poacher's still watching the farm.'

Now this man was standing in my office. Certainly, he was not there to congratulate me. He was calm and held himself with dignity. 'I would like to clarify for myself how I am to understand your statement that I am relieved of my duties,' he said, and I could not help noticing that even at this tense moment he was using the same old-fashioned, turn-of-the-century phraseology that was part of the rather irritating good manner he had always affected, and which had never improved the chemistry between us.

'You are to understand them as they were said.' I spread my arms wide.

He expanded on his question. ''Does it mean that I am discharged from the service too?'

It was not I but someone inside me who replied: 'No, not from the service but from your post. You can choose how to formalize it. You may resign, or I will issue an order.'

'Then I shall resign.' he said without hesitation. And continued: 'In that case, may I write in my letter of resignation that I ask to be relieved of the duties of First Deputy Foreign Minister and would be ready to serve in any position in which it may be found appropriate to use me?'

My God! Why wasn't he this polite and respectful with his colleagues, not to mention the Ministers of the Eastern European countries? With them he used a very different tone!

My silence told him that he had come as far as he could.

'Then one more question,' he said, after a moment of hesitation. 'May I ask if I can take a vacation now? I haven't had one for two years.'

'Of course,' I agreed readily, and could hardly keep from saying: 'And the sooner the better.'

With this we parted, deciding that the Personnel Department would carry out all the necessary formalities. Eventually Kvitsinsky as a fluent German-speaker and former Ambassador to Germany completed his post-Soviet reconversion by moving to Germany and finding work in a bank.

The Personnel Department. 'Cadres' ... Are there any other words in the Russian language that were pronounced till recently with greater awe and greater disdain? Suffice it to explain that in the Foreign Office, as in every other official body, the control of 'Cadres' – in other words selection of people for various positions from couriers and janitors to heads of department and diplomats to go abroad – lay in the hands of the Main Directorate for Personnel, or as it was usually called, 'the Cadres'. This huge Main Directorate was subdivided into ordinary directorates and departments, and supervised by the Deputy Minister, in the last years by Valentin Nikiforov. It was he who next morning submitted to me the papers on Kvitsinsky.

I received Nikiforov with mixed feelings, as I was about to give him the same news, or much the same news, that I had broken to Kvitsinsky. The difference was that sacking Kvitsinsky was my own initiative, and Gorbachev – who at the dawn of perestroika had been cordial towards him – was simply informed about the fact. In the case of Nikiforov, Gorbachev himself dropped the hint when we spoke in private on my first day in Moscow. When Yakovlev learnt about this, he added: 'If I were you I'd do it quickly.' This echoed my intentions.

Nikiforov was a real Party apparatchik, with no diplomatic background, no languages, no foreign experience – a faceless, featureless, suspicious character. He had been foisted on to the Foreign Ministry by his patron, Yegor Ligachev, and Shevardnadze had accepted him because in his Central Committee days Nikiforov had worked in Georgia. He was a

135

staff man who was really tuned in to the old apparat, so he did have certain uses. He could be polite but ruthless in the service of his boss, but when Ligachev's influence began to decline, Nikiforov made no bones about switching his allegiance to Shevardnadze.

Nikiforov was not surprised by what I said. His request was quite different. He asked me to have a word with 'the relevant bodies' to ensure that his wife, who was suffering from a kidney disease, would not be 'detached' from her 'spetspoliklinika', the privileged clinic where she was being treated.

It is no accident that I have to put so many words into inverted commas here. To me, all this terminology sounded humiliating and disgusting, and no doubt my interlocutor did not at all enjoy having to use it. But there were no other words in the modern Russian language in which he could have expressed his request.

The existence of these special clinics meant that 'privileged people', that is the families of those who held relatively high official positions, were treated in special medical institutions. But they were 'detached' from these as soon as there was any serious check to the career of the head of the family. In other words, after enjoying all the benefits of modern medicine, you could be stripped of these, even if you were at death's door, if luck should desert the head of family. This is what Nikiforov's wife was now facing, because she had been dependent for many years on an imported dialyser. In our country we had dozens, hundreds, thousands fewer than there were people who needed them. No matter what I felt about Nikiforov, I promised to do everything I could for his wife, or at least to try to. It was easy to guess that there were people at the Ministry who only yesterday would have rushed to fulfil his every request, let alone outright order, but who today would obstruct anything he might ask for now that he had become 'Mr Nobody'.

There may be people who, irrespective of the practical outcome of his work, would perceive someone of the rank of Nikiforov as a monster of Party rule, who could use all his power and influence only for evil purposes. But it was no monster who stood in front of me, but a living human being who was trying to preserve at least a semblance of self-respect and dignity under stress. While the compassion I felt was not for him but for his ailing wife, I did not feel any anger against him. He was so much a product of his own epoch that he might have been chosen by Providence itself to embody it.

Nikiforov was a 'draftee of perestroika' who had come from the Central Committee to the Foreign Ministry with the express task of cleansing the Ministry of all traces of stagnation. He was one of the ambivalent and faceless types on whom was thrust the incongruous task of implementing reform – a figure who was completely unsuited to the task both by temperament and experience. It is boring to depict all these bureaucratic nuances, but without them one would not understand what was and, alas, is still happening to us, and not only in the Foreign Ministry.

Unlike the succession of the Burgermeisters of Stupidville, as described by our famous nineteenth-century satirist Mikhail Saltykov-Shchedrin, Valentin Mikhailovich Nikiforov did not mark his ascent to the throne of the Cadre Service with any outstanding heroic deeds. That is what makes him an exemplary figure. With diligence and zeal he mechanically translated into the language of Foreign Ministry statutes and regulations those numerous and large-scale campaigns that the first months and years of perestroika were celebrated for.

To begin with, the Foreign Ministry joined the whole country in combating the 'green serpent', that is alcoholism. Irrational and harmful in itself (how many vineyards were cut down, and how many imported prefabricated breweries converted for soft drinks products that they were incapable of producing?), this campaign became a mockery in the diplomatic sphere. The order banning strong drink, including vodka, at diplomatic receptions and other protocol events survived three ministers – I too failed to cancel it, for lack of time. The anecdotes of the time became part of diplomatic folklore. 'Should the whisky heavily diluted with soda and ice which is customarily served at receptions in countries with hot climates be regarded as strong alcoholic drink?' asked the Ambassador to one Central African country, so the legend goes. 'Come to Moscow, we'll discuss this,' replied Nikiforov. The unfortunate Ambassador never returned to his post.

Next on the agenda (in line with moves towards democratization and social justice) came the campaign against nepotism and patronage. Among its victims were not only relatives (certainly there were plenty of these) but even people with the same surname. The Ivanovs, Petrovs and Sidorovs – the most common Russian names – suffered most. 'Working dynasties' – something that we were supposed to be proud of in blue-collar workers' families – turned out in the case of diplomats to mean nepotism and a violation of socialist morality. We know no measure in anything. The hurricane of demented reform tore through departments and overseas missions of the Foreign Ministry as well as through its educational institutions. 'Graduate of the Institute of International Relations' automatically began to sound like 'Somebody's son or daughter, a corrupt person and toady'. A policy of 'drafting from the workers' and peasants' ranks' into the higher education institutions of international relations and linguistic specialization was considered in all seriousness.

In the end a different solution was devised to bring in new blood. Having decided that proletarian conscription would be anachronistic, it was resolved to draw upon the 'gold reserve' of the Party and Komsomol cadres. There had been no shortage of these in the past either, but then they used to sneak into the diplomatic service when Gromyko or his deputy for personnel succumbed to pressure from some Party boss. Now they were marching in ranks through the Diplomatic Academy. This was proclaimed to be a long overdue and beneficial measure absolutely in line with the spirit of perestroika, which, as everybody knew, put barriers in the path of the unworthy.

Here let me mention a curious detail. Soon after his appointment as Deputy Foreign Minister, Nikiforov came to Stockholm to inspect the Embassy. There I organized for him some diplomatic functions like a visit to the Swedish Foreign Ministry, as well as a press conference. This annoyed and irritated him. 'I'm not a diplomat,' he reprimanded me. 'I'm a Party official. It's your job to handle the Foreign Ministry and the press.' But I insisted, and it is my hope now that whatever experience he picked up on that visit proved useful to him as Vice-Consul in Hamburg, where we posted him in consideration of his wife's poor health.

The one group which was immune from the relentless march of mindless 'reform' in the heady early days of perestroika was the intelligence community – the KGB and GRU people working at the Ministry and our embassies abroad. They were a law unto themselves, and if there were no vacancies for them, new posts were created. What this could lead to, I had come to know from my nine years' experience in Stockholm and Prague. At one point, despairing of gaining any support at the Foreign Ministry for my attempts to stop this invasion, I tried telephoning Kryuchkov while I was visiting Moscow. At that time he was First Deputy Chairman of the KGB in charge of external intelligence. He listened to me very attentively, even sympathetically, promised me solemnly that they would not build up their presence in Sweden, and wished me a safe trip to Stockholm and the best of luck.

After that, my life, or the part of it that went on inside the Embassy compound, ran into a bureaucratic minefield. To begin with, the 'close' and 'distant' neighbours who made up more than half of the Embassy staff twice on separate occasions voted me down at the elections to Partcom, the Embassy Communist Party cell.

Here I had better explain the basic power structure that used to prevail in Soviet Embassies. Every Embassy was divided between Foreign Ministry diplomats and the KGB, 'the neighbours'. The Ambassador was of course in charge of the Embassy, but in reality the Communist Party wielded enormous influence there through resident Party Secretaries appointed by the Central Committee and beyond the control of either the Foreign Ministry or the KGB. They carried a diplomatic rank, usually at Counsellor level, and had their own small staff. Relations with Party Secretaries were always nervous. Nobody respected them – neither the diplomats nor the 'neighbours' – because they tended to be overbearing Party hacks, but it was always wise to keep on their right side. Embassy Partcom (Communist Party) meetings usually took place twice a month, and were chaired by the Party Secretary, who presided over a Partcom Committee on which the Ambassador sat just as an ordinary member. Election to the Committee was by secret ballot, and there was always a danger that as Ambassador you would not be elected. If that happened, it would not be long before you were recalled to Moscow. It was an effective tool for Party pressure on diplomats everywhere.

In my case the well-oiled machinery did not work. On the first occasion I was bailed out by Yakovlev, who was in charge of the International Department of the Central Committee. During his term in Canada he had fallen under the same steamroller and understood my quandary very well. On the second occasion, the high farce of 'Embassy opinion' was staged in my absence, at the moment when the Supreme Soviet was confirming my nomination to Czechoslovakia. Somebody was late in starting the engine, and the rusty engine ground onwards in a very Kafkaesque way, flailing the air when the victim was already out of reach. Or perhaps the action was undertaken to prevent my appointment to Prague?

New surprises awaited me in Prague, just as they awaited those of my colleagues who were dispatched to the countries of Eastern and Central Europe – as Shevardnadze put it, 'the most qualified and experienced diplomats who could assist our country's leadership in forming and implementing policies in this important sphere'. But while this was an 'important sphere' for the Minister, Kvitsinsky, the First Deputy Foreign Minister and the Ministry apparatchiks saw Eastern Europe as the soft underbelly of the Soviet Union which needed protection at all costs. So they were more concerned with how to put the leash on those new leaders who allowed themselves too many liberties – and on our Ambassadors who pandered to those leaders too.

It took me half a year to secure the appointment of Alexander Lebedev as my Counsellor-Minister, and that was the first and only 'cadre' achievement that I can boast of. The neighbours meanwhile were sitting pretty, although I began to urge reductions in their numbers almost from day one of my stay in Prague.

Having disposed of Kvitsinsky and Nikiforov I could now get to grips with the others.

My main concern and headache were the Ambassadors. The newspapers were digging into the immediate past, and almost every day brought new examples of the opportunistic if not shameful behaviour of high-ranking Soviet diplomats during the coup. What was to be done?

Seven ambassadors were recalled to Moscow for consultations, which so far amounted to their hanging around in deputy ministers' ante-rooms and cautiously asking to be received by me. But I didn't have the nerve. What could I tell them? Again and again I leafed through the 'Ambassadors' file. It burned my fingers.

Loginov, Vadim Loginov. God knows how long I had known him. Since the 'thaw' of the early 1960s. He was Second Secretary of the Komsomol Central Committee, I was the editor of *Komsomolka* ... Inevitable clashes ... He called for the paper to be converted into a kind of house magazine singing the praises of the Komsomol, its heroic deeds and its leaders. That was normal. But it was no less galling.

Later Loginov went to the Diplomatic Academy, which combined the functions of a cesspool for Party and Komsomol cadres and a nursery for diplomats to be. Vadim Loginov grew into a Minister-Counsellor in our Embassy to the United States, then head of the Department of Socialist Countries in the Foreign Ministry, then Ambassador to Angola. Later, during the perestroika years, he went as Ambassador to Yugoslavia, preserving his rank of First Deputy Minister. (I believe Shevardnadze knew him from the Komsomol years.)

I read the official report:

On 20 August during the coup d'état he took a decision to

141

remove from the central lobby of the Embassy the official portrait of the President of the USSR. This action, described by him as 'incorrect', was widely covered by the Soviet and foreign press and discredited both the Ambassador and the Embassy. The attitude towards him among the Embassy staff varies from cool to sharply negative. A situation has emerged that precludes his effectively carrying out the duties of Ambassador and plenipotentiary representative of his country.

The case of Loginov seemed obvious enough, so I decided to start with him.

He entered my office and I could hardly recognize him. Where was that arrogant bearing and those broad shoulders? His snub nose had grown heavy, his eyes lifeless. He walked like an old man. He tried to explain what had happened – unfortunate coincidence, circumstances beyond his control. But finally he conceded helplessly: yes, the President's portrait was absent from the hall for two days. 'Will my career end in this shameful way?' he asked.

'The best thing for you is to decide for yourself whether you can remain an Ambassador now,' I said. Deep in his eyes a glimmer shone. He thought for a second and then asked to be allowed to go to Belgrade, to bid farewell to the country's leadership, the diplomatic corps, the Embassy staff.

'I'll tell them what really happened,' he summed up, and that was that. Since leaving the service, he has joined the business world.

Leonid Mitrofanovich Zamyatin, Ambassador to the UK and another old acquaintance of mine. The file on him contained a whole selection of clippings from the Soviet and foreign, mainly British, press. When Nikolai Uspensky moved to Stockholm, people at the Ministry said that he was on the left flank of our Ambassador corps and Zamyatin on the right. Zamyatin's career began under Foreign Minister Andrei Vyshinsky, a notorious henchman of Stalin. He prospered under Khrushchev, following him all around the world as a member of his press group, whose duty it was to transform Khrushchev's disjointed off-the-cuff pronouncements into meaningful statements and speeches for publication. In the role of spokesman, 'Zyama', as he was called behind his back, became a true alter ego of Leonid Ilyich. It seemed that he knew much better than the General Secretary himself what was good or bad for the country and for his boss's image. His first move after his appointment as General Director of TASS was to put this previously governmental news agency under the supervision of the Central Committee of the Communist Party. (In those times everyone knew what this meant.) Wasting no time, he then pushed through the Politburo a decision mandating all Soviet newspapers to carry out every instruction from TASS and to publish – even on *Komsomolka*'s meagre four pages – any matter that TASS prescribed. One simple bureaucratic ploy put all of the press under the Central Committee's, in other words Zyama's, control. My imprudent quip that if we were to take all TASS instructions literally then *Komsomolka* would turn into a TASS newsletter made us some powerful enemies.

While my stock was falling that of my opponent was rising, especially after he co-wrote with my former deputy at *Komsomolka*, Vitaly Ignatenko, a lengthy documentary, *The Story of a Communist,* that is of Brezhnev. (They were awarded the Lenin Prize for that.) Rumours spread that Zyama was soon to become Secretary of the Central Committee, talk which he certainly did not discourage.

As far as our relationship was concerned, I sometimes had the feeling that his sole purpose in acquiring the trappings of power was to devise ever new ways to persecute me. When I was appointed Ambassador, it was Zyama who showed up at VAAP to announce the news to the staff. Before leaving he ordered my former first deputy to lock my office and not to let anybody in, including the previous occupant. The deputy could not figure out why, but I understood. The office was equipped with special government telephone lines. It was one of these that I had used to telephone Andropov, who had just moved from the Lubyanka Square KGB headquarters to Staray Square to become Secretary of the Central Committee on Ideology. I had complained to him that my 'distinguished mission' to Sweden was being publicly interpreted by people in his entourage as a straight dismissal. Zamyatin, who was sent to VAAP to 'clarify the misunderstanding', undertook the clarification in his own manner.

But all this was ancient news. Now I read the report on Ambassador Zamyatin (he had been appointed to London by Gorbachev): 'On 19 August 1991, during the coup d'état, he justified the deposition of the President of the USSR as a constitutional measure. He attempted to justify himself later, and was accused by the British press of distorting the facts. His credibility in the eyes of the British government is objectively under question.'

A stack of newspaper clippings and documents from the Embassy confirmed this conclusion. I knew already that the Counsellor at our London Embassy, Alexander Galitsin, had told journalists that the events in Moscow were nothing but an adventurist putsch. Now I learned that Zamyatin had virtually kicked out of his office a diplomat who had tried to persuade him to condemn the putschists.

But one thing couldn't be denied – he fought to the end, as his battles with the British press confirmed. In keeping with the old Bolshevik principle that you can prove anything if you only try hard enough, on 26 August (!) Zamyatin wrote a letter to the *Independent* reprimanding it along with the rest of the British and world press. Among the accused was the UPI news agency, which had reported Zamyatin as saying that the attempted coup was legitimate and supporting the allegations of the coup leaders that Gorbachev was ill and could not govern the country.

In response, British television predictably replayed the tape of his press conference, and the newspapers printed lavish quotations from his statement. The habits of the Central Committee counter-propagandist, not used to being contradicted, let Zamyatin down. What about his convictions? In supporting the putsch leaders, and accusing the British press of always being on the side of Yeltsin, he remained true to himself.

Fortunately, in his conversation with me he had enough common sense to recognize defeat. Our meeting was short and brisk. He didn't argue, just asked to be allowed to retire of his own volition, and so save face. Nevertheless his returning to London to pack and say goodbye shocked the British Foreign Office. Douglas Hurd, when he came to Moscow for the second time in ten days to attend the Human Rights Conference, asked me directly what the return of Zamyatin meant. He breathed a sigh of relief when I explained the situation. The reasons for his retirement were plain enough to the Soviet and Western media. One of our newspapers bade him farewell with the headline: 'The brontosaurs depart'. It also added: 'Public prosecutor must act', but that is another story.

Yuri Vladimirovich Dubinin, famous diplomat. Once he used to run 'First Europe', the department that handled relations with French- and Spanish-speaking countries. Then, a rapid climb. Ambassador to the UN, to the United States, to France. His dossier on the three days of the putsch was thicker than, say, Loginov's, but the case seemed much more complicated. Take for instance the clipping from *Pravda*'s correspondent in France, headed 'A coup in our souls'. He branded the Ambassador 'Homo Sovieticus', by which he meant someone who always obediently applauded authority, no matter who, and supported all its decisions, no matter what. According to the *Pravda* article Dubinin forbade Soviet correspondents in Paris from giving interviews, and went in person to the Elysée Palace to deliver the junta's message.

I had known the journalist, Vladimir Bolshakov, for a long time. He used to work for *Komsomolka,* and never had a reputation as a free-thinker, or a stickler for facts. So he might be overstating the case against Dubinin. Perhaps he was simply getting even with the Ambassador for some old grudge: Ambassadors and journalists rarely have good relations.

So I turned to the *Komsomolskaya Pravda* clipping, which was an interview with my colleague, the Russian Foreign Minister Andrei Kozyrev. It was entitled: 'I feared I would be arrested

145

in Paris'. On the second day of the coup the Russian government dispatched Kozyrev abroad to secure support for the anti-putschist forces and to maintain communication with Western governments.

'Did you meet our Ambassador during the trip?' asked the correspondent.

'No. From conversations with the French I knew that our Ambassador to France was enthusiastically expounding the GKCP's policies. Secondly, no one met me at the airport. And most important, I feared I would be arrested on Embassy ground. If I had gone to the Embassy I might have walked into a trap.'

'A wretched service Ambassador Dubinin gave to our country,' wrote another newspaper. 'An experienced diplomat, this time he backed the wrong horse. In the first hours of the putsch it was he who convinced the Elysée Palace that Gorbachev was really ill, and so persuaded François Mitterrand to adopt a temporizing position.' Apparently it was at Mitterrand's request that Gorbachev quickly recalled the Ambassador.

Dubinin too was not his old self when he appeared in my office. A handsome man with silver curly hair, how he had changed! Unlike Loginov, he did not recognize any wrongdoing. He had only delivered documents, the whole process had not lasted more than a couple of minutes, a pure formality that he had performed automatically. He had not known about Kozyrev's arrival, and next day had located him in Budapest and telephoned him.

It seemed odd that Dubinin couldn't find Kozyrev in Paris where he lived, but as soon as the air had finally cleared, there he was on the phone to Budapest! In the event he was relieved from his post as our Paris Ambassador. But ironically, it was Kozyrev who subsequently appointed this same Dubinin Russia's Ambassador-at-large. The skills of the professional diplomat were still a valuable commodity.

Bessmertnykh was a case different from the likes of Kvitsinsky and Zamyatin who at least had convictions. With his excellent training, discipline, caution, reserve, and suave and unemotional front, Bessmertnykh appeared to personify the professional diplomat. Perhaps that is why he was selected by Gorbachev to become Foreign Minister when Shevardnadze resigned in December 1990. Actually he was the total apparatchik, and very much a bore. Scratch his surface and you scraped away the essence of his personality.

As Foreign Minister, Bessmertnykh set out by following the Shevardnadze line of 'new thinking', but gradually foreign policy began to drift to the right. His going to ground with an illness was typical of his basic spinelessness. 'The Boss sneezed and the whole Foreign Ministry caught cold,' one Moscow newspaper jeered. Nor did his miraculous recovery to stand witlessly beaming at the foot of the steps when Gorbachev's plane brought him back to Moscow do anything to convince either Gorbachev or Yeltsin of his reliability.

After his dismissal, Bessmertnykh gave a number of interviews protesting his democratic credentials, but he only succeeded in further irritating Gorbachev, and so disqualifying himself from other senior appointments. Things turned to farce when he found himself homeless following his dismissal. His Moscow flat was being redecorated, and his official dacha had to be vacated now that he had lost his post. So among the many affairs of State that had to be settled in the aftermath of the putsch was whether the former Foreign Minister should be allowed to stay a bit longer in his dacha. He was.

Finally we come to the bulk of the Foreign Ministry's personnel, the 'silent majority'.

To speak only when spoken to, and to toe the bosses' line was, I suppose, the prime characteristic of a Soviet apparatchik no matter who he was: Central Committee clerk, head of department of the regional Party committee, trade union functionary, or diplomat. For diplomats though, this corporate subservience was further accentuated by diplomatic traditions and rules of behaviour.

What was the duty of a Soviet Ambassador before

147

perestroika? For twenty-four hours a day, it was to explain and justify everything that went on in his country, or, to be more precise, what its leaders were doing inside and outside the one-sixth of the planet which was the Soviet Union. Were SS-20 missiles a threat to peace, destabilizing the nuclear balance? Nothing of the kind! They were purely a response to Western provocations. These were missiles of peace, the guarantee of European security, the nuclear shield of a Communist paradise. Political prisoners? Dissidents in psychiatric hospitals? Pure slander! There could be no political prisoners in our country. We didn't even have clauses for political crime in our penal codes.

Spies under the cover of our embassies? How could you even imagine such a thing? Not a single Soviet diplomat in Norway, France, Canada or Sweden did anything incompatible with the Vienna Convention on Diplomatic Relations.

Restrictions on Jewish immigration to Israel? Certainly not! All Soviet citizens were free to go where they pleased – provided, of course, that they followed established procedures. Jews actually occupied a privileged position.

Submarines? Not a single submarine.

Streams of instructions flowed from the 'Centre' to Soviet Embassies in the world's capitals: explain, deny, declare, hand a note ... And for decades Ambassadors did go out and declare, deny, preach, and look Ministers, Premiers and Presidents in the eye with a clear conscience.

'At least you have no notebook with you,' Olof Palme once joked. 'Your predecessor is remembered for his thick notebook with a black vinyl cover, which he would open and read out instructions and explanations received from Moscow. Sometimes I tried to tell him – to save time – that I'd already received this information from our Embassy in Moscow. "Then I have to add ..." he would say, and reach for his black notebook.'

In the perestroika years these routine lies diminished in number, but they did not disappear altogether. Instructions came from the Central Committee, the KGB, the Ministry of

Defence (which became more open, thus producing even more misinformation than before), and from other bodies. I would not like to overstate the point by suggesting that it was only Ambassadors from the USSR and other socialist countries who had to perform this kind of duty, but there is no denying that our workload in churning out the babble that came from our masters was heavier than anyone else's.

Some Ambassadors, like the owner of the black notebook, may have believed in what they were supposed to say. Some performed these duties automatically, not even trying to understand what they proclaimed. Still others treated these lies like a necessary evil, inevitable excesses of their profession that did not impinge upon their mind and soul. I ask myself whether it wasn't in this spirit that my colleagues visited government offices in the days of the coup. Of course, there was nothing to be proud of, but nor had there been any concerted effort to do harm to the new Soviet State.

A furious media campaign called for a major purge in the Foreign Ministry, as if the readiness to shed diplomatic blood would demonstrate my loyalty. Certainly there had been far too many spineless or discreditable responses to the putsch from the Soviet diplomatic corps, ranging from mere passive non-intervention to active collaboration. And my own career had been plagued by the unprincipled opportunists and apparatchik time-servers who had found cosy berths in our embassies. Yet it was my very resentment, and eagerness to take drastic measures, that made me think twice. There was something in the atmosphere of those days, this very special period in our life, that made people consciously refuse to see the multi-coloured picture of the world, and instead distinguish only between two colours – black and white. Were you or were you not on the barricades? This question caused some people to straighten their shoulders and raise their heads proudly, others to look down in despondency.

Yet after all, our foreign policy had made such strides during the years of perestroika. Significant results were achieved by the dialogue on conventional and nuclear disarmament initiated in

149

our country. The doctrine of military confrontation was replaced by a doctrine of defensive sufficiency. The Cold War ended. East and West became partners. The Berlin Wall fell, the nations of the so-called socialist community threw off the chains of totalitarianism, Soviet troops left or were leaving Hungary, Czechoslovakia, Poland, Germany, Mongolia ... Of course there was another point of view that would call such achievements a catalogue of failure, the humiliation of a once-great power.

So for me the situation looked like this. The right wing were attacking our foreign policy, while their opponents from the democratic camp bayed for the blood of those who were conducting this foreign policy. Wasn't it possible that the purge in the Foreign Ministry that would satisfy the democrats would actually play into the hands of the right wing?

There was something of a case to be made in favour of those who had failed to make a stand. First, in the confusion of the coup it had been hard to tell from abroad what was happening in Moscow, and there was a deep-seated reflex in such circumstances to sit tight and wait and see. Second, although the putschists had declared a state of emergency it had been in the name of 'the preservation of truly diplomatic processes and continuation of the policies of reform leading to the renewal of the Motherland'. There had been no direct intimidation, no mass arrests or disappearances. When Pinochet bombarded the Presidential Palace, Yanayev had called a press conference – and what a nervous performance he gave, sitting alongside Boris Pugo, Vassily Starodubtsev and Oleg Baklanov, telling a pack of hostile and sceptical journalists that his good friend Gorbachev had been feeling rather tired but would soon get better and resume his duties, and meanwhile he and his companions intended to obey any decision of the Supreme Soviet, no matter what it laid down – no question of dissolving parliament, no loud alarm signals given.

In the heyday of perestroika, with its reputation still unstained, the famous Soviet film director Tengiz Abuladze came to Stockholm for the showing of his film *Repentance*.

'Who in your opinion is the main opponent of perestroika?' he was asked.

'The nomenklatura,' he said instantly, as if this was self-evident.

'How many of them are there?'

'Eighteen million,' he responded. 'But those are only the individual members. They have families, relatives, friends, so you have to multiply by ten.'

It was dangerous nonsense to believe that we could simply uproot and discard the past. We needed stability, and we needed the pool of experience represented by our diplomatic corps. Even though they had sharp lessons to learn, and I was prepared to teach them, I was not inclined to organize a 'night of the long knives' at the Ministry.

However important in themselves were the events at the Foreign Ministry, they only mirrored broader events and developments in the country at large.

The *Izvestia* columnist Stanislav Kondrashov quoted the words of high-ranking officials in the Russian government, who said that Smolenskaya Square, the seat of the Soviet Foreign Ministry, would soon follow in the path of Staraya Square. This needs to be explained. Staraya Ploschad (Square), in the centre of Moscow, had always housed the Central Committee headquarters. The Secretariat, numerous departments, and other Central Committee bodies were situated there. After the defeat of the putsch and the outlawing of the Communist Party, the Russian government moved in there.

While Kondrashov was writing about Staraya Square, my mind recalled events in the neighbouring Lubyanka Square, where the KGB headquarters were situated. On 22 August a raging crowd pulled down the monument to Dzerzhinsky, the founder of the Cheka. The celebration of this well-deserved triumph soon degenerated into a riot, with brawling hooligans, calls for pogroms, and stones flying against shop windows. Democracy was turning into the rule of the mob.

Weren't there people who longed to turn the skyscraper in

151

Smolenskaya Square into another fallen monument? 'There are moments,' I told myself, 'when going against the current, even if it is a revolutionary and democratic current, is more justified and requires more courage than just following the stream.' Kondrashov wrote: 'To prevent a witch-hunt in the Smolenskaya skyscraper is plainly an important task that the new Minister is setting himself.'

Yes, too many passions were boiling around our skyscraper. So it was essential to demonstrate what direction I intended to take.

The Main Personnel Directorate was dispersed and replaced by a more compact Personnel Service, with KGB officers withdrawn from its ranks. I received the consent of the President to start negotiations with the new heads of the Ministry of Defence, Marshal Shaposhnikov, and the KGB, Chairman Vadim Bakatin, concerning the future of their people working under diplomatic cover.

The removal of the KGB from the Foreign Ministry was sealed with an incident which explains a lot about the nature and character of the KGB. The story is especially well worth telling because – in contrast to the Soviet Union – it would be premature to announce the KGB's disappearance, even though it has been several times disbanded, recast and transformed since August 1991.

One evening in early September I was informed that Leonid Shebarshin was in the reception room.

'Shebarshin?' I asked myself. The Shebarshin who immediately after the putsch, and prior to Bakatin's appointment, had been the KGB acting Chairman, and was now First Deputy to Bakatin? Yes, the very same man. I remembered that I had met him a few times at receptions and in official circles. They called him a rising star of the intelligence service: he had graduated from the Moscow Institute of International Relations, worked as a diplomat, then took up other work in the 'organs' – the vernacular for the Committee for State Security. Before the putsch he had been First Deputy Head under Kryuchkov, responsible for international activities.

That evening – and here I have to resort once again to this comparison – an entirely different person walked into my office. It seemed as if he had shrunk to half his former size: an obliterated face with no hollows or elevations, unsteady gait and faltering voice. After all, he had devoted his life to the KGB.

I invited Shebarshin to take a seat at the customary small table that in 'important offices' adjoins the desk, but as I was about to sit down opposite him, I saw a glimmer of surprise and confusion in his eyes. 'No, no,' he whispered. 'This is where you have to be,' and he pointed to the armchair where I usually sat at my ministerial desk. It was not until I returned there that he started to speak. Only when the distance was restored did he get to the point. It turned out that he had come to inform me that the KGB had consented to my proposal for drastic cuts in the number of its representatives abroad who worked under Embassy cover. He personally was also in agreement with my basic reasons. Yes indeed, they had overdone it. They had basked in the Central Committee's good graces, had taken a 'no-holds-barred' attitude, and sent their people to the Embassies regardless of expense. In such circumstances, quality and professionalism were not essential. Their relatives and friends had come too: the main thing was to get the visa granted. Then, when they arrived – 'You are absolutely right here. Those people considered themselves the masters of the situation. They abused their official position. We have already taken steps to cut staff numbers. Some thirty per cent as a first approximation. We have recalled every one of our people from certain "stations". Here, have a look.'

He passed across the table a large sheet of paper – a 'blanket' as we used to call them. I was stunned: it listed all their Embassy 'stations', and the number of their agents, both the previous figure and the reduced one. The entire intelligence network was on that single sheet of paper. I pushed it aside feeling – strange as it seemed – disconcerted. 'It's up to you to decide where and how many.'

As I was seeing Shebarshin off, I reminded him of his

telegram to the Prague Embassy, which I had been reading when Gorbachev called to send for me. As I have already related, immediately after the collapse of the coup I had sent a telegram to 'the leadership'. (Soviet diplomatic telegrams were never addressed to an individual: even highly sensitive communications intended for the President were always sent to a collective recipient.) In it I had urged the dismissal of all Foreign Ministry and KGB personnel who had supported the coup. The telegram was routinely passed to Shebarshin, acting head of the KGB, and instead of sending his reply direct to me or through Foreign Ministry channels, he had sent it to Prague through the KGB network – the very people I was trying to get fired! An awkward situation inevitably followed when the KGB's Prague Resident, Victor Titov, came in stony-faced to deliver that reply.

It took Shebarshin a moment or two to recall the incident, and when he did he looked embarrassed. 'Oh yes, of course, we did indeed convey the reply through the people it concerned. We may have let you down there. I quite agree, we ought to have forwarded it through Foreign Ministry channels.'

'And the content should have been different,' I took care to point out.

'Yes of course,' he hastened to agree.

'By the way,' I went on, 'your people are still working in the Foreign Ministry's personnel department, even though I ordered them withdrawn several days ago.'

This time too Shebarshin looked stunned and perplexed. 'It can't be. I gave the order straight away.'

Late that night, during our usual summary of the day's events, Igor Sergeyevich Ivanov, the head of the Foreign Ministry's Secretariat, told me: 'The neighbours have just vanished into thin air. It happened an hour after Shebarshin left.' In a flash, they had packed up their papers and melted away.

Next day came the news that my recent visitor had resigned from his post as First Deputy to the KGB Chairman. Obviously his visit to me had been a last attempt to mend fences, to lobby, maybe even to establish some personal rapport. He wanted to demonstrate that the KGB and the Foreign Ministry no longer needed to be rivals and antagonists. But I had seen too much in my career to be tempted to help out a KGB boss.

Following his resignation Shebarshin became a leading consultant on commercial intelligence and security. He is also a leading figure in the KGB Veterans Society.

8

Sentimental Journeys

I have been focusing on domestic politics. In those days no Russian could ignore them. But ministers of foreign affairs are appointed to carry out foreign policy, and it is time to return to these priorities. The forty-sixth session of the UN General Assembly was to open in New York on 17 September 1991. There was much to do to prepare for it. The focus of international activities was shifting from Moscow, where the CSCE Human Rights Conference continued, to New York.

A key tradition in the world community ordains that the rostrum at the UN headquarters on the East River is the site from which a country can speak about itself and its place in the world. The first week of each session is a gala parade of Presidents, Prime Ministers and Foreign Ministers. According to another tradition, as he travelled to and from New York the Foreign Minister of the USSR always visited one or two States en route. I was not going to break with this tradition, especially as during the Moscow Conference I had received invitations from almost all of the other Foreign Ministers present. Besides, my predecessors had left many obligations still unfulfilled. No matter how much Shevardnadze and Bessmertnykh travelled around the world, there were countries, even in Europe, where the Soviet Foreign Minister had never set foot.

I chose Sweden and Czechoslovakia. Today I am myself surprised both by the boldness of my decision and by the understanding it received both from my closest aides and, more importantly, from Gorbachev and Yeltsin. In the old days, what a storm of questions this choice would have raised.

Summer 1980. The Hungarian poet and novelist Antal Hidas dies in Budapest. In 1937 he and his wife had been thrown into the Gulag, and they were released only towards the end of the Second World War through the efforts of the Chairman of the Writers Union, Alexander Fadeyev. Hidas and his wife Agnes, the daughter of Bela Kun, the leader of the Hungarian Communist Revolution of 1918, were much older than we were – another generation. But we became friends, and were later admitted to their Moscow circle, people like Margarita Aliger, Leonid Martynov and Sergei Narovchatov, all famous and outstanding writers, and all victims of the Gulag now bonded together by the friendship and mutual support born in those terrible years.

When Hidas died of cancer at the age of eighty-one, Agnes was left alone in the world. I felt compelled to go to Agnes, so I went to Mikhail Zimyanin, the Central Committee Secretary on ideology. A person of my rank (I was then Chairman of the Soviet Copyright Agency, VAAP) was not supposed to leave Moscow without permission. Inside the country I ignored these restrictions, although I had to explain myself quite often before the departments of the Central Committee. But there was absolutely no way I could go abroad without a decision from the top – that is, the Central Committee.

Zimyanin certainly knew about Hidas and Agnes Kun. Even by his standards they were devoted friends of our country. Of course, after the Gulag they had no Communist beliefs left in them, but this he did not know.

157

'I have to fly to Budapest for the funeral of Antal Hidas.' Zimyanin looked past me. 'I have to go to Budapest,' I repeated. 'Agnes can't be left alone now. She has always lived with the idea of dying together with Hidas.'

No reaction, as if he was waiting for me to realize what nonsense I was talking. I insisted. Only then did he explain:

'Was there a decision of the Central Committee? No. Was there an invitation from the Hungarian side? No. You are an official person: the Chairman of VAAP, almost a State Committee Chairman.' (Usually when I tried to take questions to the Central Committee, they put me in my place: VAAP was a non-governmental body, this or that was outside my remit.) 'Besides, the Hungarian leadership has mixed feelings towards this couple. Your showing up there may be misunderstood.'

'But this will be a private visit.'

'I see no difference,' Zimyanin cut the conversation short. He made up for his small height with categorical judgements.

As Ambassador to Stockholm in the 1980s I twice tried to visit Agnes and twice was forbidden, first by Gromyko then by Shevardnadze. 'It's not our custom,' Gromyko told me delicately. 'Why do you want to provoke envy and gossip?' shrugged Shevardnadze (this was in the early years of his ministerial career).

The world and my position had now changed. Gorbachev only nodded approvingly when he signed the document confirming my route, the Foreign Ministry staff made ready for the visit, and I could only feel happy that we had come to saner times.

Although the Swedish press labelled the visit a sentimental journey, it was more than just sentiment that took me to these two countries. There were serious considerations that went to the heart of our foreign policy. Would it remain too wedded to the United States, or would a more significant place be found in it for Europe? As a former Ambassador to two 'small countries', would I introduce changes in our priorities? I did not regard Czechoslovakia or Sweden as small countries, but I did hope that my seemingly eccentric choice of destinations for these first official visits would make it clear that we were reassessing our whole foreign policy posture.

All the same, it would be wrong to pretend that it was only diplomacy I was interested in as I prepared to set off. No, I was extremely curious about my responses to flying by special plane, and leaving from the government Vnukovo-2 airport, which is known to the majority of my compatriots only through TV reports. What would I feel when the envoys of three countries – Sweden, the United States and Czechoslovakia – came to see me off in the full glare of TV cameras and flash guns?

Mercifully the mandatory public ritual of joyful kisses and hugs from Politburo members at Vnukovo airport as ministers and Party leaders came and went was now a thing of the past. (An old joke ran: First the smack of kisses, then the roar of engines – what is it? Answer: the Party/government delegation off on an official visit. First the roar of engines, then the smack of kisses – what is it? Answer: the same Party/government delegation returning home.)

Everything went like clockwork. The black Zil whisked me from the Foreign Ministry to Vnukovo, I shook hands with Ambassador Slansky of Czechoslovakia, greeted the Chargés d'Affaires of the United States and Sweden (the Ambassadors had already flown to their respective countries), exchanged words with the press and that was that. A few minutes later the engines revved up, the plane took off, and I looked around. The plane was identical to Gorbachev's in layout and design. I was sitting in a spacious cabin equipped with comfortable armchairs, a sofa and a desk. There was also a bedroom, dining-room, and excellent working quarters. The staff were housed at the back.

In the first minutes my solitude was broken only by stewardesses offering tea or fruit, which I declined. I wanted peace and quiet in which to ponder over what lay behind me and what lay ahead. The flight from Moscow to Stockholm lasts an hour and forty minutes. Regular flights may sometimes arrive earlier, but not ours. 'The doors will open at such and such an hour and minute,' on the dot.

So I had an hour and a half completely to myself.

159

Sweden. In autumn Sweden is yellow-blue, like the colours of its national flag. I had visited the country three or four times as Chairman of the Soviet Copyright Agency, but it was in September 1982 that it became part of my life, and the life of my whole family. In the sixteen months since I had left my ambassadorial post in Stockholm there had been Moscow, Prague in the grip of the 'Velvet Revolution', and Moscow again, but Sweden was still with me and in me. I can't deny that there was an element of nostalgia in my decision to start my round of official visits with the land of the Vikings, King Gustav Vasa, Alfred Nobel, Olof Palme and Abba.

When I arrived in Stockholm as Ambassador in 1982 the Swedish press enjoyed itself discussing whether this appointment was more of a promotion or a demotion for me. They did remember that the new arrival had been promoting artists of a semi-dissident nature – Yuri Trifonov, Vassily Shukshin, Chingiz Aitmakov, Feodor Abramov, Valentin Rasputin, Mikhail Roshin, Vladimir Makanin in literature, and Alfred Shnitke, Edison Denisov, Sofia Gubaidullina, Boris Tishenko in music – but my honeymoon with the Swedish press did not last longer than a month. It ended when the report of the Special Government Commission on 'violation of Swedish territorial waters by foreign submarines' was published. No real proof of the violations was produced, and no hard facts. The exception was one well-known case in 1981 when technical problems had forced a Soviet submarine to stray into Swedish waters, but that was past history. Now there was some 'circumstantial evidence' which, the Commission was convinced, pointed to the USSR.

Olof Palme decided to personally summon the Soviet Ambassador and hand him a note and the Commission's report. 'I felt it necessary to yell myself, and so disarm the loudest shouters,' he told me later in a moment of frankness. The press and the public interpreted him in a different way: there must be something in it if the Prime Minister himself was tackling the matter. The spacious lobby of the Prime Minister's Chancery, Rosenbud, was packed with journalists when I emerged after the audience with Palme. Cameras and microphones quizzed me from all sides, and we practically rolled down the broad stone steps.

Damn those submarines! Did they exist or didn't they? I knew it would be one of the first questions I would face on this visit, this time as Foreign Minister. In my first two or three years as Ambassador there had been regular protests, notes, quarterly reports of the Commission (usually before the vote on the defence budget was due to come up in the Riksdag, as some people joked). There was something surrealistic in all this. No one could tell truth from fiction. No one knew who was serious and who was making fools of everyone. The *Dagens Nyheter* – a serious liberal newspaper – once came out with a double-page spread with photographs of objects resembling periscopes sticking out of the water right in front of the Royal Palace.

The wise Olof Palme said to me: 'The Soviets say there are no submarines, we say there are submarines. No one can prove anything yet. We've just got to live with it.'

Another feature of my ambassadorship were the State funerals in our country. Brezhnev, Andropov, Chernenko in less than three years. Black crepe in the Embassy Hall, books of condolences, delegations, representatives ... Three times Palme flew to Moscow, each time he would leave early in the morning on a small jet plane and return late in the evening of the same day.

The first time I came to see him off, I couldn't find him straight away, and that was also the first time I noticed the genuine modesty of the Swedish Premier. No escort, no government lounge, he and his group simply got out of their Volvos, walked to the plane, shook hands with the Soviet Ambassador (once he managed to find them in the morning darkness), and off they went. My assistant and I were the only people left standing on the airfield.

Funerals are a sad business, but each time Palme returned from Moscow he was more optimistic. Especially the third time, in March 1985. He told me that he had exchanged a few words with Gorbachev, and I am sure that this physically small political giant felt that extraordinary changes were due in the Soviet Union. The tragedy is that he saw only a beginning of them before his murder by an unknown hand in 1986.

Ten days before his death we had lunch in my residence. By that time, in spite of the submarines and many other things, I venture to say that we had become friends. It was on the basis of this friendship and the informality between us that I believe Palme developed an intuitive understanding of how the Soviet Union was changing in the mid-1980s. After all he only had to observe the demeanour of the Ambassador and some of his colleagues (some, not all) to spot the internal dynamics of the new Soviet policies at that time. The struggle between the old taboos and the new attitudes was taking place right under his nose at the Soviet Embassy in Stockholm.

And how many small taboos I violated: making myself accessible, giving a news conference, making a speech at the Rotary Club, putting in an appearance (the first Soviet diplomat ever!) at a gathering of the Salvation Army that for many years was described at home as a synonym for bourgeois hypocrisy and deceiving the masses. All very trivial in today's climate, but in those days these were major departures from the dour image that Soviet apparatchiks cultivated. And the Swedish press picked up these changes avidly. Just getting out of the car to walk from the Foreign Ministry to the Embassy buying a frankfurter at a kiosk along the way and eating it with obvious relish – and in the morning the newspapers would be full of it: see, he is just like us. Or give an autograph, without stopping to think, to a schoolboy who approached you in the Gamla Stan (Old Town), and the reward was the triumphant shouts of his classmates, who wanted to test how the Soviet Ambassador known from his picture in the papers would behave in this situation.

Didn't this mean that to be a politician you first had to be a human being? Not if you listened to reactions in the Embassy, or the 'Soviet colony' as we used to call it. At first, my behaviour was put down to inexperience. They tried to correct me, and warn me to be careful. My poor driver! Although he had nothing to do with the 'services', he too had his instructions: watch the Ambassador. But how could he watch when every now and then the Ambassador would let the car go and walk off along the street, all by himself?

And if the Ambassador spoke with an émigré from Latvia or Estonia at a reception, or, God forbid, invited him to a reception at the Embassy, then this would surely warrant a coded report and dispatch by 'them' through channels. Just to be on the safe side.

'They' were hated but feared – they might do anything. Sad experience taught that if one of 'them' held a grudge against you, the Ambassador would not be able to protect you. One of my drivers confided that a security guard at the Embassy had reprimanded him for not reporting where the Ambassador was going: 'We have to know everything.'

Almost two years had passed since I left Sweden, but I still could not forget how many insulting and bitter situations I had found myself in. Not from the Swedes but from ourselves. They first put it about that the Ambassador lacked experience. Then it was that he fancied himself, wanted to be special, to be liked. This was provoked by my interviews, and contacts with 'dubious elements'. Anyone who did not belong to the Swedish government or the Foreign Ministry belonged to this category. These too, of course, were under suspicion, but contact with them had to be tolerated.

The longer I stayed the worse my reputation became. In October 1987 my article on the Swedish political model appeared in *Moscow News*. It caused a lot of interest in the Swedish press. My message was that it was high time we stopped branding social democrats as 'social traitors'. This met with much unrestrained sneering from among Embassy staff – let the poor innocent churn out his prose. But when I had them work on a detailed report about the Swedish experience, at the request of the most popular economists of the period, Leonid Abalkin and Abel Aganbegyan, they were on the verge of a rebellion: why should they work for those semi-enemies of the people?

The memory of those bleak days watching my back as the Soviet Ambassador in Sweden almost literally brought me down to earth, as the plane flew into Stockholm.

No sooner had we landed than I was faced with a barrage of questions from the Swedish media: was there a danger of a new coup? What kind of a State was the Soviet Union now? And what of the KGB? The KGB ... The KGB ... Would these three wretched letters be with us always?

Yet this seemingly morbid interest in the KGB really came as no surprise, because while I and the entire Soviet and Russian political leadership were adamant that there could never be a return to the old ways, our opponents were using tried and tested methods to protect themselves. And their best defence was attack. Not long before I left for Sweden, an interview with a retired KGB official, Major-General Vassily Solomatin, had appeared in the press. To be sure, it suited the spirit of the time. He condemned the uncontrolled and provocative practices of the secret services in the past, and expressed optimism about plans for reforms after the putsch. But he did not miss an opportunity to snipe at my public statements and actions.

Pankin's gestures, he was saying, look noble and courageous on the surface, but in fact he has the logic of an ordinary Ambassador for whom the presence of intelligence personnel at the Embassy disturbs his peace of mind. Pankin's statements are nothing more than evidence of the naturally tense relations, to put it mildly, between Ambassadors and resident intelligence officers. So for Solomatin all this talk of reducing the presence of intelligence officials in Soviet embassies looked like the belated revenge of the Foreign Minister on the KGB.

Another ex-resident also took the 'Pankin plan' to task: 'The Minister for Foreign Affairs said that foreign intelligence will be denied the right to use diplomatic cover. Declarations of this kind coming from such a level defy comprehension. In fact Boris Pankin's actions are aimed at dismantling our intelligence.'

It was amazing how many loquacious 'ex-residents' suddenly

began to appear out of the woodwork. And all so informative in their polemics too. How many times had I been instructed from Moscow to protest, in response to having some of our diplomats declared 'persona non grata', that Soviet diplomats did not 'engage in activities incompatible with their position'? Now these same people were admitting that they did use the cover of our Embassies.

I understood very well how sensitive and delicate was the area that I was tackling, how much prejudice and pride, how many false priorities and hurt feelings were involved. But I was determined to see it through, and now used my presence in Stockholm to reiterate my intentions: the number of KGB officers, who together with those of the GRU then made up about a half of all Embassy staff, was to be radically reduced, by at least half. Intelligence activities would be carried out in accordance with international norms and domestic legislation (yet to be worked out). Surveillance over diplomats abroad was to be terminated, and violations prosecuted.

I have to confess that in the months that passed after my official visit to Stockholm, and after the press conference where I summed up my views on espionage, my beliefs became far more radical. If we believe that espionage is necessary in the world of today, let us at least admit that it is a necessary evil, an evil institution, no matter how deep its roots in history. In a world where one country after another, like our own, recognizes the priority of universal human values and the sovereignty of the individual, where Russia and the United States are moving from animosity and nuclear confrontation to partnership and even friendship, and where nations that only recently belonged to opposing blocs are now burying the hatchets of war, rather than each other – in this world I see no room for espionage. In this world I have no time for this bloated, self-serving, self-obsessed culture of intelligence which more often than not does little besides providing employment at taxpayers' expense to bureaucratic mediocrities. And despicable though I find the KGB arch-defector Oleg Gordievsky, his description of KGB agents feathering their nests and sending home spurious reports to further their careers was entirely accurate.

Of all types of intelligence activities the most disgusting in my opinion – and here you may call me a typical Ambassador – is the kind that is conducted under the cover of diplomatic missions. The so-called covert agents, or moles, are at least risking their lives and freedom. That is not true of those who possess diplomatic rank, have access to the newest technologies, and drive around in cars with diplomatic numberplates. What do they risk? Just the chance of a corrupting cushy life.

Intelligence officers are a curious type – the nature of their work obviously attracts a strange breed of individuals who thrive on secrecy, deception and a cosmetic romanticism that must hide deep personality flaws. In the case of the KGB, even their professional activity had a double sting. For example, everybody in a Soviet Embassy knew the identity of the KGB 'neighbours'. They made no attempt to hold themselves apart, and they and their wives would socialize very normally with everyone else, making every effort to blend into the normal workings of the Embassy. And yet in the Stockholm Embassy, for example, everybody also knew that the man posing as the Embassy's Third Secretary – whom I can now name as the KGB agent Vladimir Kozhemyakin – as well as making contacts outside the Embassy also kept an eye on the people inside it, and frequently tried to turn diplomats into informers, mostly against me, who was known as a liberal in Stockholm.

Kozhemyakin, who was eventually expelled from Sweden but was later to be elected as a member of the Russian Duma (Parliament), has since his Moscow days revealed the corrupt and corrupting dimensions of a KGB field officer's work. 'Like all Soviet public servants,' he has said, 'I am guilty of *pripiskas* [deliberate distortion of results achieved].' I realize that it is difficult to translate this purely Soviet notion into English, but Kozhemyakin himself went on to illustrate the point: 'In my reports from Stockholm to the Centre, I used to resort to the following ploy. By way of analysing information flows I would dig up valuable and reliable information and attribute it to a concrete "source", that is to a foreigner who was being "worked up".' In other words if you lived in London or Stockholm you might not even have suspected that because it suited some foreign agent to claim to have recruited or suborned you, you were listed as an agent of his country, and a 'source' of top-grade information.

A blatant example of *pripiskas* most recently came to light when Oleg Gordievsky named a number of prominent Britons, including ex-Labour Party leader Michael Foot, as having been KGB contacts. It was clear that whatever contact the KGB may have had with these individuals was entirely without their knowledge and that their names were falsely used to provide credit and credibility to the worthless reports filed by the KGB agents. All of which goes to demonstrate that once you are trained or inclined to deceive, your own side is no more safe than the opposition.

If the agents posing as diplomats are dirty, the weirdest of them all are the double agents. From the standpoint of an individual's personality makeup, the step between a straight intelligence agent and a double agent is not a long one. The same deviousness and ability to deceive, the same adrenaline flow triggered by the string of deceptions – these are the common features to both regular spies and double agents. They have much more in common with each other than with the rest of humanity. This is a point worth remembering when we with one breath demonize one set of double agents while with a second breath we eulogize another lot.

My own encounter with a double-agent was a curious one. I was having lunch one day at the Atheneum Club in London while I was Russian Ambassador there. My companion, a British journalist, spotted Gordievsky in a corner and offered to introduce us. Before I had the opportunity to answer the good KGB colonel made himself scarce. It was clearly a disappearing act at which he was quite skilled. The last time I had come across his name had been some months earlier as Foreign Minister, when I and Vadim Bakatin, the new post-coup KGB chief, had agreed to approve an exit visa from the Soviet Union for Gordievsky's wife. Gorbachev had no objection and her exit

167

application was processed in a matter of days, allowing her to keep Soviet citizenship even after joining him.

If the principal purpose of my visit to Stockholm was pragmatic rather than just a sentimental journey down memory lane – obtaining aid, arguing for soft credits, securing guarantees for investments – the most time was spent dealing with the concerns raised by the Swedish media. Apart from general interest in the KGB and the state of the Soviet Union, the most painful issue was of course the fate of Raoul Wallenberg, the Swedish diplomat who went missing when Soviet troops reached Budapest in 1945, and was never seen again in the West. Wallenberg had saved thousands of Hungarian Jews during the Second World War by procuring Soviet passports for them, and had inexplicably been arrested by Soviet soldiers in Budapest. After twelve years of flatly denying any knowledge of the name, the Soviet side then spent more than three decades reiterating a version given in a 1957 note, which alleged that prisoner Raoul Wallenberg had been arrested as a spy in January 1945 in Budapest and transferred to Moscow. He had been kept in the Lubyanka Prison and died there of a coronary thrombosis on 17 July 1947. This story came from a report submitted by the head of the prison's medical service, Colonel Smoltsov, to the all-powerful chief of the MGB, Victor Abakumov (he and Beria were executed for their crimes after the death of Stalin).

Throughout these years, a Swedish committee named after the hero who had saved so many from Hitler's gas chambers refused to believe the Soviet version, and even entertained hopes that Wallenberg might still be alive in the Gulag. While I was Ambassador to Sweden, my wife and I were approached by Wallenberg's half-sister, Nina Lagergren, during one of the traditional Royal dinners for diplomats. 'Save Raoul,' she pleaded. 'Tell the truth about him and God will bless you. You will go down in history.'

I did not believe that Raoul Wallenberg could have survived for so many years in Soviet labour camps and prisons, but I understood how important it was for his family and relatives, and for the committee, to know everything there was to know about his ordeal after arrest and his eventual fate.

I also received official enquiries about the case from Olof Palme, and in my turn I bombarded Moscow with telegrams. But only when perestroika took over, and when Palme's successor Ingvar Carlsson put an enquiry to Nikolai Ryzhkov during his visit to Stockholm, did we manage to organize a trip to Moscow for Nina Lagergren, Raoul's half-brother Guy Dardel, and Sonya Sonnenfeldt, the executive secretary of the Wallenberg Committee. Perestroika was attempting to shine a glimmer of light on this bitter and shameful case.

In Moscow following their conversations in the Foreign Ministry and with the KGB they had been handed some documents and Raoul's personal belongings. There was nothing new for them in those papers, which echoed the official Soviet version, but the belongings were precious: a notebook, a wallet, some banknotes, identification cards.

After the first trip followed a second and a third. They were admitted to the Lubyanka, and to the archives of Vladimirskaya and Lefortovo prisons, where Raoul had supposedly been seen by other prisoners. I listened to these tireless travellers (each of them over seventy) with mixed feelings. Every new discovery made me happy for them, but I was tormented by the thought that they would not be told the whole truth, whatever it was.

So, what did I bring to Stockholm now? Only a firm promise from Vadim Bakatin that everything that could be found would be found, and the whole truth about the fate of Wallenberg disclosed. And as for the Foreign Ministry, I had instructed its History and Archives Department to submit to me everything they had on the Wallenberg affair. But the atmosphere was such in those days that even this small offering was received with plaudits in Stockholm.

It happened that my last act as Foreign Minister two and a half months after this visit to Stockholm was to hand over documents on the Wallenberg affair from the Foreign Ministry archives to the Swedish Ambassador to Moscow, Örjan Berner, in fulfilment of a promise given in Stockholm. It was an emotional moment as the documents changed hands one by one. He said that a special commission would examine them immediately in Stockholm and the Riksdag would issue a special statement afterwards.

The documents that were given to the Swedes represented correspondence between Molotov and Abakumov, the Foreign Ministry and the Ministry of State Security. It was clear from them that by 1947 the Wallenberg affair had become a hot potato for the top leadership, including Stalin. If they were to admit that Wallenberg was in Moscow they would have to explain first, why a citizen of a neutral country, an anti-Nazi who had saved thousands of human lives, had been arrested; second, why he had been detained so long without reason; and third, why the governments of the Allied nations had been lied to. Of course Stalin could not allow this, and Stalin knew how to solve such problems. His favourite saying was: 'A person is always a problem. No person, no problem.' Molotov, the then Minister of Foreign Affairs, was one of his keenest henchmen. No, the correspondence that I handed to the Ambassador did not contain a death sentence, or a certificate of its execution, but it left no doubt that the orders were given, and that there was no way that Raoul Wallenberg could still be alive.

At least in this respect the Soviet side was not lying in 1957 when, in response to a direct appeal from Prime Minister Tage Erlander, Khrushchev ordered a note to be presented about the death of the 'prisoner of the Lubyanka inner prison' that had occurred on 17 July 1947 – that is ten years before it was officially acknowledged. Except that this tragic victim of Stalin's Cold War paranoia died not from a heart attack, as the prison doctor reported to Abakumov, but beaten to death in his cell, or shot through the head. And having taken that callous step, somehow the Stalin regime condemned all Soviet governments, all the way up to Gorbachev, to collude in the resulting cover-up.

Since 1991 I have not seen Nina, Sonya, Guy Dardel or Pehr Angren, who had been in Budapest with Raoul, but I can imagine what they felt. The search for Raoul had given meaning to their lives. Now it was no use trying to find him among the living. It only remained for them to try to unearth the circumstances of his martyr's death.

Not a word in the bundle of documents that I handed to Ambassador Berner on 20 November 1991 was written by Wallenberg himself, so perhaps they do not say much about their subject, but what a lot they say, indeed cry out, about the tormentors who killed him perhaps by shooting, or perhaps merely by keeping him in prison without trial, cut off from the outside world, and without hope.

Wallenberg's story is a tragedy told between the lines of dry, bureaucratic correspondence. A special kind of purposeful, schematic ignorance saturates these documents, which make it so utterly obvious that their authors had not the slightest notion of morality, honour, compassion or sincerity. A human being was no more precious for them than a spent Swedish match. Their names are infamous: Vyacheslav Molotov, Andrei Vyshinsky, Ivan Serov, Victor Abakumov. Perhaps their very bureaucratic language is the most clinching proof of their total inhumanity.

In a letter to Abakumov dated 7 July 1947, Deputy Foreign Minister Andrei Yanuarievich Vyshinsky refers to the 'fuss' raised by the Swedish press and the pressure from international public opinion, and asks what is known about Wallenberg after his arrest in Budapest. He also drops a hint to Abakumov when he suggests that it is important to know where Wallenberg was kept after his arrest in Budapest, and whether there was any fighting or bombing going on there. On 22 July Vyshinsky asks Abakumov to expedite his reply to the letter of 7 July. There is a handwritten note on the letter dated 22 July from which it is clear that Abakumov had already sent a letter to Molotov on 17 July. According to the Smoltsov report, it was on 17 July that Raoul Wallenberg died. Everything was done really quickly.

On 9 August of the same year Vyshinsky submitted for Molotov's approval a draft letter to the Swedish representative in Moscow. The approved version said that information about contacts between the Soviet military and Wallenberg on 14

January 1945 had been received and promptly submitted to the Swedish side, but it was not possible to verify it now, and further investigation had yielded no positive results. Besides, given that when such contacts took place, the times had been confused, 'all sorts of accidents may have occurred: unauthorized departure of Wallenberg from the positions of the Soviet military units, enemy air or artillery attack, etc.'

Bearing in mind that Smoltsov's report about Wallenberg's death from a heart attack had already been circulated (possibly even to Stalin), one can only suppose now that Vyshinsky's hint was picked up by Abakumov.

The correspondence that I handed to the Swedish side was embarrassing. Crime upon crime, lie upon lie, and generations of Soviet Ambassadors reciting the same story to the Swedish Foreign Ministry. Under Stalin, under Khrushchev, Brezhnev, Andropov, Gorbachev ...

And, finally, the notorious submarines. I knew I would be quizzed on the apparent intrusions into Swedish waters that had continued right up to the putsch, and I wasn't wrong. At my press conference on this Stockholm visit, this is what I said:

'For seven years as Soviet Ambassador I received a great many protests, declarations and complaints from the Swedish side and duly forwarded these to Moscow. And equally dutifully I passed on the official replies: that there had been no instances of intrusion by Soviet submarines into Swedish territorial waters, with the exception of one case that happened in November 1981, when due to a malfunction of navigational equipment an old diesel submarine ran aground not far from the Swedish naval base of Karlskrone. Since then, Soviet submarines have been strictly forbidden under pain of criminal prosecution to approach closer than twelve miles to Swedish territorial waters.

'In relaying those replies, and answering numerous questions from the press, I sincerely believed what I was saying – that no one in the USSR or Sweden could provide a serious reason for such violations. Besides, even if our military for reasons of national security wanted to mislead the Swedes, I felt sure they would tell the truth to their country's Ambassador. My later experience as Ambassador to Czechoslovakia, where among other things I had to work on the withdrawal of Soviet troops, and especially the events of the coup and the role played in it by the people in charge of our submarines, has made me reconsider my views.'

I ended my statement with words that astonished the *Izvestia* correspondent so much that he referred to them twice (first after the press conference, and then three months later). What I said was: 'It is possible that the people who headed the coup have been concealing facts from the national leadership.'

My words, which came so naturally to me in the post-coup atmosphere, amazed the newspeople. The *Christian Science Monitor* commented: 'Boris Pankin puzzled the audience by saying that the diplomatic service as well as the Kremlin leadership may have been misinformed on the question of whether Soviet submarines really intruded into Swedish territorial waters in the past ten years.'

If I created an enigma with my statement, it was deliberate because it reflected a necessity: I really did not know in September 1991 whether Soviet submarines had deliberately violated Swedish waters. And I am still not sure.

The second half of my sentimental journey took in Prague. Between Stockholm and Prague I had to endure almost three weeks at the United Nations in New York, but we'll come to that later.

Prague. Here I was in the city I'd had to leave in such a hurry only a month before.

Thirteen months earlier, in an interview which was published just four days before the anniversary of our shameful intervention in Czechoslovakia, I said: 'My mission as an Ambassador I regard as making amends for myself and for my country.'

The spin-off from that mission I was to recognize in the solemn circumstances of my official visit as the Foreign

Minister of the USSR in that autumn of 1991. The warmth and splendour of the reception I was given, surpassing what would usually be expected for a working visit, testified to something more personal than mere official politeness.

The talks with Czechoslovak Foreign Minister Jiri Dienstbier that began right after my arrival from New York on 2 October 1991 confirmed that both sides were prepared to reap the benefits of improved relations. On the Minister's desk lay the draft of the treaty that we were to initial tomorrow. I produced my copy in Russian. We exchanged understanding glances.

'Any amendments?'

'No,' he answered.

'Neither have I.'

This meant that the treaty was ready for signature, and that Gorbachev would visit Prague – news that I should have reserved for my meeting with the President, but that I could not withhold from Jiri Dienstbier. This long-awaited decision meant so much for him and Havel, and for myself.

On 27 February 1990, when the Soviet-Czechoslovak Declaration was signed in Moscow and Shevardnadze's telegram appointing me Ambassador in Prague reached me in Stockholm, it seemed that a new era in relations between our two countries had definitely begun. The Soviet invasion of Czechoslovakia in August 1968 was condemned, and agreement reached to withdraw our troops before 1 June 1992. I was editor of *Komsomolskaya Pravda* at the time of the invasion, and had to publish heavily in its favour – a response I have always felt ashamed of. I saw my appointment to Prague as a chance to make amends. 'If I am to be appointed Ambassador to Czechoslovakia,' I wrote to Shevardnadze, 'I will do my best to promote the unique new relations of friendship and genuine equality between our two countries and peoples. I am fully aware that it will be harder than if we had a clean sheet.'

And how right I was. The obstacles to the application of common sense and mutual respect, even in the summer of perestroika, were formidable. Centuries of old and brand-new prejudices and preconceptions, and countless acts of open and

174

covert sabotage from both sides, stood in the way of the new thinking and those working for it.

Where shall I begin the long list of mutual suspicions and antagonisms that had clouded the last couple of years? Perhaps with my going to Wenceslas Square in August 1990 to lay flowers on the memorial stone of Jan Palach, the student who had immolated himself in January 1969 in protest against the Soviet invasion five months earlier. I had gone with no escort or advance announcements. The raised eyebrows did not just come from 'the neighbours' in the Embassy. What did this act mean, asked the local politicians and the media. Was this an official Soviet statement or just a quixotic personal gesture by Pankin?

The misgivings, the distrust, the suspicions against Soviet motivations were widespread, both among the new and the older generations of Czechoslovaks. For example it took the arm-twisting of Alexander Dubcek to persuade the Mayor of Prague to invite me to a ceremony honouring several ex-Soviet citizens who had demonstrated in Red Square in 1968 against their country's invasion of Czechoslovakia – and had been stripped of their citizenship. Their names – Vadim Delone, Vassily Dremluga, Larissa Bogoraz, Konstantin Babitsky, Viktor Feinberg, Pavel Litvinov and Natalia Gorbanevskaya – were now to be inscribed in the Book of the Honorary Citizens of Prague.

My arrival at the ceremony (again without escort and unannounced) clearly stunned everybody who recognized me, and a hush descended on the throng. The protocol officers at the City Hall were totally confused and had no idea how to handle my presence. Only Dubcek seemed openly pleased to see me. He stepped forward with a broad smile and shook my hand enthusiastically. His warm gesture of reconciliation gripped me emotionally and brought a tear to me eye. It was enough to break the ice, and soon I was shaking the hands of these Soviet – or alas, ex-Soviet – heroes and inviting them to visit the Soviet Embassy the next day.

The following morning passed for me in agonizing

175

anticipation. Would they or would they not show up, these brave but resentful former dissidents? In the event Larissa Bogoraz and Konstantin Babitsky with his wife did arrive, half an hour late. They made excuses for the others, but for me it would have been enough to have even one former Soviet dissident back on Soviet territory having a normal discussion with a senior Soviet official.

These events of course did not go unnoticed with some of my more unreconstructed colleagues and 'the neighbours' in the Embassy. These were the days when I had few allies among my staff while Kvitsinsky and Nikiforov back home were in no hurry to see my proposals to put Soviet relations with Czechoslovakia on a different footing implemented. 'Is it really advisable to go down on your knees before them?' asked one of 'the neighbours' referring to my laying flowers at the Palach memorial. 'They'll only get bolder.'

Trying to calm and re-channel the choppy waters of Moscow–Prague relations often had curious twists. One of the contentious issues between our two countries was the continuing presence of Soviet troops in Czechoslovakia. In 1990, our government had finally agreed to a withdrawal of troops, and a delegation of the Supreme Soviet Committee on Defence and Security was dispatched to Prague to work out the details. Once in Prague, and just before they were due to meet their Czechoslovak counterparts, the Deputy Chairman of the Committee, Colonel Valery Ochirov, dropped a bombshell. Shevardnadze, he announced, had signed this agreement without consulting anyone, and the Soviet side could not possibly agree to an immediate withdrawal. Besides, where would all the withdrawn officers and men be housed? No, the implementation of this agreement would have to be delayed for eighteen months.

I froze. To say this to Czechoslovaks was like dropping a lighted match into a petrol tank. The radical press, which saw even Dubcek as merely a Quisling, was full of warnings that the Russians were not to be trusted, and that any day now they might suspend their troops' withdrawal. Ochirov's remarks now

176

posed a threat to the entire system of our new relationship with Czechoslovakia, so painstakingly built up. Even without this interference there were problems enough on both sides.

I made up my mind that we were going to thrash this matter out between ourselves. Meetings with the Czechoslovak deputies and the press would have to wait.

The crux of the matter did indeed turn out to be the banal issue of housing. Where would all these Soviet officers and men be housed once back in the Soviet Union? Of course no one had bothered to think of housing when we poured 50,000 troops into Czechoslovakia during three days in 1968, but now that they were due to go back to where they had always belonged, we were asking for another eighteen months to find somewhere for them to live.

We arrived at our solution when we secured from the Czechoslovaks a promise to supply us on favourable terms thousands of 'Czech cottages', prefabricated wooden housing that could simply be shipped into the Soviet Union. But our problems were not over. The senior military staff of the Ministry of Defence discovered that these Czech cottages lacked certain seemingly essential features like fancy bathroom tiles and bidets. So the subject of negotiations eventually switched from Czech cottages to construction materials and equipment so that our rehoused colonels and generals could install their own bidets. Of course these very real concerns for the ablution facilities available to our heroic officer corps were inevitably interpreted in the suspicious atmosphere of Prague as the devious delaying tactics of a Soviet Union reluctant to draw in its imperial tentacles.

My entire period of work as Ambassador in Czechoslovakia had been like this – one step forward, one step back. (In the event, the matter of housing was resolved by the Russian–Czech Treaty of 1992, with Czech cottages acquired at a discount, and no bidets.)

It would be wrong to think that only our side was responsible for every problem. There were enough extremists in Czechoslovakia too, and they never missed a chance to have their say just when it was looking as if the sun was coming out from behind the clouds. At one point they would demand the removal of the Soviet tank that stood as a memorial to the liberation of Prague from the German occupation. At another they would introduce a bill in Parliament declaring null and void all diplomas received from Soviet universities. To speak out against these stupidities meant the risk of being branded a Brezhnevite or a stooge. And once again sane and moderate people found themselves hostages to right-wing or left-wing extremists.

With the defeat of the coup, it was as if the evil spell that continued to cast a shadow over our relations was broken. A new Soviet–Czechoslovak treaty resolving all contentious issues between us was quickly negotiated, agreed and now initialled by me in Prague on this second half of my sentimental journey. It was all set to be signed by Gorbachev on his coming visit to Prague. But as things turned out it never was signed. While Mikhail Sergeyevich was still preparing himself for his visit, the meeting of the Russian, Ukrainian and Belarus presidents in Belovezhskaya Pusha sealed its fate. Events overtook our best intentions. And once again Mikhail Sergeyevich was late off the mark.

Of course on this baking autumn afternoon when I initialled the treaty and later drank a toast with President Vaclav Havel, I had no notion that our efforts would be wasted. But perhaps they were not wasted, for the following year when it was Russia that was concluding its treaty with Prague, and I was sitting in London as the Russian Ambassador there, I was gratified to learn that the wording and all the elements of the treaty on which I had worked so hard while Soviet Foreign Minister had been preserved virtually intact in the document that was eventually signed in 1992.

9

The UN
General Assembly

Between my days in Stockholm and Prague, I immersed myself in three gruelling weeks at the General Assembly in New York – the main purpose of my trip abroad. Here was the new Soviet Foreign Minister, expected to perform tasks large and small in the cockpit of diplomacy.

Nowadays I sometimes leaf through my New York notes, or reread press clippings, or the minutes of my dozens of meetings with Foreign Ministers, Prime Ministers and Presidents. Nowhere among these do I find the slightest hint of awareness that the Soviet Union had no more than three months remaining as a single entity. Looking through my own speeches, interviews, statements for the press, articles – all these the fruits of activities that seem incredible now – I find banner headlines: 'Our goal is to speak the language of the new Union born after the coup'; 'Our country will never be the same'; 'The Soviet Union after the putsch on the way to democracy and the rule-of-law society'; 'We have made a choice.'

The General Assembly of the United Nations is the kind of

event where no word spoken by the Foreign Minister of a great power goes unnoticed, and you will always be taken to task by contemporaries and historians for what you do and say.

At that time I may have been mistaken on many accounts, but now I have to look back and measure my words and deeds by the standards of today.

The first question I was asked at the New York airport was: What new initiatives have you brought with you? The experienced Petrovsky had warned me about this particular question. It seems that everybody was accustomed to a practice exploited under Gorbachev even more than in previous times by a host of our diplomats. First they would push some initiative through the Foreign Minister, then present it to an international forum as a far-reaching and inspiring idea, and then defend it in the constant round of conferences, symposia and workshops held in various pleasant corners of the world.

I had to disappoint the journalists. I brought no new initiatives, only a need to tell the world what sort of country had been born at the barricades at the White House in Moscow, and in those round-the-clock debates of the Congress of People's Deputies. What did it stand for, this country that was starting a new era in its thousand-year history? Our victory over the putsch had washed away the crust of dictatorship and revealed to the world the true and beautiful image of a people ready to defend its right to democracy and freedom, that privilege of the wise and the brave.

The failure of the coup aiming at the restoration of totalitarianism was further underlined by the revolutionary transformation that swept away the last pillars of the bankrupt regime. Zdenek Mlynar, one of the heroes of the Prague Spring, told me after the coup: 'They wanted to repeat the 21st of August, 1968 in Moscow, but they got the Prague 17th of November, 1989.'

The defeat of the putsch was a triumph of good over the 'evil empire'. The whole world needed our victory. Only by combining our efforts could we prevent a return to the Cold War. From the first hour we felt a powerful tide of sympathy from the outside world. The active opposition of people who had tasted freedom, buoyed up by support from the outside, allowed them to bring down the regime that the putschists were defending. They opened the way to creating a State based upon the rule of law.

The Extraordinary Congress of People's Deputies responded to the challenge of the time by creating a State structure within which the constituent republics could have as much sovereignty 'as they could swallow', to use Yeltsin's phrase. The governing bodies constituted by the Congress were designed to provide a common economic defence and foreign policy environment. In other words the engine was started and the course charted. Hopefully there would be enough fuel to make the voyage.

In these circumstances we turned to the world community in the hope that at this stage of our transformation, as in the critical days and hours of the coup, it would provide the help we needed to get us through the transitional period as quickly and painlessly as possible, and make our country a normal, respectable member of the world community.

Everyone who favoured freedom and democracy agreed on the broad outlines of the country that we wanted to have: the rule of law, civil society, parliamentary democracy and a market economy. The Soviet Union needed support from the international community in this decisive and hazardous stage of our transformation, but the world community in its turn should be genuinely interested in our success, because it would be a necessary condition for the formation of stable, civilized, democratic world order.

This was the gist of the concept that I outlined from the rostrum of the forty-sixth UN General Assembly. The flesh for these bare bones was to be added by my activities at the session. In these activities I was to be supported by a number of individuals like the UN Secretary-General and Western ministers all willing us on to complete our transition to democracy successfully.

One useful ally in persuading the West to adopt a new attitude to the Soviet Union was Margaret Thatcher, whom I met at this

181

session of the General Assembly, where she had come as a private citizen. As she saw the situation, it had cost the world community tens of millions of human lives and colossal material efforts to destroy Nazism in Germany and militarism in Japan, and then to restore things to normal in both countries. The fall of Communism in the Soviet Union cost the West neither blood nor money. The people of the Soviet Union did it themselves, and almost without sacrifice. So, she explained to everybody who would listen, it would be wrong not to mobilize the economic might of the West to assist them.

I had previously met Mrs Thatcher while I was Ambassador in Prague, when she addressed the Czechoslovak National Assembly. Although her speech was a tirade against the Communist State that I still represented, I found myself admiring her. She looked like a heroic figure from one of those old Bolshevik posters from the era of absolute certainties — steely, messianic and loud. Here in New York, not long after being deposed, she was a shadow of her former self, but still managed to congratulate me rather grandly on my immediate attack on the putschists.

If there is any place on Earth where one can touch with one's bare hand what is quite abstractly called the world family, then that place is New York in the first weeks after the opening of an annual UN General Assembly session. The first impression there is that it is impossible to make sense of anything in this whirlwind of ministers, diplomats, journalists, Prime Ministers, businessmen, artists, priests, roaring traffic, leap-frogging escorts, solemn meetings, crowded receptions, and a constant succession of world-famous personalities.

But as time goes by, somehow things settle down. You get used to the working schedule that dismayed you at first, and you even manage to find windows in it, although these windows are closed at once by ruthless assistants who are not entitled to compassion because they themselves live under an unbearable pressure of requests and demands for appointments. As the new Foreign Minister of a newly respectable Soviet Union you sense that all New York, which now contains the whole world, wants to see you. You now personify your country, with all the opportunities and problems that people see in it. This is when you almost physically sense how great your country is, and how the world needs it. And at every meeting, in every conversation, you have to take decisions that will bear out your own words from the rostrum: on democracy, law, freedom, good will, disarmament. You feel that the political weight, prestige and influence of your country, which has once again turned into a great unknown for the world, depends on how you talk with your current interlocutor. And everyone wants to talk to you personally, to the minister who got his appointment under such extraordinary circumstances.

Somewhere beneath this sympathy lies the fear that things might have turned out in a different way, and your huge country might have made an about-face. You feel how great is this fear, how intense was the revulsion against what your country used to be only six years ago, and how fragile is the trust that was born with perestroika.

The pattern of the conversation has a protocol of its own. First, what you come to think of as the set programme. None of your counterparts will move on before you rehearse the coup and its defeat, the outcome of the Congress, the new structures, political and economic reforms, relations between the Centre and the republics, Gorbachev and Yeltsin. You have to reassure them that all your country's obligations will be honoured, its nuclear weapons are under reliable control, the armed forces will remain loyal and united, and foreign debt will be serviced. I was convinced that that was the way it was going to be, and my reasons sounded cogent.

Now the 'free programme' can begin: all of your interlocutors have their own problems, and they want your support and sympathy. Some expect these from you because your country has changed, while others watch jealously to see whether in turning to new friends you are not rejecting the old ones.

In my speech at the UN I advocated reconsidering the notorious UN resolution of 1975 that equated Zionism with racism. This was a short passage, but it went off like a bombshell. Early each morning the members of the Soviet delegation and the expert advisers would meet in my office at the Soviet UN mission to discuss our plan for the day. On the day of my speech, each of them had a draft copy of what I meant to say in a few hours' time. The Foreign Minister of Turkmenistan was a member of the delegation, as well as his colleagues from Azerbaijan and Kirghizstan, who were also present at the meeting. He took the floor.

'Was the Minister's speech discussed "at the top"?' he asked.

A buzz went through the audience. This was a question from the past, when literally every paragraph of a Foreign Minister's speech was laboriously discussed at Politburo meetings. As a result, even under Shevardnadze vital passages could be deleted.

I reminded the speaker that the 'top' in its old sense was non-existent, but told him that I had informed President Gorbachev and some other members of the State Council about the main topics of my speech. Unfortunately, in the heat of events I had not had time to have a word with Saparmurat Niyazov, the Turkmen leader.

'Then I suggest that this paragraph be omitted,' said the Foreign Minister. 'It may antagonize the Muslim States, and many in Turkmenistan will not be happy about it.'

The buzz in the audience grew louder. On the one hand, those present saw in this intervention a remnant of the past. We had declared the principle of de-ideologization in our policy, and here we faced a golden opportunity to substantiate our declarations. On the other hand, this too would follow the tradition of a repudiated past. We could not simply ignore the remark of our Turkmen colleague – he represented a young sovereign State that was entitled to adopt its own position, and we must not be oblivious of that.

The Ukrainian and Belarussian Ministers supported my position. The Ministers of Kirghizstan and Azerbaijan looked at each other not knowing what to say. The final decision was up to me.

The situation was complicated by the fact that this matter had not been discussed in Moscow at all. The passage on Zionism did not appear in the text prepared at home. It had emerged in the light of discussions conducted here in New York. The idea came from Sergei Lavrov, head of the Directorate of International Organizations (later Deputy Foreign Minister of Russia). Yuli Vorontsov, our Ambassador to the United Nations, supported him. The 1975 resolution was bound to be raised and probably reversed, they said, and I agreed with them. Even many of the Arab States understood this. Bush would certainly argue against the 1975 resolution in his speech. So why should the Americans reap all the benefits once again? Weren't we, as I said in my speech, a new country now?

George Bush, of course, never missed an opportunity to denounce the resolution on Zionism. But for me this was not a decisive factor. Nor would it come as a surprise to anybody. In 1975 they had voted against the resolution: their pro-Israeli leanings were well known. Our own pronouncement on this subject, on the other hand, would be completely unexpected. Again and again I had to weigh the consequences.

'Consequences for whom?' I then asked myself. 'For me personally? Will the President disapprove? Will members of the State Council from the Central Asian republics complain to him? Judging from the remarks of my Turkmen colleague this was certainly to be expected, and I would have to take some criticism, because if I retained the passage it would mean breaking with a lot of rules governing both the style and substance of the way we made our foreign policy. On the other hand, dropping the passage would mean leaving everything as it was. It was one thing to speak about de-ideologization, and another to act on this principle. Should I call Moscow? Too late. And anyway this was not a matter for a phone call.

Well, there was a time for discussion and a time for decisions. Yes, there was a risk, but a necessary and therefore justified risk. So in my UN speech I took the plunge: 'We have to renounce once and for all the heritage of the "glacial period", such as the notorious resolution equating Zionism with racism.'

Next morning the *Washington Post* and other newspapers picked up the full significance of what I had said: that the

Soviet Union had started a process of restoring full diplomatic relations with Israel. By apparent coincidence, a meeting with Israeli Foreign Minister David Levy planned long in advance took place that very day, several hours after my speech. With journalists packing the lobby of the hotel where he was staying, he met me, metaphorically speaking, with open arms. He said how closely the Israelis had watched the developments of the coup, and how they had celebrated the victory of democracy. Our denouncing of the resolution on Zionism he took as a natural expression of this victory. He finished by proposing that we sign an accord on the restoration of diplomatic relations between our countries right away, and said what an honour it would be for him to see me as his co-signatory – 'What more could I ask? A Soviet Minister who is a democrat, an intellectual, a humanitarian.'

Frankly, I felt a little uneasy. Apart from reacting to Levy's gushing flattery, I did not want my statement to be regarded as a gift to Israel. It had other objectives. It would further our relations with the United States, with their special affection for Israel, and it had benefits for us because we would be seen as a more even-handed contributor to a Middle East peace process. As far as diplomatic relations were concerned, I proposed to discuss these a little later, when the issue of convening a conference on the Middle East settlement was clearer. He was disappointed, but tried not to show it, and as he was seeing me off he gave me a strong handshake, invited me to Israel, and smiled broadly for the press. Three weeks later we would meet again in Israel.

The behaviour of many of my colleagues from the Arab States was quite different. The traditions of Middle Eastern etiquette did not permit them to declare their displeasure openly, but the language of Arab diplomacy knows hundreds of ways to convey the subtlest shades of opinion. All the same, I noticed to my relief that no united front existed between the different Arab delegations.

With the Latin Americans we discussed the Cuba situation, as their attention focused on the forthcoming withdrawal of the

186

Soviet military training brigade from the island. Once the *enfant terrible* of the continent, Cuba had now become its sick man. When one of my high-ranking Latin American interlocutors, once very close to Fidel Castro, told me that the 'Romanian variant' was possible there, I shuddered. Lately I had been giving much thought to the future fate of the regime and its leader, but the possibility of such an outcome had never occurred to me.

How is it that a freedom fighter can turn into a dictator? What cruel laws are at work here?

In the Sixties, all of us 'Children of the Thaw' felt very romantic about Cuba. In discussions between Khrushchev and Castro we took the side of the unbending Fidel. *Komsomolka* devoted pages of prose and verse by popular authors like Yevgeni Yevtushenko, Konstantin Simonov and Robert Rozhdestvensky to his reforms in education, and the fight against poverty, unemployment and prostitution. In 1963 I visited Cuba, Chile and Uruguay. After the slums, bidonvilles, masses of unemployed and swarms of unwashed kids in Santiago and Montevideo, the singing, dancing and marching to the sound of revolutionary songs that I found in Havana – green uniforms on a background of blue sea and white mansions – seemed a realization of the human dream of happiness.

At first our attempts to teach the proud and courageous Cubans to copy our ways seemed a curious nuisance, a well-meaning excess of internationalism. So did Castro's uneven but close interest in our forms of political organization. But years went by, illusions disappeared, and I came to understand what was happening in my country. Yet even today it was psychologically difficult to put the bearded giant Fidel on a par with Ceauşescu or Pinochet, although now even in appearance (with his baggy uniform, and locks of grizzled beard straggling down his chest) he looked more like an ageing demon than the eagle of thirty years past.

My colleagues in New York agreed that dictatorships and dictators were beginning to feel uneasy on the planet. There weren't so many left, in any case, and the sooner they understood that the best way out for them was reforms, the better for themselves and for their countries. Even for those of our partners from Latin America who, like me, had paid their youthful dues to the heroes of the Cuban revolution, the withdrawal of our brigade seemed an appropriate, timely and mainly symbolic gesture. Castro did need reminding from the Soviet side that our unconditional support for him could not last forever.

At this point the conversation would usually move on to Afghanistan and Najibullah, another dictator and another regime whose days were obviously numbered. But how far would these 'last days' stretch in terms of real life, and how much more blood would be spilled along the way? My meeting with the mujaheddin was another New York 'event'. The prospects of settling this conflict now seemed brighter. Accurate reports of the meeting were fogged by rumours, but all observers agreed on one thing: the post-coup Soviet Union was starting to show its hand.

The signals we were sending did not go unheard. The world responded to them, and the most powerful response came from the Bush administration, with its initiative on sharp unilateral reductions of tactical nuclear weapons. Bush would open his address on this matter by referring to the dramatic events in the Soviet Union and saying that its domestic and foreign policy made it possible to abandon the Cold War period forever, and to move away from the relations of confrontation and nuclear competition towards partnership and friendship.

Back in Moscow weeks earlier, when James Baker had sprung his five principles on us, I had announced that I was going to recommend at least two more: the reduction or even elimination of tactical nuclear weapons, and the move to a comprehensive test ban. Our General Staff had explained the urgent need to get rid of tactical nuclear weapons in very practical terms: both sides had accumulated too many of these weapons, and unauthorized access to them presented certain dangers. Besides, they were stationed on territories that were fast becoming risk zones: the former GDR, and some Soviet republics. Nuclear testing presented us with certain purely domestic problems. Kazakhstan had by now closed the Semipalatinsk test sites on its territory, and Russia was not enthusiastic about conducting tests in Novaya Zemlya.

In Moscow my proposal to include these two topics in the agenda of the disarmament talks that we were working on had not enthused James Baker. Nevertheless we kept up our pressure, and when I now approached George Bush in New York his reaction was milder. He said with an enigmatic smile that he was aware of our interests, and understood our motives, and besides the same concerns were shared by the Federal Republic of Germany, and had been voiced by Hans-Dietrich Genscher.

'This has to do with his East German background,' he added with a thin smile, referring to Genscher's birthplace. Next day, heartened by the reaction from President Bush, I returned to this issue in a conversation with James Baker. He paused for a moment, exchanged a few words with his aides, and asked me if we could get together in private the following morning for about half an hour.

I looked at my diary. At 9 o'clock I had a meeting with the group of Foreign Ministers of the Persian Gulf States, at 11.30 an appointment with the Turkish Foreign Minister. We could make some time in between.

We met at 10 o'clock in the Waldorf-Astoria Hotel, which housed the American delegation. Baker produced some sheets of typed paper from his pocket and said that he wanted to inform me about an initiative that President Bush planned to announce in a televised speech. It took us thirty minutes, with Baker reading aloud while I wrote down his words. This was the now famous Bush initiative on unilateral reductions of tactical nuclear weapons. Baker added that before he made his announcement Bush intended to telephone Gorbachev and Yeltsin.

Baker looked at me with the triumphant smile of a teenager who has just bested his pal in a game. Of course the United States would expect us to reciprocate, but this was a unilateral initiative. They would carry it through in any case, though naturally hoping for a positive and constructive response. 'You must be pleased,' he concluded mildly. 'Isn't this much better than getting involved in endless tiresome negotiations?'

My first instinct was to play the ball back into his court by pointing out that he had not mentioned the tests, but I checked myself.

On 27 September 1991, the day of the Bush speech, I was dining with Jiri Dienstbier, and we stopped talking and turned on the TV. When it was over, my guest took his leave without waiting for coffee and dessert. I walked him to the lobby of our mission, where several journalists were always on watch, and they let me see off the visitor before plying me with questions – 'What is your reaction? Weren't you taken by surprise?'

I had already sent to Moscow a summary and first analysis of the American initiative, along with my ideas about our possible reaction. As yet I had received no answer, but I decided to tell the press more or less what I had told Moscow.

'No,' I said wearily, 'the Bush proposals didn't take me by surprise because the American side had briefed us in advance.'

From the torrent of reaction to the Bush proposals, the political observers singled out responses from Gorbachev, Yeltsin and me. They noted that while Yeltsin and Pankin gave their unequivocal support to the proposals, the Soviet President's reaction was more cautious. In his opinion, 'the Bush initiative raises many questions and requires further discussion.' The Soviet leader's remark that the initiative was an extension of the process begun in Geneva and continued in Reykjavik, Malta, Moscow and Washington was also interpreted as an attempt to play down the initiative. Judging from the reaction of Baker, whom we were meeting every day, I felt that the Americans were disappointed by this cautious response. If two days ago Baker had looked like a naughty boy, now he seemed to me like the same boy feeling aggrieved over failing to receive his due reward. I tried to reassure him by saying that it was bound to take time to study such a complicated matter, knowing full well that some of the remaining hawks had been looking over Gorbachev's shoulder. That made me all the more glad to have supported the Americans unequivocally. It evened the balance.

The issue was quickly settled. We agreed that one of Baker's deputies, Reginald Bartholomew, should go urgently to Moscow. Gorbachev in Moscow set up a commission to work out our response to the initiative. It was headed by Ivan Silayev, and consisted of Yevgeni Shaposhnikov, Vladimir Lobov, Yuri Ryzhov, Vadim Bakatin and myself. When after strenuous discussions we came to an agreement, I advised the President to put it out fast on TV. He sent Shaposhnikov and Petrovsky to Yeltsin, who was on vacation by the Black Sea, and we all sat down to put the final touches to his speech. Yeltsin approved the document.

Thus after Gorbachev's speech, the press response was to assert that the eight days between the two speeches had closed a gap of forty years. A single leap transformed the arms race into a disarmament race. The world became a rather better place to live in.

Maybe it was precisely our move towards disarmament so impetuously carried out, or maybe it was the conspicuous success of a putsch-resistant Soviet Union hailed all over the world, that soon prompted us to take one more daring step, and this time in an area where unhappily the world community's fingers were all thumbs. The case in point was the then still existing Yugoslavia, which as it turned out was living through its final months.

Let me remind my readers that this was early October 1991. Following the expiry of the three-month moratorium on political and military confrontation stipulated by the so-called 'Brioni Accord', now half-forgotten but then headline news, Croatia followed Slovenia in declaring its independence. The focus of tensions now shifted to Croatia. (The leadership of the federal republic of Yugoslavia had more or less reconciled itself to the loss of Slovenia.) The situation was now transformed by the outbreak of large-scale hostilities between the regular army

191

forces, equipped with aircraft and tanks, and the Croatian armed formations.

Regular night bombings were laying Dubrovnik, the pearl of the Adriatic coast, in ruins, and I felt haunted every day by the idea that something must be done. All this time the ciphered telegrams from our Ambassadors, newspaper and TV reports, not to mention the appeals and reproaches of my close relatives, were reminding me of the drama that was unfolding.

Today I still have faith in personal diplomacy, but my faith was greater then. I consulted my experts and proposed to Gorbachev that we invite Slobodan Milosevic and Franjo Tudjman, the Serb and Croat leaders, to Moscow with a view to defusing the growing tensions. He instantly agreed, but Anatoly Chernyaev, his senior aide (and a 'blood brother' after the Foros events), took against my proposal. He was convinced that the President should not become involved in such a hopeless enterprise. Yet the diplomatic machinery started working, and within a few hours we received the consent of both Belgrade and Zagreb. However, while the two leaders agreed to meet with Gorbachev, they left open the issue of possible direct contacts between themselves.

News about the forthcoming meeting raised the hopes of the world on a scale matched only by the growing senselessness of the carnage raging between the peoples of long-suffering Yugoslavia. Since the fighting had no other reasons than political and ethnic ambitions which as I saw it had affected only a relatively small number of intellectuals and politicians, I felt that a resolute effort to appeal to the reason and feelings of the protagonists could still achieve results.

It seemed that things were moving in exactly that direction when our guests reached Moscow on 15 October 1991. After long and heated discussions with Gorbachev in which I too took part, of course (as did Chernyaev), both Tudjman and Milosevic agreed to meet face-to-face. The Serb who represented the central government trod cautiously. He feared that his meeting with Tudjman might be interpreted as recognition of Croatia's legitimate right to secede, and he made the face-to-face meeting conditional on Gorbachev being there, as if this would somehow dilute any implication of Croatian recognition. Gorbachev in turn requested me to be present.

At first the two Yugoslavs were reserved and glowering, but very soon they became more talkative and open. It turned out that they had known each other for a long time, and had even studied at the same university.

'Oh, Franiu, Franiu,' Milosevic would lament from time to time. 'Oh, Franiu, Franiu ...'

Maybe it was precisely that familiar form of address on the part of the explosive Milosevic to his dedicated opponent that inspired the greatest hope. It seemed that it might be contact on the human level between these wily warlords that could prevent bloodshed in the Balkans.

At one point Gorbachev leaned over to me: 'Could you arrange a dinner at the Foreign Ministry? Say, for ten people?' This was his natural and human impulse to consolidate in friendly, easygoing conversation what was now taking place at the negotiating table.

The notion that absolutely everything is preconcerted for meetings at the 'highest level' is only superficially valid. It may apply in normal circumstances, but in this particular case everything – starting with the very idea of the meeting – was improvised. It was this improvisation that promised a successful outcome.

It was agreed in Gorbachev's office to issue a trilateral communiqué stating the need to cease all armed conflicts immediately, to start negotiations on all issues that were the sources of contradictions and dissensions within a month, and to conduct them in the light of the common interests of the peoples of Yugoslavia. The Presidents of Serbia and Croatia would look to the USSR, the United States and the European Community for their good offices in organizing and conducting the negotiating process.

The Presidents – each with his own escort – drove to the Foreign Ministry mansion in Alexei Tolstoy Street, then washed their hands and stretched their legs, after being seated for a long time. Meanwhile I and Chernyaev, who now candidly conceded he had been wrong to oppose these negotiations, were drafting the communiqué. The leaders signed it and shook hands, but not in the textbook manner. Instead, on an impulse, the three men locked their hands together, with Gorbachev's on top.

After that meeting, during which I thought Gorbachev had agreed on all points with Milosevic, he turned to me as Milosevic left the room and said: 'Look at him. Another Boris Nikolayevich [Yeltsin], but much cleverer.'

Despite their theatrical performances, neither of our guests was easy to approach. Milosevic struck me as tough and decisive but also wary and capricious, always on his guard, and looking to take offence. Tudjman was more silent and reserved, very Byzantine, almost too clever. I found him less trustworthy than Milosevic, if only because Milosevic seemed straightforward even when he raged and bullied – you knew where you stood with him. Despite our best efforts, Milosevic looked to us as protectors, though I think he felt less comfortable with Gorbachev than with Yeltsin's more similar temperament.

The day after the meeting, the memorandum issued by the three was broadcast all over the world, and it seemed that it might usher in a new era in the settlement of the Yugloslav crisis. Two days later, in the wake of the Moscow agreements, the USSR, the United States and the EC made their statement in support. Yet on the same day the parliament of Bosnia-Herzegovina voted for independence. The deputies representing the areas populated by Serbs walked out of the conference room. The domino effect resumed its lethal function.

Soviet policy had all along been to preserve the integrity of Yugoslavia, but with our hands full of problems at home, and the disintegration of the Warsaw Pact on our doorstep, we had neither the influence nor the will to stand up to the European – or I should say the German – inclination to let Yugoslavia fall apart.

194

10

Towards a Middle Eastern Settlement

Even before I left New York it had become clear that my next journey would take me to the Middle East. Israelis, Arabs, Palestinians, Americans – nobody asked me *whether* I would go, they only asked when. The Bush–Gorbachev initiative on nuclear disarmament was a great achievement, but it had more to do with the nuclear club, the five permanent members of the UN Security Council. At the same time dozens of nations near and far from the River Jordan were expecting us to involve ourselves in launching the peace process in the Middle East. Each of these nations had its own understanding of our role, but the general feeling was that the world did not want to be left without a second superpower. In all my conversations with world leaders, even in Europe, this was a recurring theme. Certainly the idea of a pair of superpowers who could be played off one against the other was bound to have its attractions for smaller, weaker States – especially in the Middle East.

According to the Israeli Foreign Minister, the restoration of diplomatic relations between our two countries would be a long overdue reversal of the mistakes of the past. On the other hand, according to Farooq ash-Shar', my colleague from Syria, my visit to the region could reverse the mistake we had made in 1987 when we signed a consular agreement with Israel.

As they examined the style and felt the pulse of our post-coup diplomacy, both sides sensed that the role of the personal factor in our foreign policy-making had increased. In the very first days of my appointment the Western press had predicted that one of my first steps would be to restore diplomatic relations with Israel, because in contrast to Gorbachev's chief adviser on the Middle East, Yevgeni Primakov, I allegedly had pro-Israeli leanings. Nevertheless, the invitations that I received from my colleagues to visit Syria, Jordan, Egypt and other Arab States provided me with an excellent opportunity to listen to all sides in the Middle East conflict, to be exposed to the full spectrum of opinion and to allay any fears of bias to one side or another.

Jerusalem was my first destination. James Baker was due there at the same time, and in case of success we were to become co-chairs of the peace conference on the Middle East. In Jerusalem we could negotiate simultaneously with the Israelis and Palestinians, while savouring a sense past of millennia, hearing the voices of three religions, and attempting to comprehend the complexity of the conflict that ravaged that mysterious and beautiful land.

So, two weeks after returning from the UN in New York, I was back at Vnukovo-2 airport. Four hours' flying and we were in the Holy Land. From Ben Gurion Airport at Lod, a motorcade almost five hundred metres long escorted us to Jerusalem, where we stayed at the King David Hotel.

As I write, I am holding the programme of my visit, a thin booklet on chalky paper, in my hands, and I can hardly believe my eyes. The visit lasted little more than a day. Arrival, 1 pm, 17 October; departure, 6 pm next day (with two hours' delay) to Damascus, to be greeted by the Syrian Foreign Minister, ash-Shar'.

Less than four years later it is impossible to conceive how a single day could embrace so many dramatic events and fateful decisions. So many things came together during those few hours: historical imperatives and mere coincidence, clashes of events and individuals, personal and national interests.

On the eve of my departure to Jerusalem I visited Mikhail Sergeyevich. Lying on his desk was my memo on the situation in the Middle East, which stated that the world community and the region expected us to play a positive role in preparing for the peace conference. Its current formula, as yet far from perfect, had been drafted in talks between the Soviet and American Presidents in Helsinki, and then in Moscow about a month before the coup. Since Israel rejected out of hand the mere idea of a 1973-type conference with numerous participating States, under the patronage of the United Nations, a plan was devised to proceed with a combination of bilateral negotiations between Israel and its neighbours and multilateral negotiations chaired by the two great powers. Neither Israel nor the Arabs rejected this idea at first sight, and it had become the focus of our diplomatic activity.

However, the participation of the two great powers had not been even-handed. In recent times James Baker had paid eight visits to the Middle East to Alexander Bessmertnykh's one. It was clear that the formula would work only if the principle of co-chairmanship was sustained. Those who were interested in our participation were moved by something more than a love of symmetry. We had a long and complex history of relations with the countries of the region, their interests were intertwined with ours, and we couldn't afford to drop out of the game. This was true even from the most pragmatic and utilitarian point of view. The situation in the region depended on developments in our country, and vice versa. There were more than half a million of our compatriots living in Israel.

This was the message of my memo. When I raised with the President the necessity for me to go to the region, and listed the countries that I planned to visit, there was no need to explain the importance of my mission. He understood that we had to prove our status as a great power, which was also crucial from the domestic point of view.

197

We recognized that the most difficult problem still remained the restoration of diplomatic relations with Israel. It was attending the conference with apparent great reluctance, and setting a whole series of preliminary conditions that were far from satisfying the other likely parties concerned. The main stumbling-block now was the formula for the involvement of the Palestinians. On that we had work to do, both with the Israelis and with the Arab States. The role of the sponsors was to convince the adversaries to come to the negotiating table and then let them reach the agreements they saw fit. Like the Americans, we had our own views on each of the contradictions that were disrupting the region, as well as on the situation in general. Our position was based on the need to implement Security Council resolutions 242 and 338.

Israel had to be convinced that it did have to come to the negotiating table, and the Arabs must understand that Israel's mere consent to do so was a count in its favour. In the past, Israel had refused to acknowledge that there was any matter for discussion, since the stake at the conference was the territories it would have to return – 'Peace for land.' Land is something that you can touch, while peace ... This notion still needed substance. In other words, if the conference was to open at all, each of the participants, and not only the Arabs and Israelis, would have to sacrifice something. The Americans and ourselves had different kinds of leverage over Israel. The Americans could use sticks, we only had carrots. The US administration had already proposed to the Congress to postpone indefinitely the provision of guarantees for a ten-billion-dollar loan towards resettling émigrés, mainly from the Soviet Union. Our 'instrument of peace' was diplomatic relations with Israel, but the peculiarity of the situation was that our own need for these relations was hardly less than theirs, so it was not that simple to use this lever. Thus once in Israel, I would have to delay the signature of our new diplomatic agreement as long as I could, or the Israelis would have what *they* wanted without giving us what *we* wanted, which was a Palestinian presence at the peace conference. But besides the

198

Palestinian dimension we judged that establishing relations with Israel would further open the doors of good will towards us in the USA.

'Act according to your memo,' Gorbachev summed up. 'We will announce the restoration of relations a couple of days before the conference – if, of course, you manage to agree on it. And if you need to play for time you can discuss with Levy the text of the letters that we'll be exchanging. Spin it out as long as you can.'

He shook my hand in his usual energetic manner, and I was halfway to the door of his big room when he said: 'Listen, Boris Dimitrievich, you're going in three days, aren't you? Why don't we circulate your memo among the members of the State Council? To be on the safe side, eh? And you'll feel more secure.'

Momentarily I recalled the discussion in New York before my speech at the UN. This grinding process of coordination was familiar to me from the old days. Someone would think that a comma was out of place, and everything would bog down.

'Mikhail Sergeyevich!' I exclaimed. 'Please don't! I take the risk upon myself. I have reported to the State Council on the outcome of our work at the UN General Assembly, and particularly on our talk with Levy. There were no objections. The restoration of relations is already on the agenda.'

I saw relief in his eyes. That was not the first time that he was glad to be talked out of one of his own suggestions.

'Not that it worries me,' he said. 'I ... Well, all right, you go ahead then. Give my regards to those who deserve ...' he finished hurriedly, as if fearing that to continue the conversation might lead us into new and undesirable complications.

Once again I saw how strong were the old prejudices in him, and how hard it was for him to break with them. No, it was not the approval of this or that State Council member he was after. He seemed always to be contending with the way the future would deal with him, how history would assess him, the things he had and had not done.

Yeltsin seemed to be more resolute in this respect,

199

unencumbered by worries about his position in history. For example his reputation as the man who completed the break-up of the Soviet Union troubles him not one whit.

It didn't require a prophet to foresee that from the moment of my arrival at Ben Gurion airport David Levy would resume the pressure on me. What should I say? My intention was to propose discussing a draft letter whose text ran as follows:

> The Union of Soviet Socialist Republics and the State of Israel, guided by their wish for cooperation and mutual understanding in the interests of the peoples of the two countries, resolve to restore their diplomatic relations commencing from the date of publication of this Joint Statement, and to exchange diplomatic representatives at ambassadorial level.
>
> The two sides declare their readiness to build their bilateral relations in accordance with the UN Charter and the norms of international law, and on the basis of the principles of equality, mutual respect, sovereignty and non-interference in each other's domestic affairs.
>
> Both sides express their confidence that the restoration of full diplomatic relations between the USSR and the State of Israel fully responds to the task of a comprehensive Middle East settlement, and the promotion of enduring peace and stability in the region, developing and strengthening international cooperation.

What more was there to say? It was a good document, and ready for signing, as Levy was likely to agree provided that he had no objections to the last paragraph. So what followed?

I had little room for manoeuvre, but I could not complain. I had limited the document deliberately as the price of the chance to take a decision that was long overdue.

We parted with Levy after a short meeting at the airport, to meet again after moving into Jerusalem's prestigious King David Hotel, famous for having been blown up in 1946 by the Jewish terrorist organization Irgun Zvai Leumi, with the deaths of more than ninety people. It was neither the first nor the last explosion in Jerusalem, and the bloodshed continued. At this very moment the city was in a state of emergency owing to Baker's and my visits. There were so many policemen, soldiers, jeeps and motorcyclists on the ground and helicopters in the sky that even we, in whose honour all this was organized, had difficulty making our way through the welter of people and vehicles.

The first thing I saw when I entered the hotel, standing with a group of journalists and ready to ask me a question, was the corpulent frame of Alexander Bovin. My wife and I had discussed Bovin on the plane to Israel. She is an orientalist, and she reminded me that for years Bovin's articles in the government daily *Izvestia* had been an almost unique source of objective information about Israel, in which he had dared to put forward the idea of re-establishing diplomatic relations. Bovin was a brave and principled man who had displayed courage in the most trying circumstances, including most recently his dismissive, sneering questioning of the coup plotters in their televised press conference which was beamed around the world on 19 August. I need hardly say what price he would have had to pay if the coup plotters had emerged victorious.

When I saw this man at the King David Hotel, I went over and whispered to him: 'Do you know what my wife and I were saying on the plane? That you are the most suitable candidate to be our Ambassador to Israel.' My words didn't take him by surprise. 'Why not?' he said. 'Frankly, I'm sick of writing about politics. Let's try to make politics instead.' Bovin was to become Soviet Ambassador to Israel in November 1991.

My suite, or rather residence, at the King David was situated on three levels. On the first floor there was a hall and living-room, below it a bathroom with a small pool, above it a bedroom. We were told that this was the best suite in the hotel, bigger than the one where Baker was staying. (He had arrived the day before.) A great honour, of course, but very inconvenient, as I realized from the very first moments, when I let a tie fall here, a jacket there, and then had to dash between the floors to look for them. You could use a lift, but that would look ridiculous. Still, I would only be staying for a day, and no

201

more than a few hours in the suite itself.

Now it was time to go. The corridor was jammed with Soviet and Israeli security guards, but I was starting to get used to this. After New York there were few surprises left.

It turned out that our plans had changed. An extraordinary meeting of the Israeli Cabinet had begun, with Levy in attendance. Clearly it was devoted to our visit. Fine! I thought. That gives us an unexpected opportunity for sight-seeing. We sent for our cars and diligently looked around us as we sped through the city. The Holy City is a familiar sight on millions of TV screens, so I won't dwell on the tour, except to recall our surprise at hearing so much Russian spoken around us when we left the car. It reminded me of the joke that a *Komsomolka* correspondent passed on to me as an example of Jerusalem humour: 'What will be the second official language in Israel? – Russian!'

I don't think the crowds that thronged around us as we walked had been prerehearsed: our tour was unscheduled. Both sets of bodyguards worked hard to keep us clear of interference, but everywhere people stretched out their arms and cried out: 'Welcome!' 'When do we start diplomatic relations?' 'Mr Pankin, give us back our homeland! Give us peace!'

The same *Komsomolka* correspondent would write (not without a drop of acid): 'When the new Minister left the car to speak to the people in the best tradition of recent Soviet leaders, he was greeted at the Wailing Wall by thousands of people shouting in Russian: "Good luck!"'

The meetings were brief and the exchanges momentary, but they lasted long enough for me to understand that we had half a million compatriots living here, with another three or four million relatives still living in every corner of our huge country. For those who devised the regulations about the automatic removal of Soviet citizenship from those who emigrated to Israel, they were deserters. But I felt that for them, or quite a lot of them, the country left behind was still their homeland. They were still immersed in its affairs, and watched everything that happened there. Someone remarked, only half jokingly, that since the Soviet Union was moving to a market economy, the expertise of the Jews who had gone through the tough Israeli school of business was priceless. They didn't even have to learn the language, in either country. Thus the issue of diplomatic relations took on a human dimension.

The feeling of closeness grew after our visit to the most terrible place in Jerusalem, the Yad Vashem Memorial to the six million Jews murdered by Hitler's Germany, a testimony to the Holocaust. Here we saw photographs, replicas of the gas chambers, shabby clothes with big yellow stars of David sewn on to them, ashes, the remains of bones, gold from dentures, and some of the other familiar horrors that have haunted the minds of my generation ever since the Forties. And many, many figures: the number of prisoners hanged, shot, gassed, burnt, dead from starvation. The largest number of victims came from the USSR and Poland. To the sound of Jewish prayers we laid a wreath at the eternal flame.

It occurred to me now that our hosts had proposed the visit to Yad Vashem with a certain hesitation. Why? They said that it was not on the programme, and that Soviet officials had been reluctant to come here in the past. Yet so many of the people who died had been our compatriots! Even the design of the monument resembled some of the endless memorials in our own bitter land.

Time was running out, and we were already late for our visit to the Foreign Ministry, which consists of a series of one-storey pavilions resembling a military barracks. David Levy was fresh from the Cabinet meeting. He smiled broadly and opened his arms to me, but in his eyes I could still see the smoulder of recent argument. As I thought, the meeting had been devoted to the peace conference, and hence to the imminent talks with the Soviet Foreign Minister.

The alignment of forces was as follows, he began to explain. He, Levy, was the keenest supporter of Israeli participation in the conference. Prime Minister Yitzhak Shamir was sceptical about the outcome but thought it worth a try. And there were some small but influential right-wing parties that were categorically opposed to any conferences or negotiations. They had few votes in the Knesset and only a couple of ministerial posts, but on the other hand, Likud had a very fragile majority. The right-wing parties were threatening to quit the coalition, which meant the resignation of the government and possibly new general elections. One of the arguments of the opponents of the conference was the absence of diplomatic relations with the USSR. How could it work if one party to negotiations and one co-chairman had no diplomatic relations? It was both insulting and impractical.

The Minister was only explaining the views of the unidentified opponents of the conference, but I could tell from his voice that he agreed with them on one point at least: the urgent need to restore diplomatic relations.

One of my experts interjected that following the October War in 1973 we had been co-chairs at the subsequent conference without having diplomatic relations. Levy's face lit up. This argument favoured him, he said. Wasn't that one of the reasons why the conference had yielded no result?

I took out the draft of our prepared letter and passed it across the table. Levy pounced on the text and devoured it with his eyes. As I more or less expected, he had no objections. He liked the text and was prepared to sign it right away. An awkward pause ensued. My experts came to the rescue of their boss and began to propose editorial amendments to our own text. The Israeli accepted them all. Once again the move was ours. In chess this is called zugzwang.

I proposed to proceed to discussion of the conference and outline our position. Fortunately time was running out. Next meeting was in the evening, at a dinner at the King David.

My next appointment was with the Palestinians, but the Israeli side wanted nothing to do with it. They hadn't even included it in the printed programme of the visit, although of course they were well aware of it.

I knew that talks with the Palestinians would be no easier than with the Israelis. This was clear from the contacts we had had with them in the few weeks since taking the decision to step up our preparations for the conference. In Moscow I had received Farukh Kadummi, a close aide of Arafat's with a reputation as a moderate. After that our Ambassador to Tunisia had delivered to the PLO leader a message from Gorbachev, and I too had entered into correspondence with him. We were discussing the formula for Palestinian participation in the conference.

On this point Israel took a tough line. First, the Palestinians were not to have a separate delegation at the conference, but should form a part of the Jordanian-Palestinian delegation. Second, the Palestine Liberation Organization, which was regarded by Israel as a terrorist organization that did not recognize Israel, must not be officially represented in the delegation. The Palestinian part of the joint delegation should comprise Palestinians permanently residing on the occupied West Bank of the River Jordan and in the Gaza Strip. The participation of the Palestinian diaspora and residents of East Jerusalem (where we were to meet with them) was also unacceptable.

Of course, those were unjustified demands, but they had to be taken into account if we wanted to bring the Israelis to the negotiating table. And this was important because Israel's decision to participate in the conference would signify that it recognized the existence of the problem of occupied territories, which was something that the right wing rejected.

Thus the situation was so confused that even for the USSR and the US as the mediators it was difficult at times to tell a real concession from an artificially inflated demand. And each side, naturally, depicted its own situation in the gloomiest colours and that of its opponents in the brightest hues. It was only logical that in this respect the Americans had more problems than we with the Israelis, who were used to regarding them as natural allies, while we conversely came under more pressure from the Palestinians and the Arab States.

I set myself a dual task in the negotiations with the Palestinians at the National Palace Hotel in East Jerusalem. First, to bridge the gap between the participants and the co-chairs over the formula for Palestinian participation in the conference. Second, to test their reaction to the possibility of establishing diplomatic relations with Israel. My experts advised me to have plenty of patience and not to despair, especially in the first half-hour. Then things would go more smoothly.

To begin with, more Palestinians came to the talks than we expected, and still more kept arriving as we talked. Again and again we had to go back to basics, because each newcomer represented an individual organization and regarded himself as an independent party to the negotiations, not as a member of the delegation, and thus demanded special attention. That was a matter of style. In substance too, our interlocutors wanted to start from the basics, as if they had never previously had protracted negotiations with us and the Americans, or as if all the correspondence between Gorbachev, myself and Yasser Arafat had never happened.

I could understand their position. This was an opportunity for them to spell out all the genuine grievances and problems that had accumulated down the years, to share their hopes with a representative of the country they had always regarded as their natural and unconditional ally. I picked up the conversation at that point, saying that we were indeed their friends. There was a sigh of relief, before a voice piped up: 'Then why did you ... ?' and the whole thing started all over again, with our side resuming its explanations in the most detailed and respectful manner.

'Why do we have to pretend that our leaders, the PLO, are not taking part in the conference?'

'For the very same reason that Israel pretends that the PLO is not taking part, even though it's obvious to everyone that this formula is only a fig-leaf.'

Slowly, one by one, without any interruption (although I was already hopelessly late for the dinner with Levy), the sides outlined their positions. Passions cooled, and we entered into a very practical and businesslike dialogue with a group of people for whom a long period of discussions, agreements, negotiations and ultimatums lay ahead.

Among them was an elderly medical doctor, Heidar Abdel

206

Shafi, one of the founders of the Palestine National Council and known for his sober and moderate position. Several days later Arafat appointed him head of the Palestinian section of the Jordanian-Palestinian delegation. I was to meet him many times in Madrid. With him were Hannan Ashrawi and Feisal Husseini. They let us know that they would have to report the results of our negotiations to the PLO in Tunisia, but their feeling was that a consensus would be reached and the conference could begin its work. The outcome was another matter. The Palestinians were ready for tactical concessions, but swore to be uncompromising on principle. Their right to self-determination must be acknowledged, and here they trusted that they could rely on our support. As to our restoration of diplomatic relations with Israel, why not, if it could promote their cause?

When I arrived at the King David Hotel, journalists bombarded me with questions about our negotiations with Levy. From a communiqué they already knew that we had discussed bilateral relations. Meanwhile Levy had revealed that the Soviet delegation had brought the draft of a joint declaration of a long-awaited step, and I too had no intention of concealing this development. I was still under the influence of the warm closing atmosphere of our conversation with the Palestinians. My aides remarked that as a non-expert in Middle East affairs I had not resorted to the traditional clichés but had spoken in normal human terms. Thank God I hadn't had time to master the jargon, I thought. In answering the journalists I had only one thing to add to the communiqué: 'If the negotiations continue in the same spirit, they too may be brought to a successful conclusion.'

Early next morning, a Friday, came a call from the Israeli Foreign Ministry: 'Will the Soviet side object if journalists are invited to your meeting with Levy today?' Yesterday the talks had been conducted behind closed doors. This meant that the Israelis had interpreted our signal in a very positive way. There was now no going back. I was firmly convinced of this after the previous day's meeting with the Palestinians.

207

A conversation with Baker, whom I had not seen since New York, only confirmed my belief. His escort, even more numerous than mine, had made so many sallies through the crowded streets of Jerusalem that the newspapers had been wondering when these Foreign Ministers had time to sleep. The city was seething with expectation, and this affected everyone: participants in the negotiations, informed observers and even casual onlookers.

Before he met me Baker had had time to talk with the Palestinians, and he confirmed that they had softened their positions. Only a handful of technicalities remained, bearing mainly on American–Palestinian relations. His people were working through them right now with Shafi and Hannan Ashrawi. He thought that in a couple of hours he would be able to telephone Shamir and inform him that the Palestinian part of the delegation would be made up as provisionally agreed.

The newspapers claimed that he was going to send a list of the Palestinian conference participants to Shamir, but this was not so, he assured me. There was an understanding – of which the Palestinians were well aware – that he would simply make a telephone call. Thus by committing nothing to paper, face could be saved.

There were no details in the tapestry that both of us were weaving that were too insignificant. If we neglected the tiniest knot, the whole design might unravel.

Baker said further that he had information that the Israelis had been thoroughly impressed by our yesterday's meeting, so if the restoration of diplomatic relations really was to be announced today (here a questioning look at me) that would strip the right wing of all their trump cards and Shamir (Baker looked at me slyly) would have no way back.

We rubbed our hands conspiratorially and got down to editing the official text of an invitation to the conference. If things went well, as they now seemed set to do, it would be announced today at our joint press conference and then dispatched in the name of Gorbachev and Bush to the heads of State of the participating countries, namely to King Hussein of Jordan, Presidents Assad of Syria and Mubarak of Egypt, and to the leaders of Israel and Lebanon. These were the main participants, those who would sit down at the negotiating table right after the closing of the plenary session of the conference.

A word here about the workings of the Soviet and American delegations. Throughout the Israeli visit, the atmosphere between myself and Baker was very informal and workmanlike. Although for the sake of appearances we had to give the impression that we were acting quite separately from one another, in fact our every move was coordinated. The Soviet and American parties were in constant touch with each other behind the scenes, exchanging views and information on every development. Our meetings with the Palestinians and Israelis were kept separate because both of these sides were anxious to have private talks with their erstwhile protectors. The Palestinians would say things to us that they could never have said in front of the Americans, and the Israelis could confer more comfortably alone with the Americans. This afforded both of them the opportunity to test out negotiating points without any obligation to follow them through or to take up rigid positions to save face.

As we were working on the conference invitation, Baker asked for a few words in private. He told me in a whisper that the negotiations he was conducting on behalf of our two countries showed that the most suitable place to hold the conference would be Madrid. This was the preliminary view of the eventual participants, and the Spanish government was prepared to cover the costs. Okay, let it be Madrid. I had no special preferences here. I did make some attempt to lobby for Prague, which had also applied, but it was difficult as yet for Prague to compete with Madrid.

Everything was going smoothly, and I was feeling more and more persuaded that I would not be violating the President's instructions if I were to sign the declaration today. The most important thing here was not the date but the conviction that this really would help to bring about the conference, and I had no doubt about that.

At this point our privacy was interrupted by Baker's closest assistants, Dennis Ross and Margaret Tatweiler, who excused themselves and whispered in Baker's ear. My own chief experts, Vassily Kolotusha and Andrei Derkovsky, came back. Gloomily, Baker explained what had happened. They had failed to finalize the 'technical details' of attendance at the conference with the Palestinians. Without this he could not make the telephone call to Shamir, and without this call, as had been agreed with President Bush, the American side could not make an announcement about the conference.

So, it looked as if our castle was built on sand.

But this was not all. My aides had a surprise in store for me too. One of them handed me that day's edition of the Israeli Russian-language newspaper *Den* (The Day). Its banner headline shouted 'Peres in Moscow' above a story that the Israeli leader of the opposition had had a two-hour meeting with Gorbachev in which he was informed that 'diplomatic relations will be restored as soon as the date for convening the regional conference on the Middle East becomes known'!

Only ten minutes previously, this would have been good news. Gorbachev had taken a step forward from our conversation in the Kremlin, and the resumption of diplomatic links was now to take place, not a day or two before the opening of the conference, but on the day of its announcement. This tallied with what I was now about to do, and relieved me of any possible reproach. Of course it was odd, to say the least, for Gorbachev to have granted an audience to Peres without informing his Foreign Minister. With his domestic influence draining away it was reassuring for Gorbachev to talk to a high-ranking foreign personality who took him seriously. As he was growing more and more politically isolated at home, he increasingly took refuge in foreign affairs. So any prominent foreigner coming to Moscow found it quite easy to be granted an audience.

I translated the article I was holding for Baker. He understood without further explanations, then asked what I was going to do now. I said inconclusively that in any case I would go to see Levy now. The negotiations were scheduled to begin in thirty minutes. In the long silence that followed, we both felt too upset and frustrated to speak. To cap it all, the Sabbath was approaching, restricting the transaction of any serious business for at least twenty-four hours.

Once again I was faced with a situation in which there were drawbacks to both of my possible choices. While I was in Prague I came across a little-known article by the former Czechoslovak President, Edvard Beneš, who came to power after the Second World War and was forced into retirement as a result of a quiet Communist takeover in February 1948. The article was called 'Democracy and Diplomacy'. Beneš wrote that there were two types of diplomats: the 'artist' who is moved by emotions and intuition, which verges on adventurism, and the 'scientist' who concentrates or over-concentrates on the analysis of facts, and as a result can often make no decision at all. At that particular moment I had to muster all my intuition and all my analytical capabilities.

I had to do what my sense of duty, my 'inner voice', told me to do. I had no doubt that it would advance the cause that brought me here. And after that, we should see ...

I entered the car and the convoy set off to the Israeli Foreign Ministry, accompanied by the wailing of police sirens. The meeting went well. We confirmed that the text of the declaration restoring diplomatic relations satisfied both sides, and that each of us was ready to sign it, then we sat down at the table and added our signatures. Under the camera flash we shook hands several times. Even though the expression on my face, despite my best efforts, was not adequate to the occasion, deep in my heart I felt no less triumphant than Levy. Perhaps this was the first time in my life when I thought about history: no matter what happened next, my signature would always be on this document.

When after a brief celebration we went back to the table and began to discuss the practical implementation of what we had just agreed upon, a note was placed face down in front of me. I picked it up and read it. Good old Baker! He was resolved, if I had no objections, that he and I together would announce the convening of the conference. Tonight! He took it upon himself to make all necessary arrangements with the Palestinians and Israel. The unresolved details truly were purely technical, and could actually be ignored. The press was waiting, but we'd have to hurry because of the Sabbath.

I hardly need say what a relief it was for me, and how enthusiastically I emerged from the Israeli Foreign Ministry. When I returned to the huge lobby of the King David, I found Baker waiting for me, smiling and impatient to keep the ball rolling. He showed me the text of the joint statement about sending invitations to the Madrid Conference, which had been drawn up in my absence. We had long ago decided that it would open on 30 October, and the Presidents of the two countries that were to open it had arranged their schedules accordingly. When we took our seats at the table in front of a huge crowd of journalists, I jokingly whispered to James not to forget to mention that this was a joint statement. Then we answered questions, though there weren't too many of these. The journalists were in a hurry to report the story that so many people had longed to hear.

But I did have time to add one more thing that was very important to me. I said that we had succeeded in reaching an agreement because all sides had proved willing to compromise. The attitudes of the two co-chairs had also changed. Gone was the stereotype of an a priori anti-Israeli USSR, and an anti-Arab USA.

For several days the press made much of this statement of mine, but there was a journalist from the *New York Times* who latched on to something else. The supersensitive microphones had picked up my would-be humorous remark to Baker about the credit for the document he was reading out. It provoked this reporter into observations about the 'subordinate role' of Soviet diplomacy – the Soviet Foreign Minister hadn't even had a copy of the text in his hands. The comment struck a chord with me and I reacted to it in Madrid. When Baker and I were giving a press conference there on the results of the plenary session, we agreed to switch roles. I read out our joint statement, he made comments. I drew the attention of the press to this switch, and they burst out laughing, but actually that keen-eared reporter had a point. I *had* wanted to convey to Baker that he should not be too eager to have his country hog the limelight. With the Americans so obviously setting the pace and making the running, the potential domestic benefits from the peace process for the Soviet Union might rebound against us if our conservative opponents could accuse us of merely tagging along behind the American juggernaut.

Our business in Israel had gone well, and between us we and the Americans had managed to bring Yitzhak Shamir some way towards the conference table. This tough little fighter with a mean streak had all the inclinations of a terrorist (which he had been in Israel's fight for statehood) to use all weapons at his disposal to achieve his goals. This included whatever he had in his personal armoury – controlled mood-swings, rhetoric, manipulations through attempts at charm. He even used his physical appearance to good effect. He was a small man, smaller even than I had expected, and oddly proportioned, with a large head merging into a bull neck set above a tiny body. I was struck when I met him by the way that all of his movements and gestures were calculated to project toughness and bravado: he had the symptoms of a Napoleonic complex. I always felt that he was less interested in achieving real results than in giving the Americans and a section of his domestic public opinion the impression of flexibility. At heart he was utterly unwilling to make concessions, but the momentum of events took hold of him, and he was no longer able to control them.

David Levy was the complete contrast to Shamir. He too was not a diplomat by temperament, but his style was to seem open, talkative, friendly and flattering – almost cloyingly so. He liked to give the impression of being very straight, but there was a strong devious streak in him, and like all people who try too hard to appear straight, he didn't fool anybody.

213

Two hours after the press conference at the King David Hotel the Soviet delegation landed in Damascus. In the plane that took us there we all lived again and again through the sequence of events in Jerusalem. There are moments in life when elation reigns, and even those who only yesterday were on opposite sides of the barricades feel like one team. That was the feeling on board the plane to Damascus on 18 October. The journalists were trying to coax some missing details out of the diplomats and the latter were unusually talkative. An aura of success hung around us.

No matter how active the American diplomacy in the region, it would have been impossible to convince all sides to come to the negotiating table without our participation, declared our chief expert on the Middle East. Someone else added that the concerted efforts of the two great powers in making the conference happen marked a new stage in the remaking of Soviet–American relations.

The most lively discussions were about the resumption of diplomatic relations. There were no sceptics on the plane. They had either stayed in Jerusalem or were waiting for us further along the route. One of them, the *Pravda* correspondent in Cairo, had warned against this step in a recent article called 'Let's keep some trumps in reserve'.

Someone remarked how stupid it was to have broken off relations in 1967, for the third time in twelve years – even Stalin, for all his anti-Semitism, was smart enough to be one of the first world leaders to vote for the creation of the Jewish and Palestinian States and to establish diplomatic relations with Israel. When we broke them off, we shut ourselves out of the process for many years to come.

I shared the delight on the plane, but I knew that we were flying into stormier weather. Although Syria was the Soviet Union's principal client State in the Middle East, we had decided to forgo the courtesy of notifying them in advance about our intentions in Israel. Their opposition was predictable and we wanted to preempt it. We had to create solid facts, and quickly. From our perspective it was important to achieve a breakthrough in the Middle East for which the Soviet Union

214

could be seen to deserve credit. Success would strengthen our hand in domestic political terms. Internationally it would demonstrate to the Americans and the West in general – with whom we needed better economic relations – that we were reliable partners who could deliver. Delivering our ally Syria to the negotiating table, even kicking and screaming, was a price we were happy to pay, but I felt that I had better temper the general exuberance by reminding us all of James Baker's words at the press conference: 'There's a long way still to go. Suspicions won't vanish overnight.'

They were prophetic words. When Farooq ash-Shar' greeted me off the plane, and then while we sat on a sofa in the VIP lounge fielding questions from the media, my Syrian colleague kept up appearances, but as soon as we got into a car he virtually assaulted me.

'How could you establish relations at such a moment? Why didn't you consult with us? Why couldn't you postpone it? I daren't imagine what tomorrow's press will say!'

The spate of exclamations and rhetorical questions, expressed in a language not suited to diplomacy, let alone to Middle Eastern courtesy, did not let up until I proposed half-seriously to my colleague that I should go back to the airport. That calmed him down a little, and after a few minutes we began to discuss the programme of the visit. Here too there were problems. Only yesterday my assistant had told me that all details had been cleared with the Syrian Foreign Ministry. Now it seemed that the programme consisted mainly of question-marks, although he explained all the changes by our two hours' delay in arriving.

'We planned an official dinner but it had to be cancelled. There's no time left for negotiations, so we'll have to begin tomorrow morning. Because of that the visit to the President will take place later.'

Clearly he was stalling. The news from Jerusalem had taken our hosts by surprise, and they needed time to work out a position.

Next morning my guess proved right. When after breakfast

we were ready to drive off at 9.45, the flustered Syrian chief of protocol asked us to wait a little. The Minister had been delayed on official business. For roughly an hour, our delegation – all clad in black suits – strolled solemnly about the hotel admiring the surrounding mountain peaks. Someone pointed to a big green grove on a slope of one of the mountains. This was the President's new residence, where he received only the heads of States and governments.

Where did he intend to receive us? And would he receive us at all?

The minutes dragged. More and more alarming thoughts were entering my head. But there was no panic, and in fact the delay gave us time to reflect on the whole situation. Yesterday's reception and this morning's delays gave me reason enough for that. Now I could see for myself what our experts on the Middle East had often told me in the course of preparing for the trip, namely how unceremoniously our best friends could treat us, even at my level. One might have thought that it was they who had been helping us, providing us with weapons and subsidies, sharing know-how, sending experts and advisers. It was as if we owed a debt to them, and not the other way round. And for this we had no one to blame but ourselves.

This stupidity dated back to Khrushchev's time, when it sufficed for a leader or regime to call themselves 'socialist' and they automatically became our bosom friends. We would support them at the UN, exchange lavish State visits, stage costly festivals of friendship, throw dollars at them, and disregard their cruelty to their own people.

Who, for example, was Mengistu Haile Mariam of Ethiopia but a total bandit, a butcher? Yet we supported him as a true revolutionary.

And this had lasted until recent times. Once when I was visiting Moscow from Stockholm I had been sitting in Shevardnadze's office when a call came on the internal telephone and he looked at his watch.

'I have to go to the airport to meet Mengistu. Yesterday he asked Mikhail Sergeyevich to receive him here in private.'

216

'Isn't it time we stopped supporting Mengistu?'

'But how can we?' Shevardnadze looked at me condescendingly. 'He's our friend.'

So here we were in Damascus preparing to be excoriated by another 'friend'.

Meanwhile time was passing. At last, after something like an hour and a half during which time we strolled around the hotel, came inside and then went out again, an animated chief of protocol showed up. 'The Minister will be here in a moment and you will go straight to see the President.' I sighed with relief but did not show it.

'Won't we be having talks with the Minister before going to the President?' I asked. The chief of protocol could only make a silent gesture – 'I don't understand what's going on' – but I saw from his mood that things were improving.

Enter ash-Shar'. Not a trace of yesterday's indignation. With the air of a man who was bestowing a great favour, he confirmed that the President expected us in twenty minutes at his new residence. ('Aha!' I thought.) So if we were ready and had nothing better to do, then we could go. The residence was high up in the mountains and we were short of time.

The experts were holding their folders. The traditional gifts (photograph albums and crystal-ware) were stowed in the boots of the cars. We could go ahead.

Viewed from the hotel, the residence seemed to loom up above us, but we had to cross half of Damascus merely to get to the foot of the mountain.

In the afternoon we would have time to walk in the Old Town of Damascus, the city of legend, but the quarters we were passing through now resembled our own new boroughs. Here I could see the hand of Soviet architects who under every foreign sky, and no matter how ancient the host civilization, had obeyed their instructions and churned out the same boring high-rises of glass, steel and concrete – so many gestures of cultural vandalism. Only in the outlines of balconies and windows could you see the slightest tribute paid to local traditions and climate.

Finally the city lay behind us and the long climb to the

residence began. Past massive gates the road led us far up to the main entrance, where we were conducted through a spacious lobby with an opulent rug and walls of glass, towards a huge hall. Standing in the doorway, President Hafez al-Assad welcomed us in a simple and easygoing manner.

We were seated in armchairs obligingly offered by our host, who also suggested tea, coffee, fruit. Apologies with a good-natured smile for changes in the programme. How was your first night in Damascus? Is this your first trip to the Middle East? What are your impressions of Jerusalem? Slowly we approached the matters that brought me to Damascus and the other capitals of the region.

During my years as editor of *Komsomolka* and as VAAP chairman I had quite often visited our Central Asian republics and met their leaders. Here I noticed many similarities in the style of receiving a guest. Eastern traditions.

I knew that it cost Assad great pains to give his consent to the conference, even though, as Baker repeatedly complained to me, there were so many conditions and reservations along the way that you never knew whether it was happening or not. In fact we still had not yet been informed that the invitation to Syria had been accepted. But the President's warm welcome looked encouraging.

Putting myself in the President's shoes, I felt it made sense for him to decide that what's done is done, and to put a brave face on things could only enhance his prestige as a statesman. No matter how sceptical he was about the conference at the early stages, there were forces in Syria that adopted an even more negative attitude, and they viewed the President as too soft and yielding under pressure from the West and Israel. Assad could not ignore them. On the other hand he understood that he needed to change his image as a hawk and dictator. He did not want to be viewed in the same light as Castro or, worse still, Saddam Hussein.

His image was vital to Hafez al-Assad. Everything was designed to foster the idea that he was one of history's great men. The personality cult around him was worthy of Stalin –

pictures, placards, hoardings, banners all over town proclaiming his wisdom, integrity and inspired leadership. His entourage was comprehensively servile, further projecting his power.

Yet all these trappings, and the grandiose style of his palace, were belied by his very modest manner. Physically he was out of the ordinary, with a head shaped to a design that I had never seen before. When speaking in his soft voice he had a gentle if rather wooden smile, and refrained from sweeping gestures. I had been warned that conversations with Assad could take hours, and he did go on at some length, but he made his points very rationally, and with a cold logic. He avoided grand tours d'horizon, and did not waste time waltzing around irrelevant issues.

In purpose, Assad was the mirror of Shamir. Both men wanted to create the impression of being cooperative negotiators, willing to make concessions. Both men intended never to give an inch.

The conference afforded Assad a good way to solve many problems at once. It was worth while to agree to it, despite the opposition from extremists, and to show that he was ready for constructive steps. But once in attendance he would take a tough and uncompromising line, and this would be a good lesson for the sceptics inside the country. The fact that the USSR – their old, true and reliable friend, as the communiqué from the Syrian side would say – was a co-chairman of the conference was another indication that they were doing everything right. But how could a country act as a co-chair when it had no relations with one of the parties to the conflict? The action of the new Soviet Foreign Minister in Jerusalem furthered the overall preparation of the conference, so the Soviet Union could be congratulated on such an excellent move.

The President spoke the last phrase out loud, and I could not help darting a glance at Shar'. Right then there was no one in the world who agreed more zealously with his President's assessment of the wisdom of the Soviet moves in Jerusalem!

'Yes, a very good response to your visit to Israel,' he said cheerfully. 'Our press has had a lot to say about it.'

In return I outlined our position at some length.

The meeting with Assad was decisive. The leader of the country that was most sceptical about this gathering had finally given his firm consent in conversation with the Soviet Foreign Minister. On the same day Shar' received the Soviet and American Ambassadors and accepted the invitation to Madrid. This was included in the Syrian communiqué on the results of my visit.

An hour after his meeting with me, Assad received Yasser Arafat and reaffirmed his acceptance. That was their first meeting in many years, which was a good sign too.

After those three critical days in Jerusalem and Damascus, I recall the visits to Amman and Cairo, for all their intensity, and with no more than four or five hours' sleep, as a time of relaxation when business mixed harmoniously with pleasure. King Hussein was a likeable man of obvious integrity, who spoke at length in very measured tones. President Mubarak reminded me of an apparatchik from one of our Central Asian republics. He struck me as an intelligent fellow who had made his way astutely from the provinces to success in the big city without being quite convinced that he belonged there. I had long talks with both men, and their Prime Ministers and Foreign Ministers. There were also sightseeing tours of the pyramids, museums and tombs, and visits to the Dead Sea, the banks of the Jordan, mosques, temples and bazaars.

In Amman we discussed with Foreign Minister Abu Jaber the course of debate on the conference within the Israeli government. The Soviet-Israeli Declaration, as was expected, had strengthened Shamir's positions. By a vote of 16 to 3, the Cabinet decided for participation in the conference.

The extremists in both camps were outraged, and expressed their opposition with action as well as speeches. Twenty-two Palestinians were wounded in clashes with Israeli forces in the occupied territories. The Muslim Brotherhood staged a mass rally of protest against the concept of the conference, and called for jihad, a holy war.

220

President Mubarak told me that the interested Arab States would be meeting to coordinate their efforts. President Assad had mentioned the idea three days before. The meeting would take place any day now (time was precious) in Damascus.

From Tehran came the news that a four-day conference in support of the 'Islamic revolution of the people of Palestine' had opened there. The General Secretary of the extremist Hezbollah group declared at its inauguration that everything possible would be done to disrupt the conference. The dissenting members of the Israeli Cabinet threatened to quit the government. Similar statements came from several extremist Palestinian organizations within the PLO.

The Madrid Conference on the Middle East. Only five days ago it meant nothing. Now the whole world was talking about it.

Meanwhile the newspeople were trying to solve a riddle: Yasser Arafat was travelling along the same route as I was. His small plane had been taking off or landing at the airports in Damascus, Amman and Cairo an hour before or after ours. And each time the press predicted that a meeting between Pankin and Arafat was certain to take place. It was known that Arafat had asked for a meeting before I left for the Middle East and I had replied that I would be ready to see him in any of the capitals on the way. But he kept postponing the meeting until at last he named Paris, where we would both be attending the International Peace Conference on Cambodia.

The first thing I learned when I arrived at the Soviet Ambassador's residence in the rue de Grenelle on 22 October for the conference in Paris was that Arafat was already waiting for me. We recalled our first meeting in 1983, when he was in Stockholm at the invitation of Olof Palme. Arafat told me in the politest Middle Eastern tones that he had heard a lot of good things about me from his representatives in Prague and Stockholm, that he was proud of the quality of Palestinian-Soviet relations and continued to rely upon the firm support of the Soviet Union for the just cause of the Palestinian people. I chose not to remind him of his pronouncements in support of the coup and, earlier, of Saddam Hussein, and I saw that he was grateful for that. My discretion bore fruit when he informed me that the decision on Palestinian participation in the conference had been taken, and the formula – although unjust and imposed on them – accepted.

We parted at the doorway of the residence under the eyes of numerous journalists, and Arafat made a statement: 'We highly appreciate the efforts made by the USSR and the United States towards convening the conference in Madrid. This very important conference will definitely take place in Madrid at the end of this month and, as we hope, will promote a peaceful settlement in the region according to the principles of international law.'

I felt that this statement, bland though it was, would make Baker's life easier as he worked out the remaining technical details that had so worried him in Jerusalem.

Following this final touch to my trip to the Middle East, it was also decided that the opening of the conference would be immediately preceded by another important event: a summit meeting in Madrid between the Presidents of the USSR and the USA. This one would have a special significance because it would be Gorbachev's first journey abroad since the putsch.

No one could know that it would also be his last foreign visit as head of State, and that the State itself would cease to exist in exactly two months' time.

11

Madrid: the Arab-Israeli Dialogue Begins

The last days of October, late autumn, Indian summer. Madrid was in a festive mood as distinguished guests poured in from all over the world. The royal residence, the Oriente palace, was solemnly decorated. At 10 am Middle European time, 30 October 1991, the Madrid Conference on the Middle East was scheduled to open there.

An elegiac mood prevailed in our delegation, headed by the President of the Soviet Union, Mikhail Sergeyevich Gorbachev. The strange, ambivalent feeling returns to me even now, as I write these lines.

There were reasons enough to celebrate. Generations had been marked by animosities, hatred, intolerance, confrontation, and suddenly, for the first time in half a century, a ray of hope appeared. The enemies were to sit down at a negotiating table that was even designed on purpose so as to ensure the proximity of the most intractable opponents, the Palestinians and the Israelis.

Until the last hour, last minute and very last moment before

223

my gavel banged on the table and the conference was declared open, worries still lingered that the whole thing might yet be disrupted, and collapse like the tower of Babel into the abyss of pride and prejudice. Even the most thorough sceptics and cynics among the journalists tried to restrain themselves so as not to cause unexpected harm, though some of them found a special meaning in the fact that the conference was taking place in the land of Don Quixote.

The co-chairmanship of the two great powers whose previous rivalry in the region had only added fuel to the flames was now regarded as a guarantee of success. No one, of course, expected immediate solutions, but the mere fact that the conference started at all, and that no one left the negotiating table permanently while it continued, although there were plenty of pretexts to do just that, was viewed as a historic achievement. Things that no one dared to think about in the past were now discussed in all seriousness, at least in the press: demilitarization of the Golan Heights, a transitional government in the occupied territories of the West Bank and the Gaza Strip, East Jerusalem as the capital of a self-governing Palestine, Israel's withdrawal from southern Lebanon. Whispers, rumours, guesses, leaks. Everything seemed within reach, and looking closely into the faces of Jews and Arabs, people recalled that Palestinians and Jews are half-brothers.

My optimism was bolstered by the fact that the role of the Soviet Union was duly appreciated by the press. Previously the Soviet Union, for various reasons, had been viewed as playing a subordinate role to Uncle Sam. Now the emphasis was on our participation. The *New York Times* came close to striking the proper balance when it stated: 'The most significant Soviet contribution to the conference lay not in twisting the arms of the Arabs, but in providing them with what they most needed – a symbolic cover. The Arabs would never have accepted a diplomatic initiative stamped "Made in the USA" because Washington has always taken a pro-Israeli stance. They would never have participated in an all-American show. The Soviet Union supported them, and thus gave them an opportunity to agree to negotiations.'

Once again you could read between the lines that the world would be the loser if one of the superpowers dropped out. Even the temporary weakening of our country could be turned to our advantage, according to the press. Was the Soviet Union now following the American lead after ceasing its unconditional support for all Arab demands? But then again, hadn't the United States dropped their unconditional support for Israel? Both sides had discarded their ideological blinkers. The wind of cooperation, compromise and reconciliation was blowing in Madrid.

I believe that the conference gained a great deal from following the Soviet–American summit. Gorbachev came to Madrid on the evening of 28 October. Bush reached the Spanish capital early next morning. They had a round of talks over breakfast at the Soviet Embassy, and later that day the two Presidents were received by King Juan Carlos in an audience attended by the Spanish Prime Minister, Felipe Gonzalez. Gorbachev came back late at night to the Embassy where we were all staying, had me hauled out of bed, and following the interpreter's notes began excitedly to recount his long conversation in the King's country residence. Only a few days later he would be describing the same meeting to the State Council in Moscow.

The proceedings and the results of the conference in Madrid are well known to the smallest detail. CNN broadcast it live from first to last, and hundreds of correspondents covered it. So I will focus upon a few seemingly marginal details that may nevertheless convey the tensions that reigned in the opulent royal palace, under the eyes of hundreds of journalists and observers, all as keenly aware as the delegates themselves of the historic nature of the moment.

In the evening that Gorbachev and Bush spent at the King's country house, I went to the Oriente Palace. The problem was that the Spanish and our chiefs of protocol gave me, as the chairman of the opening session, such an elaborate explanation of its procedures – when the guests would come, the order of appearance and places at the table of Presidents and Ministers – that they got me absolutely confused. Having the usual Ambassador's syndrome, an obsession with detail, I asked for explanations on the spot.

Gradually it began to sink in. The King, Prime Minister and Foreign Minister of Spain would await their main visitors in the Throne Room, two passages away from the meeting room. First to arrive would be Bush and Baker. The Spaniards would greet them, and they would then all wait for us. We were to arrive exactly four minutes later. More greetings and instructions. Then the three Foreign Ministers were to leave the King, the Prime Minister and the Presidents and proceed to the meeting hall, where they would take their seats to the right-hand side of the rostrum. Five minutes later they would be followed by the heads of States and governments. Once they were seated to the left of the rostrum I was to bang a gavel on the table and say: 'The Conference is open.'

Next morning Gorbachev and I, accompanied by a flock of protocol officials, walked up the ceremonial steps to the Throne Room, where portraits of Spanish kings looked down at us from the wall. While we were walking I explained the procedure to Gorbachev, adding that we were honoured by the order of appearance: the Americans were greeted only by the Spaniards, while we were to be greeted by both.

'They explained it differently to the Americans,' Gorbachev grinned, and as he spoke we entered the Throne Room, where to my great surprise I saw only our hosts. The Americans weren't there. 'They've changed the order at the last minute,' I thought, unhappy about my explanation to Gorbachev. Then came the greetings, handshakes, embraces. For me this was my first encounter with the King and Gonzalez, but for Gorbachev they were now old acquaintances. The rattle and glare of cameras ... The Americans were still missing, but we were already being ushered towards the meeting hall. Another change in the ceremony? There was no one to ask: the protocol people were not allowed into this place. We entered the meeting hall and discovered (or rather I discovered, because Gorbachev was

226

not concerned) that the Americans were not there either. There
was a commotion in the hall when we appeared, then as we
reached our seats we found ourselves suddenly turned back
towards the Throne Room, and this time the Big Five were all
there: the King, Gonzalez, Fernández Ordóñez, Bush and
Baker. It turned out that they had already been to the meeting
hall, discovered the mistake in Spanish protocol, turned back to
meet us on the way ... and somehow missed us. But at least we
were reunited, and this time in full accordance with the
guidance of the overzealous Spanish protocol we went in due
sequence to the meeting hall. All this happened right in front of
the CNN cameras.

Never mind, I banged on the table right on time, Felipe
Gonzalez took the floor, Bush and Gorbachev followed him.
Thank God, we had begun!

Next day the tense but orderly proceedings of the conference
were suddenly disrupted by a bitter exchange between Prime
Minister Shamir, who led the Israeli delegation in person,
leaving my friend David Levy at home, and the Syrian Foreign
Minister Farooq ash-Shar'.

The sides were speaking for the second time. This was their
opportunity to answer critical remarks. Shamir called Syria 'one
of the worst repressive terrorist regimes in the world'. Shar'
could not let this pass, and he held up a poster dating back to
the time of the British mandate in Palestine, and naming Shamir
as being wanted by the police for his part in acts of terrorism.
Shar' read out the description of the suspect: 'Height 165 cm,
big ears, untidy appearance ...' No doubt Shamir had asked for
this, but clearly Shar' overreacted. All this was going on with
me in the chair, sitting there quite impotent and not permitted
to interfere in the course of debate, let alone take sides.

It may be that Shamir with his outburst was trying to provoke
the Syrians, the most touchy participants, into leaving the
conference. Shar' responded in kind and resorted to personal
attacks. What next?

The situation was saved by tough but level-headed speeches

by the Lebanese, Jordanians and Palestinians, but a break announced for twenty minutes lasted for more than two hours. Baker spoke to the Syrian Foreign Minister while I worked on the Israeli delegation. Then we swapped over.

Our task was to dampen the often theatrical emotions that spilled out. We all knew – mediators and antagonists alike – that most of the harsh words and insults being traded were for consumption in each delegation's home market. We had to make sure that the channels of communication were not choked by excessive histrionics. Shamir for example was constantly pretending to be insulted. Because we all knew it was impossible to insult this thick-skinned little fighter, we knew how to bypass his affectation of rage.

Baker's and my concluding remarks lowered the temperature still further.

The time came (again it fell to me) to bang the gavel and say: 'I declare the plenary session closed.' Everybody rose from their seats, but unexpectedly Shar' asked for the floor. 'The conference is not finished but just suspended, and can be resumed at any moment if the parties agree to do so,' he said. The remark of the Syrian Minister reflected the different interpretations of the status of the bilateral negotiations that were due to start after the plenary session. The Arabs viewed them as a continuation of the conference, while Israel saw them as completely separate. My formula, laboriously worked out by the co-chairs, precisely addressed the point, and Shar' certainly knew this. 'That is exactly what I said,' I told him in a conciliatory tone. 'The plenary session is closed. And I agree with the honourable speaker that it may be resumed at any time, provided there is an agreement between the parties to do so.'

The subsequent course of events is also well known. After two days of consultations, the bilateral negotiations continued in Madrid, which was the preference of the Arabs as well as the co-chairs. We agreed with Baker to have the next round of bilateral negotiations in Washington, and to conduct the next plenary in Moscow, where Gorbachev (who was already back in

Moscow himself) agreed to invite the participants after some persuasion by me. The plenary did take place there, but by then Gorbachev was no longer the USSR President and the Soviet Union had ceased to exist.

Nevertheless I can take satisfaction from the fact that the words 'Madrid peace process' are solidly incorporated into the international political language.

12

Gorbachev: Last Summit in Madrid

I mentioned in the previous chapter that at the Middle East peace conference an elegiac mood prevailed in the Soviet delegation, and it was most of all Gorbachev who felt it. There was another drama playing in Madrid: the summit meeting.

Judging from the previous summits, this one was no stranger than its predecessors, yet something very essential was missing. The press that was so euphoric about the conference on the Middle East sounded a funereal note when it turned to the summit. 'Emissary of a non-existent State' was typical of the headlines in the Moscow press.

On the surface, everything looked normal. Even the fact that the Presidents had very little time to prepare for the summit and that there was no pre-set agenda could be interpreted in a positive light. Gone were the days of pompous meetings orchestrated in advance. And the Bush initiative drew the line under tedious, long-drawn-out negotiations on nuclear disarmament. The relations between the two States and their leaders had become such that it was no longer necessary to prepare momentous documents for theatrical signing ceremonies to convey an impression of success.

Almost on the eve of our departure to Madrid the American Embassy in Moscow had delivered a letter from President Bush to Gorbachev covering nuclear disarmament. It had already been agreed that the subject would be discussed in Madrid. Now Bush was analysing the situation in connection with 'my initiative and your courageous response'. The President stated that 'impressive progress towards consolidating nuclear stability had been achieved without protracted and complex negotiations. Many obstacles have been overcome on the way to adjusting our armed forces to the new realities in relations between our two countries.'

Bush informed Gorbachev about the measures undertaken by the American side to implement their unilateral obligations. They looked impressive. Gorbachev demanded a report from the Defence Minister on actions taken on our side, and the latest information was received over the special Presidential hot line in the aircraft.

In addition to discussing Middle East affairs, Gorbachev had received a request from President Vassiliou of Cyprus (who left Moscow after a visit there just an hour before Gorbachev's plane took off) to ask President Bush to step up American efforts to settle the Cyprus problem. Gorbachev and Bush were also to review the situation in Yugoslavia, which was becoming desperate, as well as a wide range of issues connected with economic assistance to our reforms from the G-7 nations.

So the agenda was packed, forcing Anatoly Chernyaev to carry a big case stuffed with briefing documents. On the plane Gorbachev had a series of discussions with various groups of experts. The sessions went on at one end of the cabin, while at the opposite end Raisa Maximovna (I renewed my acquaintance with her) was quietly reading a book.

The Presidential Ilyushin 62 plane was not much different from the one that I had been using, except for its special communication system. There was the same long cabin with two tables and two sofas for the chief passenger, a small sleeping

231

compartment where Raisa Maximovna retired from time to time, plus two small cabins for four and six people where we were seated with the comfort of economy-class passengers. I noticed that just as in my own plane, the noisiest hottest place was the main cabin.

Before landing we were told that Prime Minister Gonzalez and his wife were to greet the Gorbachevs at the airport. I sensed that this news cheered up the President a little. It had been decided beforehand that both Presidents would be met at a working level, particularly because Bush was coming without Barbara.

The next day's meeting between the Presidents in the central lobby of the Soviet Embassy was warm, even cordial, especially while the cameras were rolling. But still there was a feeling that something was missing, like salt from a well cooked dish – it looks and smells fine, but you know that something is wrong. The same feeling persisted over luncheon, and even in the conversation in our immediate circle.

So what was missing? Certainly not topics for discussion. Of course the conversation started with the failed coup, and emotional congratulations from the Americans. It was their first meeting since the fateful events of August. The Presidents went on to exchange views about the implementation of disarmament initiatives, and here they remained satisfied. They touched upon Yugoslavia, and Bush said that this should probably be left with the EC. On Cyprus Bush groaned, looked at Baker, and said that yes, it was time to resume talks with Turkey. They weighed up the chances of success for the forthcoming Madrid Conference. Bush enquired about the state of affairs in the Soviet Union.

It gradually dawned on me what was wrong. Gorbachev was irritated and concerned by media speculation about the disintegration of the Soviet Union and his own precarious position. He knew that President Bush was receiving much the same information that he was, and he expected Bush to give some indication of support, to send some signal. But Bush sent no signal. Their conversation ended strictly on schedule, which

232

was unusual, and so did the luncheon that followed. The reporters who didn't have long to wait for their press conference were more disappointed than happy.

During the press conference there were many questions about alleged flirtations between the US administration and the republics of the Soviet Union. In denying these stories, Bush talked about his respect for Gorbachev and support for the Soviet President, but with no great air of conviction.

If it was moral support that the Soviet President needed, he did not receive it until the evening's royal reception. The King and the Spanish Prime Minister, with their first-hand experience of transforming a dictatorship into a democracy, remarked how important it was to accelerate reforms but at the same time not to surrender to anarchy. Democracy could not exist without order and discipline, otherwise it would relapse into mob rule. The remarks of the Spaniards were sometimes quite critical, but that was exactly what Gorbachev needed to rally and inspire him, and that was the impression he took home.

Late in the night of the meeting he reworked his speech for the Madrid Conference. To the surprise of the audience, the greater part of it was devoted to Soviet domestic problems. That was not a statesmanlike move. As the Madrid *El Pais* commented next morning, the delegates were surprised that Gorbachev did not use up all his allotted time, and that the major part of his speech ignored the Middle East.

I too was surprised, and disappointed. The Madrid Conference crowned our foreign policy efforts of recent months. We had passed the test for world-power status, and this had made possible the Soviet–American summit so important for Gorbachev at this particular moment. A meeting with President Mitterrand also lay ahead. All these advantages began to be undermined because of pressures in Moscow so intense that they drained our President both psychologically and spiritually, and impaired his judgement.

Here I could compare Gorbachev with President Bush, whose stock had been rising as Gorbachev's fell. Bush was every inch the consummate politician, self-confident and knowledgeable, every smile and handshake a part of the machinery. When I first met him in New York he had struck me as a rather wooden figure, posing as a world statesman. In Madrid he was even more self-confident – one might almost say self-satisfied. Obviously Gorbachev was much weaker than he had been even a few weeks earlier, and this gave Bush the chance to strut. He revelled in the role of the world mediator not to be troubled by details, and his attitude to Gorbachev was nothing short of patronizing. In this he differed from the punctilious James Baker, whose cool charm was no more rattled by success than by setbacks.

I myself had plenty of reasons to worry about what was going on at home. Between Paris, where I attended the Cambodia conference on 23 October, and Madrid I had spent only five days in Moscow. In the airport before flying to Madrid a journalist had asked me to comment on the recent statement from the Foreign Ministry of Russia that the Soviet Foreign Ministry ought in future to be cut down to no more than three hundred people, who would carry out the limited functions assigned to them by the republican ministries. Not at all bothered by the question, I said that the statement was either a slip of the tongue or the press had misinterpreted the words of Andrei Vladimirovich Kozyrev. We had only recently talked to him, and discovered that we had a lot in common in our understanding of how the responsibilities of the republican and federal foreign ministries should be distributed and the way these bodies should interact.

To Madrid, though, came the news that Boris Nikolayevich Yeltsin, speaking before the Supreme Soviet of Russia, had declared that the Soviet Foreign Ministry should be cut by 90 per cent. That was more disquieting news, but even then I decided to shrug it off with a joke. In an interview with Soviet television I said that Boris Nikolayevich must have been speaking figuratively, just as when two people meet and say that they haven't seen each other for ages, no one takes it literally. I said this in passing, since the main subject of the interview was the Madrid Conference, but that was the only part that was broadcast and then re-broadcast several times. Either it really impressed the editors, or perhaps they wanted to put me in Yeltsin's bad books.

By no means everyone enjoyed my little joke. It did not prevent a panic in the Foreign Ministry, as my First Deputies Anatoly Kovalev and Vladimir Petrovsky informed me. There were complaints that the Minister was spending time in Madrid while the roof of his house was on fire. Someone even circulated a petition. I read about it in *Izvestia* and could not believe my eyes. It seemed incredible that adult people, professional diplomats with whom we had lived through so much turbulence during these months, could be thinking like this. How could they equate a petty domestic squabble with this historic conference? My faith went unrewarded: from Moscow I received a coded telegram giving the text of the petition, which was signed by one of my deputies (appointed by me, incidentally) and a number of other people in high and not so high-ranking positions at the Ministry. And it did have the nerve to say that rather than establishing peace in the Middle East I should hurry back home and set about saving the Foreign Ministry.

That was on Thursday 31 October. The plenaries had ended. Baker and I wanted to make sure that after two days of consultations the opposing sides would open the bilateral negotiations on Sunday. After that, we would go home in the evening with a sense of a mission completed.

A session of the Gossoviet, the State Council, was scheduled for Monday 4 November. One of the items on the agenda was the reorganization of the Foreign Ministry, and my comprehensive proposals on that subject had been forwarded to the State Council and to the President well in advance. I felt sure of myself: it was just a matter of coming back and presenting them at the State Council. But that was not the view of my wise deputy, and chief expert on the Middle East, Alexander Belonogov. He told me:

'Boris Dimitrievich, take my advice. Book the plane for tomorrow and fly home. You'll have two days, Sunday and Saturday, to prepare for your presentation and calm our people down. And we will somehow manage here. If you leave Madrid tomorrow afternoon you'll have time to meet the Palestinians. They've asked for an appointment.'

After a brief hesitation I agreed.

When I told James that I might have to go to Moscow earlier than scheduled he was taken aback, and very tactfully enquired why. Both he and Bush had shown a lot of concern about the future of the Soviet Foreign Ministry in their conversation with Gorbachev in Madrid. They could not understand how people in Moscow could attack the Ministry at the moment when its chief was engaged in what was after all a historic mission. This concern now encouraged me to hint to Baker about my problems. He agreed with my decision to return, and promised to ask Bush to telephone Yeltsin. I do not know whether this call was ever made.

What strange times we were living in. Here was one Foreign Minister driven to discreetly lobby with another Foreign Minister for the preservation of his own country's Foreign Ministry and diplomatic capacity.

13

Last Days of the Soviet Union

The advice of Belonogov and Baker proved invaluable. I did need time to make careful preparations for the meeting of the State Council. Fortunately those two days happened to be Saturday and Sunday, and there was less routine work to deal with.

On Saturday Gorbachev, who was already back in Moscow, called me twice: to ask about the latest news from Madrid and to cheer me up before the State Council meeting. On Sunday I was in my office on the seventh floor of the Smolenskaya skyscraper. All my deputies and aides were on alert too, supplying me with position papers, calculations, statistics, and the latest telegrams.

There was plenty to think about. Until now, until the first distant whispers of warning reached me before Madrid, I had acted as I myself saw fit. Occasional digs from the press did not bother me. Myself a journalist, I knew how to ignore them. All my proposals had found immediate support in Moscow and the quick and resolute workings of Soviet diplomacy were bringing me friends abroad. As well as having a good working relationship with democratic intellectual circles in Moscow, I was also in regular contact with Gorbachev and Yeltsin, and had no reason to doubt their sympathies. So now I was concerned not so much with my personal future, nor even with the outlook for the Foreign Ministry but with a larger issue. When journalists asked questions about the Ministry, I always answered that the future of the Soviet Foreign Ministry depended on the future of the Soviet Union.

And that was something that I needed to think about now.

At the beginning of September 1991 the so-called 10+1 Declaration at the Fifth Extraordinary Congress of People's Deputies stated that the defeat of the coup had 'created a historical opportunity to accelerate the radical transformation and renewal of the country'. I described in chapter 4 how my return to Moscow from Prague to take up the post of Foreign Minister almost coincided with the opening of that Congress's sessions. I was present when Gorbachev excitedly summarized the coming decisions to John Major, his first visitor from the West after the coup. I saw how these vague outlines were transformed by the Congress into the foundations of a new Union that was being born before my eyes. Naturally, I took a special interest in the debate on foreign policy and its institutions, and was glad when vague and amorphous notions turned into a clear mandate.

When the Congress dissolved the Supreme Soviet, which had failed to take a firm stand against the coup, I was relieved of the need to seek the approval of my new appointment by that ill-fated Parliament. This only added to my interest in the first steps taken by the State Council, newly created by the Congress. It was a structure unique in the history of our State, combining both legislative and executive powers. I participated in its first organizing meeting, when Presidents, Chairmen of Supreme Soviets and other high-ranking representatives of the republics gathered right after the closing of the Congress behind the scenes of the Kremlin's Palace of Congresses. They were

238

excited and happy, not least because three sleepless days and nights were already behind them. What I saw reminded me of molten iron cooling into a new form. Moments ago we had '10+1', meaning ten Soviet republics plus USSR. Now 10+1 had become the State Council – barely two weeks after the failed coup.

When the agenda of the first official State Council meeting was discussed the day after it was established in early September, the first item was the recognition of the independence of the Baltic States. Bureaucratically speaking, that was 'my item' because for two days I had been reminding Gorbachev that we had to settle this issue before the end of the Congress. I even prepared a draft of the decree that would need to be adopted. In his usual way the President had prevaricated for a day or two before deciding to put it on the agenda of the State Council.

I stressed to the President that already fifty States, including all the leading Western countries, had recognized the independence of Latvia, Lithuania and Estonia, and that their membership of the UN was inevitable. But the international factor, no matter how important in the current circumstances, was not decisive. The secession of these countries from the Soviet Union was a certainty, and the point of principle had been stated already by the President of the USSR and the leaders of the republics in the debate in the Congress. Rather than lag behind events, it was in our interest to act quickly.

What I meant to imply was that inconsistency, both here and in other contexts, and delays between words and deeds, could do us nothing but harm. I stressed that this decision would not provide a precedent for other sovereign republics, because recognition of the independence of Latvia, Lithuania and Estonia was connected to the very specific historical and political circumstances of their joining the Soviet Union following their occupation in 1940. Obviously the recognition of independence was linked to full-scale negotiations on such crucial problems as the army and defence, economic cooperation, border arrangements, solid guarantees of the rights

239

of national minorities, and legal protection for those citizens who chose either to stay or to leave.

At the first informal meeting of the State Council in the Kremlin Palace of Congresses I presented my draft resolution. Next day the resolution was adopted without discussion, except that the Prime Minister of Georgia asked in the tone of a spoiled child why his own republic was denied such recognition. Finding no support he left in a huff, but the fuss he raised failed to disrupt the decision on the Baltic States. The State Council authorized the Foreign Minister to make a statement for the press and passed on to the next item on the agenda.

This had been my first encounter with the State Council, immediately after it had come into being. It had been a smooth ride in early September. Now two months later, on my return to Moscow from Madrid, the situation was more murky.

Yet it all seemed so straightforward in the early days of the State Council, when I could look with unsatiable curiosity into the faces of the men who from now on were to decide the fate of the country.

Who were these unfamiliar new men of the State Council? Who were these new khans from the outer regions of the Soviet Union? On the table in front of me there always was a list of participants. Karimov of Uzbekistan, Niyazov of Turkmenistan, Dementei of Belarus, Mutalibov of Azerbaijan, Kravchuk of Ukraine ... I tried to relate these not very familiar names and faces to the names of their republics. Two of them made an immediate impression: the pleasant, dapper-looking Levon Ter-Petrosian of Armenia, and the solid Nursultan Nazarbayev of Kazakhstan. He remembered me from the *Komsomolka* years.

You could detect the Ukrainian in Kravchuk at a glance. His always upright head at once reminded me of characters in Gogol. He was plumpish, but this only added to the impression of a man with a strong sense of self-satisfaction and self-importance. Ayaz Mutalibov of Azerbaijan resembled a teenage street thug who had grown up and lost touch with his bad companions but never quite shed his old habits.

240

Saparmurat Niyazov of Turkmenistan – a chairman of a first-class collective farm. Askar Akayev of Kirghizstan – a local educator from the 1920s ...

At that time the Turkmen Niyazov behaved placidly and looked more inconspicuous than the others. I was quite surprised that his Foreign Minister turned out to be so aggressive in New York at the UN session. However, it was Niyazov himself who really distinguished himself from the rest after the break-up of the Soviet Union. He had been one of the first people whom Gorbachev promoted when in December 1985 he became the First Secretary of the Turkmenian Communist Party. Now six years later he began to reflect upon his future – what ideological foundations could he rely on when the old Communist base had completely outlived its usefulness?

But Niyazov looked back rather than forward. He found his solution in the tribal and clan traditions of the Turkmen people. Traditionally it was rulers from the Teke tribe whom the Turkmen regarded as legitimate. During the Communist years that tradition had been suppressed and no Teke occupied any position of authority. Now it was claimed that Saparmurat Niyazov was the first Soviet ruler of Turkmenia from the Teke tribe. When oppositionists asserted that he actually came from the lowly Ata tribe, a special mission from the republican archives department was dispatched to the Teke village of Gapzhag near Ashkhabad, where Niyazov was born, to find concrete evidence of his high extraction. Naturally such evidence was soon found, and thus Niyazov could officially call himself Turkmenbashi, 'chief' or 'father' of the Turkmen people. A special Saparmurat Turkmenbashi Archives Foundation was set up, and proceeded to trace his family tree.

There followed the renaming of all Soviet facilities and establishments as Turkmenbashi facilities. Buildings, cities, enterprises, kolkhozes were now named after the Turkmenbashi. But things did not stop there. A campaign was even launched in the Turkmen press to award Saparmurat the Nobel peace prize.

Although in these circumstances it came as no surprise that there were portraits of the Turkmenbashi on every building and

241

in every house, his image was also printed on the republic's banknotes, something even Stalin had shrunk from. And it was with Stalinian modesty that he informed the world that since the people had to have an ideal, and since a nationwide affection happened to have focused on his modest figure, he stood ready to sacrifice himself. Having emerged the winner in the presidential elections of 1992 with a tolerable 98.3 per cent of the votes, he could not flout the will of the Majlis, the Turkmen parliament, which resolved to hold a referendum on extending the presidential powers from five to ten years. The referendum succeeded. Under the new law, Niyazov is guaranteed to remain in power until the year 2002.

Following Turkmenia's lead, a search for pedigrees began in other newly-born States of Central Asia, formerly republics of the USSR, and soon Askar Akayev turned out to be a direct descendant of one of the last Kirghiz rulers, Khan Shiban – in other words, he was shown to be the legitimate successor to the Kirghiz throne.

Then it was the turn of Islam Karimov, the president of Uzbekistan. He himself could boast no noble pedigree, so he dug further into the past. He recalled that in the Middle Ages three cities in the territory of the republic – Bukhara, Khorezm and Kokand – were the centres of powerful States. The spirit of the formidable Timur Leng (Tamerlane) was resurrected from oblivion. His statue, many metres tall, replaced Karl Marx in the main square of Tashkent, the country's capital. At the same time Karimov rehabilitated his predecessor, Sharaf Rashidov, the First Secretary of the Uzbekistan Communist Party, Brezhnev's favourite, who was accused of corruption and shot himself in the perestroika years. Karimov called him a people's hero, proclaiming that it was the most deadly sin to speak ill of one's own past. He also banned several parties that were in opposition to him, stating as his rationale: 'First let's build our national house. We can sort out democracy later.'

The meetings of the State Council displayed not a trace of the staid old order. Gone now were the stiff set speeches, the heavily regulated entrances and exits of apparatchiks and the iron hand of that dry old pedant Mikhail Suslov, whose spirit as orchestrator of the Council of Ministers and the Central Committee had lingered even after his death while Gorbachev was trying to kick-start perestroika.

Now not a trace remained of that culture. In the ante-room people jostled in a fog of tobacco smoke. There was noise and fuss. Old friends embraced. The doors to the meeting hall were opened well in advance, and the appearance of the participants was preceded by the press, including television, with its big old-fashioned cameras that would be moved around noisily by the cameramen during the session. Gorbachev chaired. To his right sat Yeltsin, to his left Nazarbayev, Kravchuk and the other republican leaders; then we four ministers; Ivan Silayev, Chairman of the Intrarepublican Committee for the Operational Management of the Economy, and his team – Yavlinsky, Volsky, Luzhkov and others; then members of the Presidential Political Consulting Committee – Alexander and Yegor Yakovlev, Shevardnadze ...

On chairs along the walls sat the people who were invited for the discussions of different items on the agenda. They wandered in and out at will, and conducted their own separate conversations. The whole chaotic atmosphere conjured up a feeling of both extravagance and pettiness, with its easily triggered squabbles, and truculent antagonists keeping an ostentatious distance between each other.

Some people were inspired by such anarchy: they viewed it as a tangible harbinger of new democratic changes in the making. Others, including those in Yeltsin's camp and the followers of other self-proclaimed republican leaders, tended to gloat over confusion that denoted such an obvious decline in Gorbachev's authority. People no longer trembled before him, and by time-honoured Russian tradition that meant the beginning of the end, and eventually humiliation. The bureaucratic experience of our country had taught that where there is power there is order, where there is order there is power. Only two Soviet leaders, Khrushchev and Gorbachev, had broken that cast-iron rule.

What became of Khrushchev was well known. So what would become of Gorbachev? This question was not uttered out loud – it was all in the air.

With hindsight I have to say that all the republican presidents were anxious to make the Soviet Union as weak as possible, and to this end they used Yeltsin as their stick. Their goal was to create as much disruption as possible, their tactic to discuss everything, resolve nothing, and undermine Gorbachev. Yeltsin, who was to prove the bane of Gorbachev, was more than happy to oblige his republican colleagues to further this goal. And he was certainly up to the job.

At first I did not notice many of these things. I had my work to do, no one was interfering, and that was what mattered. Besides, I was often on the road and missed some meetings, and during other meetings I was mentally on my travels. On several occasions I came to a meeting straight from the airport, or had to leave to catch a plane.

I always left full of most radical intentions, came back in triumph, and genuinely believed that everything was going fine in Moscow. The issues that the State Council addressed from its very inception were very serious, and the way it was dealing with them squared with my understanding of what should be done in a country that had rid itself of totalitarianism, whose member republics had all the independence they wanted in solving their problems, and where the Centre was reduced to a minimum. That formerly ugly, all-pervading Centre was now squeezed into a single room, and a good half of it was represented by the leaders of independent republics.

After deciding in its first session to grant independence to the Baltic States, the State Council proceeded to discuss the draft treaty on economic union. The draft was prepared by a group of forward-thinking economists headed by Grigory Yavlinsky, a flamboyant young genius with playboy inclinations, whose sharp sense of humour often discomfited the lesser mortals around him, especially if they happened to be crusty old apparatchiks. But Yavlinsky's involvement also inspired hope.

244

He had good credentials. He was the author of a famous 'Five Hundred Days' programme of transition to a market economy which some time before had caused disagreements between Yeltsin and Gorbachev. Later he became the co-author of a programme of economic reforms, worked out in cooperation with a Harvard University team, which had been presented to the Group of Seven when Gorbachev met them in London in July 1991. Yavlinsky was a person who had worked with both Yeltsin and Gorbachev, and proved to both his competence and independence. Now he was focusing and integrating the interests of both.

Supporting the draft was Ivan Silayev, an old apparatchik who had been Deputy Prime Minister in Ryzhkov's government, and a long-term ally of Yeltsin. He had now been made Chairman of the Intrarepublican Committee for the Management of the Economy, on Gorbachev's recommendation. That for me was further proof of the seriousness of the draft document. Although Silayev was not an all-out reformer, he was solid and reliable. He was a man of the people, and had the solid charm of an old farmer.

It seemed very sensible for the State Council to start by reorganizing the Union's economic structure, although the documents of the Congress also mentioned political and defence unions. It is obvious that in periods of instability economic imperatives are the strongest integrating factor.

As I write I have in front of me the first draft of the treaty and Yavlinsky's note of explanation. It is dated 5 September 1991. In other words, a day after the Congress closed down this document was already tabled for consideration by the State Council, which means that work on it had been going on for some time.

'The main task of the economic union is to consolidate the efforts of the sovereign states to form a common market and to conduct a concerted economic policy as a necessary condition of overcoming the crisis,' Yavlinsky wrote. The preamble to the treaty stated that the goal was to create a market economy and integrate it into the world economy. It was stressed that joining the Economic Union was in no way conditional on signing the treaty on the Union of Sovereign States, and that each side was free to join or leave it as its government saw fit.

In the chapter called 'Free Enterprise' the revival of the economy was linked to private property and free enterprise, which would be protected by law from excessive intervention by the State. It was on the basis of these principles that the movement of goods and services, banking and monetary systems, pricing, finance and taxation, and foreign economic activities would be coordinated between the republics.

In addition to the treaty itself, a package of supplementary agreements detailed the ways and means of cooperation between the independent States in key areas.

The developments around the treaty would continue to attract outside attention for quite some time. First the treaty was approved by the State Council, then initialled and signed by the majority of the republics – in fact, by the very same people who several weeks later would go so far as to consign the Soviet Union to oblivion and rubber-stamp the creation of the insipid CIS. The verdict of experts abroad was that the treaty allowed each republic to develop its economy on the principles of private property and the free market, and in coordination with other republics. It was modelled broadly on the European Community, whose example Gorbachev constantly had in mind, though when he exaggerated the analogies with the EC some of the State Council's members would temper his enthusiasm by saying that while the EC was a rather loose entity, we, thank God, were a federation.

And naturally, there was nothing totalitarian or coercive in the treaty.

Yavlinsky never tired of repeating that after the treaty was approved by the State Council, negotiations could start with foreign countries and international organizations on massive economic assistance. This would help stabilize the economy and accelerate the pace of reforms. As for the running of this new Economic Union, both Gorbachev and Yeltsin recommended Silayev as its executive head.

As a first step it was necessary to agree upon the joint responsibility of the republics for the foreign debt and other economic obligations of the Soviet Union. That would pave the way for humanitarian assistance, short-term credits and other forms of economic cooperation, including joining the World Bank and the IMF. In the course of the debate the West was waiting to discover who it would be dealing with in the economic sphere, in the State that was now beginning to call itself the Union of Independent States. The intention was that the Vnezhekonombank, the Bank for Foreign Trade, would deal with debt problems on behalf of all republics, and the committee headed by Silayev, representing all the republics, would coordinate all forms of economic assistance.

All these matters were discussed and resolved in principle in the two State Council sessions of 5 and 16 September, so when I went to the airport to fly to the UN General Assembly session I had answers to most of the questions that might be asked, and was ready to explain with a clear conscience what my country was going to look like in the near future. I felt quite optimistic then, notwithstanding the plethora of crises that beset us at home. Revolution is revolution, even when it is peaceful, so we needed assistance in struggling through a transitional period. I was not ashamed to address the international community for help.

My account of the events in our country did impress my interlocutors at the UN, who understood that we were all in one boat, and it did prompt them to start acting, to pass from words to deeds. I remain convinced that the objective needs of our development compelled us to go in the direction that was worked out in the Congress of People's Deputies and that was initially supported by the State Council. But the State Council to which I returned from Madrid had evolved over the last weeks into a body with very different ideas.

During the two days that I sat in my office on Smolenskaya Square and prepared for the 4 November meeting of the State Council, I found good cause to believe that the fate of the

247

Foreign Ministry was only a card in the Moscow power game. The proof was soon to come.

In the long list of items on the agenda of the State Council, the reorganization of the Foreign Ministry, together with similar items on the Defence and Interior Ministries, Intelligence, etc. was one of the last. The meeting started with something that was not on the agenda. Gorbachev proposed to discuss the situation in the country. I knew that he was eager to share his impressions from his conversations with the King and Prime Minister of Spain and the US President and Secretary of State, and these conversations certainly had a direct bearing on what the State Council was to discuss.

The following account is taken from my own detailed notes, written during the session.

'The West fears the break-up of the Soviet Union,' Gorbachev declared, looking at me. 'I assure you that this was the main subject of all my talks in Madrid. They can't understand what's happening here. Just when we're finally on the road to democracy and clearing the debris of totalitarianism ... They say the Soviet Union has to be preserved as one of the pillars of the international system.

'Gonzalez put it in a very straightforward manner: Europe and the world need the Soviet Union, they need the Union of Independent States that you and the republican leaders proposed to the Congress. He raised this issue specifically because of speculation in the press concerning the Foreign Ministry, and the future of our foreign policy. They asked me: Are the State Council members changing their positions? Are they reneging on what they said and promised at the Fifth Congress?

'This is what Bush had to say: We need you. We are prepared to help you. But we need guarantees. We were told: deal with the Silayev Committee, he represents all the republics. But then your Presidents show up and each one makes his own requests.

'I informed Bush that our twelve Finance Ministers, on State Council authority, had worked out a coordinated policy on dealing with our country's foreign debt. But the next information to reach Madrid was that this agreement was phoney: this one had no mandate, that one had changed his position. The world is either laughing at us or it's scared. And so aid is suspended. There are plenty of examples. The same foot-dragging in relation to Economic Union. I want us to speak about all this.'

I did sympathize with what Gorbachev was saying, and looked forward with some relish to the replies. But they didn't reply. They just stared blankly in front of them, or shuffled their papers and kept quiet, like dunces afraid of being singled out. The impression was that they were worried about something else, and it wasn't hard to guess what that was.

The seat to the right of Gorbachev was empty. Yeltsin was expected to attend, but he was late, and Gorbachev decided to start without him. Someone (I think it was Yegor Yakovlev, head of the Soviet television corporation, appointed by Gorbachev after the coup) suggested that it was wrong to hold meetings like this in the absence of Yeltsin, but he was ignored.

Yeltsin showed up only twenty minutes later, excused himself casually, and took his seat. Gorbachev refrained from comments with obvious difficulty, merely remarking that he would have to repeat what he had said. He spoke about the recent memorable speech in the Russian Parliament in which Yeltsin had announced that Russia was embarking on economic reforms that would begin at the end of the year with a price liberalization.

Gorbachev welcomed Yeltsin's having 'finally' undertaken the reforms, and supported their main direction, but was critical of careless work on some important details. 'That's what always happens when you lag behind events,' he remarked. Those present looked at each other in amusement: the roles had switched, and now it was Gorbachev reproaching Yeltsin for wasting time. Gorbachev recalled that some time previously Yeltsin had quite justly criticized Prime Minister Ryzhkov, and now he himself had committed the same mistake by announcing the forthcoming price rise well in advance.

'And you can see the results.' The President turned to his notes. 'Here I have the statistics: sales of bread in Moscow are usually 1,800 tons a day. Yesterday sales were 2,500 tons. People are queuing up for bread, there's a shortage of it now. What people picked up from the speech was not its main theme, which I repeat is good and serious, but the news about prices. And another panic was provoked.'

Gorbachev finished speaking and once again asked for comments. Silence.

Yeltsin looked around the table. 'Let's get to the agenda.'

'Yes, the agenda!' others rumbled with relief.

'On the agenda is the situation in the country,' Gorbachev snapped. 'And I'm calling on you to speak about that!'

'And on my agenda' – a familiar hoarseness rasped in Yeltsin's voice – 'on my agenda, item one is supplementary agreements to the Treaty on Economic Union.'

'And on my agenda ...' Gorbachev began to respond, but here Nazarbayev intervened. He often acted as a mediator.

'I think, Mikhail Sergeyevich,' he said pacifically, 'that you're right in what you say. But our entire agenda is all about the situation in the country. So we will speak about that in the course of the discussion.'

'Fine,' said Gorbachev drily. 'Supplements to the Economic Union Treaty. Who is the main speaker? Yavlinsky?'

Yavlinsky came to the stand, and with his unique blend of sarcastic persuasiveness and ironic despair began to say that this was the fourth time the State Council had addressed this issue. 'Here we manage to agree on something, but when the State Council members return home, they immediately go back on their word. Take the economic treaty that Mikhail Sergeyevich was mentioning. We did come to an agreement, and decided to initial it, but now it looks as if we have to start all over again. What's the point of talking about supplementary agreements if there's no clarity about the treaty itself? Are we civilized people or not?'

As a highly organized person, an economist and mathematician who appreciated above all precision and clarity in figures, words and actions, and a man with a wonderful sense of humour that helped him cope with what was going on,

250

Yavlinsky hated these meetings where he had to speak more often than others.

'All this would be very funny if it weren't so sad.' This melancholy verdict would best convey his mood, the mood of a person convinced that he was right, but who had lost all hope that others could understand him. And many of the State Council members behaved as if they were determined to confirm his worst fears.

A typical case was the urgent issue of humanitarian aid. On one occasion when the Council discussed a draft resolution on coordinating the effort to distribute the aid that was beginning to pour into the country, Prime Minister Vitold Fokin of Ukraine solemnly intoned:

'We agree that it's necessary to adopt such a document. But we are not in a position to give a clear response now, because we haven't yet fully examined this document.'

Chairman Silayev: 'But your representative did work on the committee that was authorized to ...'

'Yes, as an observer.'

'Why couldn't you give him full status?'

'That was my mistake.'

Then there was the key matter of the Soviet Union's foreign debt. At one meeting everything seemed to be settled, with all the republics accepting joint responsibility. Then at the next meeting the Chairman of the Supreme Soviet of Uzbekistan stood up:

'How can we take responsibility when we don't know what our share is?'

Yavlinsky, bowing his head and clearly demonstrating that he was running out of patience, got up and went to the rostrum:

'I'll explain it once again. What the share of this or that republic is going to be, we do not and cannot know, because when the former Centre borrowed it didn't trouble itself with such questions. This we have to decide among ourselves. Our Western lenders are not interested in this. They expect us to confirm the joint responsibility. Without that, no one will do business with us, and then everything we've done here for the last three months will be a waste of time and effort. There'll be no humanitarian aid, no credits, no investment. That means a disaster.'

So, there in the Kremlin, they would come to decisions. Then they would retract them as soon as they got home. And at the next meeting in Moscow they would bleat about their own Supreme Soviets, pressure from the opposition, forthcoming elections, referendums and any number of other excuses.

Take Kravchuk, for example. He was an adept at stoking up the pressure in his country as a convenient pretext for muddying the waters in Moscow. Then he would explain, hand on heart, that he was obliged to insist on the creation of a Ukrainian army for tactical electoral reasons. The idea was popular in his republic and he could not leave the field open to the opposition. But when he became President (in December 1991) he grew even more enthusiastic about the idea. What he eventually got was what he really wanted.

The same frame of mind prompted him then to demand the division of the Black Sea fleet. The appetite just grew with every concession granted.

While listening to the speakers at the sessions of the State Council – all of them were or were soon to become the Presidents of independent States – I found myself recollecting their recent past. With the exception of Ter-Petrosian, a classic dissident, and Akayev, a scholar, they had all been Party functionaries. In the first years of perestroika they were all on the second or third rungs of the Party hierarchy. By the time of the putsch many had risen to the positions of First Secretaries of the Communist Parties of their republics. Nothing had changed since then in the logic of their behaviour. Schooled in zealous obedience to orders from 'above' – that is, from the republican or Moscow Party bosses on whom their personal standing depended – with equal zeal and for the same reasons they now obeyed their 'orders from below'. These orders might come from a republican parliament, an opposition party, or just a rally of people unhappy about something.

But perhaps there were forces from 'below' that had an interest in the chaos that was more and more enveloping the country. Except for those individuals and elite groups who were determined to consolidate their power at any price, who was it who gained from national clashes, the creation of customs barriers between republics, artificial local currencies, or the rupture of economic ties? Who benefited from the fact that Western leaders, seeing this disorder, postponed their decisions to provide us with economic assistance, although they themselves were convinced that it had to be done?

The sessions of the State Council were accompanied by presidential elections in the republics. If Russia had a President, why wasn't Turkmenistan or Azerbaijan entitled to have one? We were going full steam ahead for democracy, but the presidential nominees, usually ex-Party secretaries, had no opponents and were elected with 90–95 per cent of the vote.

No, I said to myself, their God is not the people, nor is it public opinion in the higher meaning of the word. Their idol is opportunism, and they worship it with the usual zeal of the Party hack.

What, then, about Boris Nikolayevich Yeltsin?

At the State Council meetings he preferred to stay silent, and he took the floor usually when all the rest had had their say. With rare exceptions he did not join in verbal duels. Sometimes I had the impression that he was observing everything that happened in that room from a long distance. During the breaks, when all the other State Council members and ministers were hurrying to the famous Kremlin canteen (although it had lost much of its past glamour) Gorbachev would drag Yeltsin off to his own offices, where they would continue to discuss urgent problems tête-à-tête over a meal.

On the one hand, this pleased Yeltsin, a man who loves attention. On the other, it made him uneasy, because there in the recesses of his Kremlin offices Gorbachev would wring out more concessions than at the crowded sessions. Yeltsin's natural environment was, and always would be, a platform, a rally, a huge crowd of admirers, but not a confined encounter. With his suggestible nature, he often loses to more cunning partners. And for all his public bluster, the old apparatchik still felt junior to Gorbachev.

But it was not only Yeltsin's nature and apparatchik background that made him content to accept a subsidiary role to the supreme leader of the Soviet State. I am convinced that Yeltsin, even if he had emerged as the top figure in a reconstituted Soviet Union, would not have promoted the overlordship of the Russian Republic. Yeltsin never had the inclination to thrust Russia forward as a neo-imperial force dominating its neighbour republics. Why do I say this?

First, Yeltsin's period of prominent opposition, when he was tossed briefly into the political wilderness in the late 1980s, produced no hint of any 'Russia-first' mentality. At the Plenum of the Central Committee of the CPSU in 1987, when Yeltsin first raised the banner of rebellion against Gorbachev, his words contained not the slightest leaning towards Russian super-sovereignty, or even any rejection of Communism. His criticisms were about the excessive adulation of Gorbachev, about his style of work and the sluggish pace of perestroika. He cast no doubts at all on the principles that were being expounded, only on the way in which they were being implemented. Yeltsin's subsequent dismissal resulted from his insubordination, not from any suspicion that he wanted to promote a super-Russia.

Of course the response to Yeltsin's insubordination went too far, but his dismissal was engineered by people whose political attitudes were formed in a culture of obedience, regardless of the new experimentation with perestroika. As Shevardnadze has said in his memoirs, 'We felt obliged to react ... We had no rudimentary idea of the rules and norms of political struggle in a civilized society. Resolute measures? Yes. The words of a General Secretary were a law to us. If he said: dismiss so-and-so from the Politburo, that was it. We were brought up that way.'

Thus perestroika, the melting of the ideological ice, was

launched by people who had themselves grown up and been raised in that spiritual permafrost that for a long time froze other people into its mould and principles. Leonid Brezhnev was a particular adherent of those principles, and it was during his rule that the would-be fathers of perestroika – Gorbachev, Shevardnadze, Yakovlev and, among others, their junior colleague Boris Pankin – made their careers. The situation of the first two was especially complicated because of the heights they had reached under the previous regime – under Brezhnev, Chernenko, Andropov. Any display of discontent, the slightest hint of disagreement at that level, could destroy one's career. Neither was it in the tradition of the Party bureaucracy to risk it. The only thing left was to share concern and doubts with one's closest friends. Gorbachev and Shevardnadze were exactly such friends: they became friends precisely because they had both been at the head of Party regional organizations. They also spent their vacations in each other's regions, since both Northern Caucasus and Georgia with its Black Sea coast were favourite resorts of the powers that be.

So, when the time came for Gorbachev to place his people in key posts, it was not professionalism and eligibility he was thinking about, but rather the dependability of his team. And when perestroika came under attack both from conservatives, who wanted to put a brake on the process, and from radicals who wanted to accelerate it, Edvard Ambrosievich demonstrated his loyalty to Gorbachev by attacking the dissenters, while Yeltsin took up the cudgels of dissent. Yeltsin was thus pushed out from the inner circle as a 'heretic' not because his ideas were unpalatable, but because he had questioned his boss. And had he not suffered such a savage rebuff at the Central Committee plenum, followed by those clumsy anti-Yeltsin campaigns (later the General Secretary and his supporters would have to swallow far worse insults!) there would have been no 'Yeltsin phenomenon'.

It was in this way that the democratic spirit awoke spontaneously in Yeltsin during his personal political drama, but once awake, and multiplied by the originality and toughness of his character, it demanded a field of action. Russia became his strategic arena because there was a vacuum to fill. Yeltsin exploited this arena, becoming a democratically elected Chairman of the Supreme Soviet of the Russian Federation, and then the President. But soon he saw that just as it was 'impossible to build Communism in a socialist setting' (as the popular joke of the stagnation period ran), so it was equally impossible to create a democracy and civic society in a single separate republic, even one the size of Russia.

He soon received the chance, provided to him by the August putsch, and if Russia had not been what it had become under Yeltsin it would have stood no chance of quelling a rebellion of the Party apparatchiks, KGB and generals. But after saving the country for democracy, Yeltsin's Russia wanted to personify the whole country. The decrees taking over the majority of Union power structures and institutions, adopted as an anti-putsch measure, were not repealed by the Russian government after the coup was defeated. Far from it. Having acquired a degree of sovereignty for Russia to counter the coup, Yeltsin now took the opportunity to neutralize the overarching supremacy of the Gorbachev team by maintaining that sovereignty. Thus democracy and the sovereignty of Russia became synonymous for millions of people.

The putschists did some of their deepest damage here. When they rebelled in defence of the Soviet Union as a single State, they made an intact Soviet Union seem tantamount to totalitarianism. The cautionary words of many people, including Henry Kissinger, that divisions between the Centre and the republics did not necessarily correspond to the distinction between totalitarianism and democracy, remained unheard.

When during his election campaign Yeltsin made a gesture towards the autonomous republics of Russia – 'Take as much sovereignty as you can swallow' – he could hardly anticipate that some time later it would boomerang against him. He was paving the way, not for those republics but for himself. But the process of building up the legitimacy and viability of Russian sovereignty contained within it the idea of Russia as legal heir to the Soviet Union, an idea that frightened democrats in other republics who had seen the sovereignty of their republics as being possible only within the Soviet Union. This fear was seized upon by former Party bosses like Mutalibov in Azerbaijan, Kravchuk in Ukraine, Snegur in Moldova, Nabiyev in Tajikistan. In playing up to separatists they could also launder their Party apparatchik past.

That is why they watched Yeltsin's behaviour so closely at State Council meetings, and he watched theirs. That is why Gorbachev's appeals for frank discussions were so futile, and the work of this potentially effective form of running the country moved in fits and starts.

This became obvious when on 14 November 1991 the State Council resumed discussion of the Union Treaty, or, in Gorbachev's favourite phrase, the Novo Ogarevo process.

In that process, work went on in a very closed circle. We ministers were invited to Novo Ogarevo late in the afternoon, around five o'clock. Our concerns, the reorganization of the Foreign Ministry, Armed Forces, Ministry of the Interior and KGB, would be kept till later.

Driving out of Moscow along the Rublevo Shosse, we turned right before 'Barvikha', a government recreation estate. Then after a couple of kilometres we noticed militia posts and army patrols. One green fence, then another ... Two two-storey houses built either of brick or wood, and in a style that has no name in architecture. Government dachas. In one of the houses, to the left of the gates, members of the State Council were now sitting. The Novo Ogarevo process was under way.

In the building to the right, the ministers were gathered. While we waited for our turn we could drink tea, play billiards, or try to compare notes about the history of this clumsy building. Some said that Andropov had lived there, others that it used to be the Gorbachevs' dacha when he was in the Politburo. Just gossip to pass the time.

At last it was the turn of the ministers, and we walked across to the neighbouring building, where the press was milling at the

257

door. Inside we found a large entrance hall and a staircase covered with a traditional red carpet, leading to the meeting-room on the second floor. Presidents were buzzing in and out of it like bees from an agitated hive, some rushing to the telephones, some to the bathroom, others conferring with their assistants. The side-rooms swarmed with security guards, aides and secretaries.

Ten minutes later everyone reassembled in the room. Judging from the restless but happy look on Gorbachev's face, the discussion had gone well. He looked confident. Maybe that is why the discussion about our organizations was quickly completed. Several references were made to a document just adopted by the State Council.

Finally Gorbachev addressed the republican leaders and suggested that they should go downstairs and hold a press conference, but this proposal excited no enthusiasm and someone (I think it was Shushkevich of Belarus) proposed authorizing Gorbachev to represent them all. Another seconded him, but Gorbachev balked and finally dragged all of them with him. Only Mutalibov remained upstairs, saying between puffs of his cigarette that he had observer status today.

I had nothing more to do here, so I sat in my car and listened to the press conference on the radio. It sounded as though they had every reason to be pleased with the results. The Presidents had approved the Union Treaty. Now they were to submit it for consideration by their parliaments. In about a week's time they would meet again in Moscow and sign it. This was encouraging news.

Later in the evening Gorbachev telephoned me, congratulated me on winning a tussle about reorganizing the Foreign Ministry, and offered a triumphant account of his own battle with the republican bosses. Seeing that he was making no headway at first, he had threatened to resign, and had even walked out of the room and left the decision to them. Later they (Yeltsin and Shushkevich, I believe) came and invited him back, and they reached an agreement. So there would be a Union.

Only six days remained before my final meeting with him.

The Union of Independent States was planned to be a federative democratic State that would exercise powers delegated to it by the constituent republics, each one of them a sovereign State. Of course it was late when we spoke, and Gorbachev was not so systematic in outlining the substance of the document, but next morning he sent me an autographed copy. For obvious reasons he emphasized in the document the points that meant that the Soviet Union was not about to break up into dozens of States but would remain – for all the independence of the constituent republics – a single political, economic and legal entity, a rather different animal from the Soviet Union, but nevertheless with the bones of Union intact.

'There will be a President, a Vice-President, a single Parliament, a State Council, a government ...' he rejoiced.

Accepting the priority of individual rights in full compliance with the Universal Declaration of Human Rights and other norms of international law, and paying tribute to the principles of civic society and democracy, the founding fathers of the new Union laid down the right of each constituent State freely to determine its own forms and structures of government and administration and to preserve and uphold its cultural traditions. In constituting the Union, the participating States established spheres of joint responsibility and signed appropriate agreements on economic cooperation, common defence and collective security, and the coordination of foreign policy.

The member States guaranteed the free development and protection of all forms of property. Land and natural resources would belong to the sovereign States, with their exploitation controlled by their national legislation.

Mikhail Sergeyevich, Boris Nikolayevich and the other State Council members could congratulate themselves on a job well done.

Alas, on 24 November, after my replacement as Foreign Minister, they would meet again to turn their backs on what they had agreed on that critical day of 14 November, and Gorbachev would be left to face the world on his own, and try with a baffled smile to convince everybody that all was not lost. He insisted that the country remained, and the joint address of the President and State Council members to the parliaments of the republics should be regarded as their signatures under a new version of the Treaty.

Meanwhile in Ukraine the republic's parliament decided on a referendum about the new Union Treaty which President Kravchuk claimed he could not resist. That referendum and its outcome (over 90 per cent against) sounded the death-knell of the Soviet Union, but the responsibility has to rest with Kravchuk, who had played a double game from first to last.

The lightning struck on 8 December 1991. After a two-day session in a dacha in Belovezhskaya Pusha, Yeltsin, Kravchuk and Shushkevich, the Belarus leader, issued a document announcing the formation of the Commonwealth of Independent Slavic States and declaring that the Soviet Union and all its institutions had 'ceased to exist'.

A new era was beginning. But as the situation evolved, I began to understand more and more about what had lain behind the in-fighting over the Soviet Foreign Ministry, starting with Yeltsin's proposal to cut it by 90 per cent, and what had happened to me. It is not my intention to dwell upon petty intrigue or injured ambitions here, but to try to concentrate on what I see as the most important issues.

Yeltsin had nothing against me personally. Our relationship, which had begun in Stockholm at a difficult moment for him and continued in Prague and Moscow, remained friendly and businesslike. But the Soviet Foreign Ministry that had become so active under its new chief, Pankin, was also becoming a serious nuisance. It was not that its line on foreign policy itself did not satisfy the Russian President. Quite the contrary: my views on de-ideologization, pragmatism and humanization appealed to the democratic leadership of Russia.

From the point of view of the Russian leadership this line had only one fault, although a serious one: it was pursued in the name of the Soviet Union and the Soviet President, and at times it was the only reminder to the world that the Soviet Union still existed and had nothing in common with the monster it used to be. While there was a strong Foreign Ministry, fully staffed and functioning, there was a visible and functioning Soviet Union. A State with no foreign policy and no diplomatic capability was no real State. Those who favoured the break-up of the Union therefore saw our active foreign policy as an impediment to the emergence of a dominant Russia. The Foreign Ministry became a football in the struggle between Russian and Soviet aspirations.

I remember Vladimir Petrovsky meeting me at the airport on my way back from the Middle East and putting into my red box a memo summarizing the events that had happened in my absence. I started to read it right there, and learned that in a conversation with Mikhail Sergeyevich, Kovalev had thanked him for overriding a decision to suspend the financing of the Foreign Ministry.

'Well, what's that all about?'

'Yes, there was such a decision by the Russian Finance Ministry,' Petrovsky explained. 'We didn't want to worry you. Mikhail Sergeyevich spoke to Boris Nikolayevich and he reversed it.'

Next day I telephoned Yeltsin to tell him about my trip, and among other things to express my surprise at what idiocies were happening in our country and how fortunate it was that there were wise statesmen who could correct the mistakes.

'Indeed, our Finance Minister Lazarev was overzealous,' said Yeltsin good-humouredly. 'Mikhail Sergeyevich called me and we changed that.'

He paused, and I was about to say goodbye when he added suddenly: 'But anyway, let this be regarded as a signal.'

'What do you mean?' I hardly had time to ask the question before he hung up.

So the proposal on a tenfold reduction of the Foreign Ministry was the second signal to a stubborn Minister.

On the morning of the State Council meeting on 4 November, the one when Yeltsin arrived late, I delivered a speech at the Collegium of the Foreign Ministry. Earlier conversations with Gorbachev and Yeltsin had partly set my mind at rest, but I could not ignore the news about panic in the Foreign Ministry – the petition, the complaints about my absence – that had greeted me on my return from Madrid. These were after all the people I defended when there was pressure from all sides to purge the Foreign Ministry after its staff behaved so cowardly during the coup. I therefore decided to call a meeting of the Collegium before the State Council session, and to speak my mind about the behaviour of my staff.

I began calmly by describing the impending reorganization of the Foreign Ministry. There was to be a Council of Foreign Ministries of the Union and republics – the supreme consultative body – which would review our long-term strategic options. For regular coordination, a permanent secretariat of the Council of Foreign Ministers was to be formed, and there would be republican representation in our Embassies. The Foreign Ministry would be amalgamated with the Ministry of Foreign Trade. Given the current problems with finance, personnel in the Foreign Ministry and the Embassies was to be cut by one third, mainly at the expense of the 'neighbours', both KGB and GRU. When making decisions about cuts we would bear in mind not only professional competence but also moral courage. Moral courage. This gave me my cue for points I wanted to get off my chest.

Today I cannot reproduce my words verbatim, but I remember my lips trembling with emotion as I spoke, which is of course unforgivable in a Minister, but as I was told later, made the strongest impression. The Foreign Ministry, I said, didn't brandish mass petitions during the putsch when the fate of the country was at stake. There wasn't much criticism of Bessmertnykh the Minister when he was taken diplomatically ill. That left the Ministry without any outside support, and now for the third month running we were still having to explain ourselves to the press. Back then, only a handful made a protest. Yet now, when people sense that their positions were threatened, we saw all the stops pulled out: mass petitions, demands to recall the Minister from the Madrid Conference where one of the most dramatic events in the history of diplomacy was going on!

I felt morally justified to pronounce these words because I had done my utmost not to allow the Foreign Ministry to be purged after the putsch, when many people saw no difference between Smolenskaya and Dzerzhinskaya squares, respectively the nerve centres of the Foreign Ministry and the KGB.

I closed the Collegium meeting without opening the debate. Petrovsky had time to whisper in my ear: 'This is what was needed! This matches Prague!'

Strangely enough, later that day at the State Council the discussion of my item passed very smoothly. I presented my proposals, Gorbachev supported them. The first to speak was Boris Nikolayevich, who said that he had had his doubts, but the Minister's presentation had dispelled them, and the proposals deserved to be approved. 'The most important thing is that the system of coordination between the central and republican Foreign Ministries is thought through. As far as cuts are concerned, one third is better than 90 per cent,' he said, smiling benevolently at me. 'And it will only do good. Let's put it straight.' Yeltsin sounded tough now. 'There are people to be sacked and people to be thrown away. From the Embassies too. What rubbish they come out with at times, and we all know how shamefully many of them behaved during the coup! I hope the new Minister will have enough willpower to carry out this line. He's got a firm hand. I know it from Prague.'

That was the end of debate. I had grasped the situation by then: democracy and equality were all very well, but few present at this top meeting dared to argue with Boris Nikolayevich. The proposals were adopted in principle, and at the next meeting ten days later they were approved in their final form.

There were new stakes in the game. I think Yeltsin took the view that if the Soviet Union survived then the reorganized Ministry would be more suited to carry out its duties, whereas if the USSR broke up, the Ministry in this form could serve an

263

independent Russia. Gorbachev on the other hand had his own calculations. He was increasingly aware that a reputable foreign policy alone was not enough to maintain the fading prestige of the Union. It was relatively easy for our foreign policy to go with the grain of world opinion. Inside the Soviet Union, there was no consensus and too many centrifugal forces. The process of fusing a foreign policy involving the republics would in his judgement bring the different republics together, contributing to and strengthening the Union. He realized however that to achieve this the Foreign Ministry would increasingly have to deal with the former republics. This was where he played his Shevardnadze card. He saw Edvard Ambrosievich, the non-Russian who had spent a significant part of his career in Georgia, as a more acceptable interlocutor with the republics. Thus ironically the Foreign Minister's drive to preserve a fully functioning Foreign Ministry created the basis for the departure of that Foreign Minister and his replacement by Shevardnadze.

True to Gorbachev's intent, the return of Shevardnadze was announced together with a planned tour of the sovereign republics of the USSR. But he never got the chance.

The meeting on 8 December 1991 in Belovezhskaya Pusha between the leaders of Russia, Ukraine and Belarus was preceded by a referendum in Ukraine in which the majority of the population voted for independence – just as a year before it had voted for the preservation of the Soviet Union. Were they really mutually exclusive, these two votes? By that time everything had become so utterly confused that any electoral results could have all sorts of interpretations. So when Yeltsin and Gorbachev repeated that they did not see a Union without Ukraine, they had different things in mind. According to Gorbachev, even after the referendum Ukraine was not entirely lost. According to Yeltsin, Russia had no alternative but to follow Ukraine.

This was the last stage of their love-hate relationship.

Nowadays, few people would venture to say that the fates of States, societies, nations and individuals are rigorously predetermined. For millions and millions of people who watched this struggle of giants from the sidelines, the course of events did seem predetermined. Some people, supporters of the Union, did not doubt the eventual success of Gorbachev. For others the victory of Yeltsin was a self-evident thing. Each side believed that its protagonist answered to the imperatives of the time. My position in the three months between August and December provided me with a unique opportunity to see how the wheels of history turn, how the clock can slow down or speed up.

While watching these events with one foot in the thick of the Gorbachev–Yeltsin battle and another in the outside world, which was anxiously following Gorbachev's last stand, I was able to develop a close sense of how the West was evaluating the struggle in Moscow. I am quite certain that right up to the moment when the thunderclap sounded from Belovezhskaya Pusha, the West continued to support Gorbachev: all its bets were on him and on the renewed democratic Union. The negotiations in Madrid were obvious proof of that position. The West was ready to tolerate both his mistakes and his slow pace of reforms. Bush in Madrid and other Western leaders in all our diplomatic contacts made no bones about their wish to see the Soviet Union continue, and for obvious reasons – that no one could predict what instability and dangers might result from an overzealous transformation of the Soviet empire. Add to all this the hints we picked up that Yeltsin was not altogether trusted as a stable and predictable leader of a Russian State.

The reasons for the West's caution in welcoming the rise of Yeltsin, however, went well beyond doubts about his stability and predictability. Yeltsin represented an unknown. And it was by no means clear to the world how the Yeltsin factor and the rise of Russia out of the ashes of the Soviet Union would work on the dreaded new phenomenon – nationalism – that was beginning to rear its head in Europe.

At the UN I had spoken about the virus of nationalism, 'which has caught all of us, or almost all of us, unprepared ... Cleansing storms have torn through Central and Eastern Europe

265

bringing their long-awaited freedom and reviving dignity and self-respect, a belief in the high destination of a human individual on the planet Earth. And it is not the pursuit of freedom that is to blame for the outbursts of ethnic hostility that have once again swept across the world like a plague of forgotten epidemics. Primordial instincts have come back to life in a new environment that was not created for them. And all this is accompanied by dangers of economic chaos, the heat of social contradictions, refugees, diseases.'

I do not consider myself a prophet. It was not my own country I was thinking of, although I knew about the tensions in Nagorno-Karabakh, South Ossetia and the Trans-Dnestr region. At that time I had in mind an image of Yugoslavia creeping slowly into civil war. As for the Soviet Union I still had no notion that it would break up into its component republics, each a new independent State, each in thrall to a kind of nationalism that served the purposes of its ruling elite.

A common feature of all the nationalist movements in the Soviet republics was that this nationalism breathed life back into the former Communist Party nomenklatura. Or was it that the nomenklatura had to rely on the new nationalism to ensure its own survival? How else to explain the re-emergence of the likes of that former internationalist Geidar Aliyev reinventing himself as the great champion of Azerbaijani nationalism?

As we examine the forces that tore the Soviet Union asunder in the late autumn of 1991, it is worth considering the position of Aliyev because he so neatly typified the attitudes of those claiming to represent the national aspiration of the republics. By tracing the zigzags of his career one can judge the real nature of the brand of nationalism that swept the Soviet Union.

A devout follower of Brezhnev (few of our leaders could please Brezhnev more than this ex-First Secretary of the Communist Party of Azerbaijan), he prospered under Andropov and Chernenko to become First Deputy Chairman of the Council of Ministers of the USSR and a full Politburo member. But he fell out of favour in the perestroika years and retired.

There used to be a belief that only Yeltsin managed to

weather the political oblivion to which the Communist regime attempted to consign him, but it turns out that the democratic system that grew out of the debris of totalitarianism succeeded in resurrecting figures of a very different kind. The old warhorse Aliyev was spurred back to life by the first signs of tensions between Armenia and Karabakh. Posing as a defender of the interests of Nagorno-Karabakh and the whole of Azerbaijan, in September 1990 he was elected to the Supreme Soviet of Azerbaijan. Then he became President of the Nakhichevan republic, where he won popularity by attempts to nationalize the property of the former USSR armed forces stationed there. By now you would find no stronger critic of the Communist regime than this ex-Politburo member.

The next stage followed when the Supreme Soviet of Azerbaijan elected Aliyev, now a champion of Azeri rights in Nagorno-Karabakh, Deputy Chairman. It was not long before Aliyev, backing a military revolt, took power in Baku. Too wily to hold power by brute force, he was quick to launch the constitutional process. He wrapped the democratic blanket around himself, and in succession was elected speaker and then President of Azerbaijan. His metamorphosis from mastermind of an armed revolt to lawfully elected President of an independent State had taken only a few months. What he had to offer was the firm hand of an ex-Chairman of the Azerbaijani KGB, the hope that he would at last establish law and order.

When I said at the UN that the eight republics that proclaimed their independence during the three weeks after the putsch were escaping, not from the Soviet Union but from the threat of seeing totalitarianism restored, some of my friends added: 'And from the threat of democracy.' I find myself compelled to agree. Men like Aliyev – and the Soviet nomenklatura produced plenty like him – were all attracted by one and the same goal – power. If there was one thing that the Bolshevik Revolution taught people in our country it was the importance of seeking and holding power. Bolshevism for me does not necessarily mean belonging to a Leninist party that has now ceased to exist. It is not even an ideology. It is a state of

267

mind. To me Bolshevism means the desire of minorities to rule over the majority at any price. Lenin was a romantic of voluntarism and the arbitrary power of the few. He deployed a mystique based on exerting an almost hypnotic effect over the majority of people that he preferred to call 'the masses'. A mass, like clay or plaster, could be moulded into any shape or form.

Bolshevism is lack of tolerance of any other opinion, the readiness to achieve your goal at any price. Stalin once explained that a socialist State had the same goals as a bourgeois parliamentary one, the difference being that the power of workers and peasants simply could not wait on all these parliamentary games such as elections, opposition, voting blocs etc., etc. The similarities between Stalin's and Hitler's evil empires were simply lost on the admirers and apologists of Bolshevism.

Could not some analogies be drawn with our own times, when it has become fashionable to applaud the break-up of the Soviet Union and to praise the creation of new States, 'sovereign, truly independent, free from the imperial yoke', not noticing that in the majority of them the same hateful features of the evil empire are restored or preserved? The Presidents who were elected uncontested with an overwhelming majority of votes do not press on with economic reform or with acknowledging the rights to private property, but they do seize opportunities to proclaim states of emergency, take emergency powers, to indefinitely postpone democratic elections, and replace democratically elected local governments with their special representatives. Are not they much the same as Lenin's and Stalin's commissars? And they offer the same rationale: right now we can't afford those democratic games. We'll get back to them when victory is ours. (Victory over whom? For what purpose?)

The ex-First Secretary of the Communist Party of Moldavia, Mircea Ion Snegur, now the President of Moldova, has imposed in his country such a draconian state of emergency, amounting to a dictatorship, that the August 1991 Moscow putsch pales in comparison. Why? Because the Russian minority in the Trans-Dnestr region wanted from Moldova the same things that

Moldova had demanded (and received) from the 'totalitarian' Centre back in November and December of 1991. This is the logic of a horse, as Khrushchev used to put it. For Moldova, independence or, more than that, joining Romania means a step forward towards democracy and freedom, while autonomy for the Gagauz and Russians in the Trans-Dnestr region means relapsing into a squalid totalitarian past.

The Leninist-Stalinist Soviet Union was welded together by uncompromising Bolshevik methods. But its Gorbachev–Yakovlev–Yeltsin (yes, Yeltsin) version was closed down in the same arbitrary Bolshevik manner, as if forgetting that behind the abstract symbols, behind the political and administrative jargon, there were millions, tens of millions, of human beings. With a stroke of a pen they were once again converted into masses, who now inhabit the immense territory of the former Soviet Union, their erstwhile Motherland, and try to find out whose citizens they are, in which army they serve, who is a native citizen, and who is a national minority.

And the Russians, as usual, were in the worst position. If the roughly 30 million of them who live outside the Russian Federation were to become refugees or émigrés, the result could only be chaos on an unprecedented scale.

Some of our politicians were angry enough when the authorities of newly free Czechoslovakia, Hungary and Poland gave us too short a time to withdraw our troops from their territories. Yet now the CIS Armed Forces found themselves in the position of occupiers in their own country: Ukraine, Belarus, Moldova. The new Chairman of the State Council of Georgia, one of the architects of perestroika, now had to speak about settling terms for the withdrawal of almost two hundred thousand troops. And where to? Of course to Russia, where already hundreds of thousands of officers and their families were homeless.

The imposed dissolution of the Soviet Union created a new set of structural problems. First, Russia was left to pick up the pieces. That meant taking over some responsibilities – such as what to do with tactical nuclear weapons – that had previously

269

been spread more evenly through the old Union. But it also meant Russia confronting a role that pre-dated the Soviet Union. It has become more and more obvious that the State that existed in the territory of the former Soviet Union was by no means an entity invented by the Bolsheviks. What the Bolsheviks did was to distort the State and transnational entity that had been forming for centuries in Euro-Asia, and was called Russia, so grotesquely that it became unrecognizable. The reaction triggered by their generations of criminal actions produced another extreme seventy-five years later when those who struggled so hard against Bolshevism threw out the baby along with the bath-water, and destroyed what our academician Lev Gumilev aptly called 'the accommodating and nurturing space' that in a natural way had united tens and hundreds of nations and nationalities by helping each of them to find its own way of living. The fact that some Russians have interpreted this vacant role in a frankly imperialist light since the fall of the Soviet Union does not invalidate the role.

The disappearance of the Union also left several of the new republics to cope with problems on a scale too great for fledgling States – problems that the old Union should have recognized and dealt with as a common task. Instead, Ukraine was left on its own with the aftermath of Chernobyl, and Kazakhstan with the tragedy of the dying Aral Sea. With so little history of democracy, the new States were prey, as we have seen, to the ambitions of powerful populist leaders, some of them trained in the old Communist school. These States also had their own imperialisms, and ex-President Kravchuk found himself at one stage claiming ownership of the entire Black Sea fleet of the old Soviet Union on behalf of Ukraine. (What could Ukraine afford to do with it?) Ukraine also faced difficulties with the Crimea, transferred to it from Russia as a free gift by Khrushchev in 1954, along with some reluctant minorities. When Russia and Ukraine were parts of one State, there was room for more differences in a larger, looser, whole. The friction arose from the break-up. Examples like these could be cited over and over.

The vacant role exists, and the fact that it came into existence explains why the disappearance of the 'all-powerful Centre' so bitterly resented both inside and outside the old Soviet Union brought no universal tranquillity to the Euro-Asian region. Both in the CIS and abroad, it was soon Russia that was called 'Big Brother'.

If there was an advantage in the creation of the CIS it was that Gorbachev was replaced by Yeltsin. Gorbachev may have been good or bad, great or small, but his capacities were plainly exhausted. It seems to me that he understood this himself right after the putsch, and now I see that the best thing he could have done then was to cede the Presidency of the Soviet Union to Yeltsin. Had he done so, there would be no CIS today. As it was, the arbitrary action taken at Belovezhskaya Pusha left many observers, and not only the Communist faithful, wondering whether this was not a new putsch, silent and bloodless. It was a fear recognized by the initiators of the Commonwealth themselves, when they introduced amendments to the original formulas of their document of 8 December and prolonged the changeover until Gorbachev and the Union Parliament formally recognized the *fait accompli* in late December. But what the decisions of November and December 1991 failed to recognize was that we have to rely on the experience of civilized countries in building a democratic society. Their experience – including that of the European Community, which has become the centre of attraction for the very countries that so recently opposed it – testifies that strength lies in unity and not in separation, in the supremacy of universal values such as parliamentary democracy and the rule of law, and not in harking back to bygone ethnic pasts.

Experience has shown that extremists both from the right and from the left would like to expunge a crucial period – those last one hundred days of the Soviet State, when we were attempting to preserve some kind of union – and pretend that it never existed. Those from the left are custodians of our Communist past in various disguises. They weep for that past, and in the

271

three memorable months from the August putsch till the meeting in Belovezhskaya Pusha they were ready to condemn every act of the new Soviet diplomacy, which they viewed as a betrayal of the public – meaning their own personal – interests. Those from the right are those who would like to claim the credit for what happened on their own behalf. My own, though not impartial, view is that during those months, to borrow a term from our nineteenth-century Foreign Minister and Chancellor, Prince Gorchakov, a great nation was *concentrating* on choosing its road to the future. The years since then bear out the proposition that the road it has since taken was not necessarily the right one.

What really matters is that life itself keeps compelling the leaders of Russia and the other CIS States to revert to the ideas and practicalities of integration. The Economic Union now being revived with the approval of Boris Yeltsin preserves the spirit of the Union put forward by Yavlinsky and Gorbachev in those meetings of the State Council in September–December 1991. The CIS is gradually acquiring coordinating bodies, and one of these is the CFM, the Council of Foreign Ministers. The need derives not from the whims and manoeuvres of ambitious leaders, but from the concrete needs of the former Soviet peoples – the need for economic and social development.

The world now has a single superpower, the United States, and I have remarked already that it does not altogether welcome the change. In 1991 Russian diplomats were too concerned to establish the independence and legitimacy of their new sovereign State to worry about the possible superpower status of the Russian Federation. In any case, the economic plight of their country forbade any grander ambitions. After the collapse of the Soviet Union, Russia's declared aim, in the words of Kozyrev, was to become a 'normal great power' (not 'superpower'). More recently the notion of Russia as a second superpower has gathered force in the Russian foreign policy establishment. This is in part a response to nationalist sentiment in Russia, and in part the result of a feeling that playing the staunch American ally has yielded few measurable dividends.

Hence the Russian inclination to play a more robust role in steering into some sort of Russian-led fold the former Soviet republics, exerting a more dynamic influence in the Balkans, and taking a more independent line on Middle Eastern issues such as relations with Iraq and Iran. Obviously there are more than enough problems to go round.

Immediately after my return from the Madrid Conference I gave an interview to Edward Kuznetsov, the former dissident and defender of human rights, now editor-in-chief of the Israeli Russian-language daily *Vremya*. He asked about my reading of the conference, and I replied: 'Now I am even more optimistic than before ... There's some sort of magic that comes with the negotiating process itself, when instead of shooting at each other the representatives of the warring forces proceed to discuss their interests and to search for a compromise while sitting at one table.'

That interview was published on the eve of my leaving for London, and a sceptical reader might question my optimism. After all, the hurdles in the way of the Madrid process have been considerable. Yet the negotiations in Oslo and the Palestine–Israeli agreement concluded in Washington would be inconceivable without the Madrid initiative that James Baker and I announced in Jerusalem in mid-October 1991. And the agreements on Cambodia that I had the honour to sign in Paris immediately after leaving the Middle East created further hopeful possibilities. I am still an optimist, and I hope that the international efforts on former Yugoslavia will also eventually bear fruit. Let both Milosevic and Tudjman recall their handshake in the Kremlin on one of the hundred days to which this book is dedicated.

When I first arrived in London a British journalist once asked me: 'Who are you for?'

'I am for my country and my people,' I replied, and I hope that I shall continue to serve them with the story of my hundred days as Foreign Minister of the Soviet Union, which also happened to coincide with the last days of the country that bore that name.

273

I would like to end this book with a quotation from one of the most radical opponents of totalitarianism, the Polish philosopher Leszek Kolakowski, writing in praise of that quality of generous inconsistency that for him is a synonym of tolerance:

> The race of inconsistent people continues to remain one of the main sources of the hope that humankind will survive. Because this is a race part of which believes in God and in the supremacy of Salvation over earthly pleasures, but does not demand the wrath of bonfires for heretics and unbelievers. And part of which does not believe in God, and accepts revolutionary change in society, but rejects actions that contradict the moral tradition in which they were raised.

Tolerance and inconsistency reflect both the contradictions that exist in the world, and the impossibility of final solutions.

INDEX

281